MW01248187

Every Life's A Story and This Is Mine

Stephen Oxley

NATIONAL
LIBRARY
OF AUSTRALIA

A catalogue record for this
book is available from the
National Library of Australia

Copyright © 2022 by Stephen Oxley

All rights reserved. No part of this book may be reproduced or transmitted in any form
or by any means, electronic or mechanical, including photocopying, recording, or by
any information storage and retrieval system, without permission in writing from the
copyright owner.

Publisher:
ASPG (Australian Self Publishing Group)
P.O. Box 159, Calwell, ACT Australia 2905
Email: publishaspg@gmail.com
http://www.inspiringpublishers.com

National Library of Australia Cataloguing-in-Publication entry

Author: Oxley, Stephen

Title: **EVERY LIFE'S A STORY AND THIS IS MINE**/*Stephen Oxley*

ISBN: 978-1-922792-99-0 (pbk)

Contents

Preface

This is my story, Stephen Leonard Oxley, created from my memories, adventures, mishaps, misfortunes, and marvels. I have jotted my thoughts in journals and poetry since I can remember, documenting the absurd through to the sombre. I am no scholar, so I tell it as I think it and hopefully through my poetic ramblings, you can get some sense of the life I have lived, the people and the places I have loved.

Tracing My Family in Australia

I n Boorowa, the names of my ancestors include Oxley, Wells, Silk, Faulkner, Venables, Howe, Clifford, and Conquest. At this time, I am the only descendant remaining in Boorowa, but my family has had a long association with the town.

My Great, Great, Great Grandmother was born in Maitland in 1816 to parents Robert and Sarah Wells. She was buried at Frogmore in 1870. Her father, Robert, was sent to Australia for 'highway robbery' from Middlesex, England in 1792. My Great, Great, Great Grandfather, William Oxley was sent to the colonies (Australia) for the term of his natural life in 1827, also for 'highway robbery,' in Nottingham. He married Sarah Wells in 1837, in Maitland and was buried in Liverpool in 1893. One of their sons, William Oxley, was born in Parramatta in 1844. He married Mary Silk in Goulburn, in 1865. He was buried in Boorowa, next to his wife, in 1922. Mary's parents are also buried in Boorowa, listed as John Silk of County Carlow and Mary Silk of County Kildare, Ireland.

William and Mary Oxley had a son John Joseph Oxley. He and his wife, Marian Faulkner (my great grandparents) are buried beside each other in the Boorowa Cemetery. John and Marian Oxley had my grandfather, William James Oxley, who married Linda Venessa Venables. Both of them are buried in Boorowa. My grandparents on my mother's side were Frederick and Elsie Maude May Howe (nee Clifford). Frederick was raised in Bundanoon and played cricket against Donald Bradman. My grandmother Linda Venables was born in the same room as Bradman, in Cootamundra.

Another Boorowa name related to me is my mother's grand-father, William Henry Norman Augustin Conquest, supposedly a descendant of William the Conqueror. He was a coach builder and supposedly worked with Hargraves, who jumped off Stanwell Tops on the South Coast, in his kite. Conquest's story within my family is that he apparently built an airplane in a barn near Boorowa, long before the Wright Brothers flew. Locals told him he was crazy, whereupon he wrecked the plane with an axe and disappeared.

Both my parents, Maxwell Leonard, and Alice Joan Oxley (nee Howe) are at rest in the cemetery wall at Boorowa. I am the third child in our family of seven children:

1. Marian
2. Ian
3. Stephen
4. Paul
5. Lewis
6. Neil
7. Caroline

Section 1

Brewarrina and Boorowa

$$\diamondsuit$$

Chapter 1

Early Years

W hen I was about three years or four years old, I lived with my Mum, Dad, older brother Ian and older sister Marian, in Brewarrina, a town in North-West New South Wales, Australia. Dad was working in the sheds, and we were on a sheep station named Merriman. For some reason, I remember a cuckoo clock in the Shearer's quarters – maybe because that seemed a strange thing to me for shearers to have, even at my young age. There was also a dirt air strip that sticks in my mind (sometime around 1955/56) and a plane would sometimes land there, I think a DC3. Me and some other kids spoke to the pilot when the plane came – he wore beady little sunglasses and would give us chewing gum.

There was a nice Aboriginal man named Felly and Mum always said she trusted him with us kids. I would get on the carrier behind the 'Fergy' tractor and Felly would drive to the first gate from the homestead, where I would jump off and open the gate, and after Felly drove through, I would shut the gate and walk back to the homestead. There were times I remember chasing wild pigs which could frighten me, as when the little pigs were chased, their mother would charge my dad and I feared he would get hurt.

I think we came back to Boorowa in 1956, driving through flood-waters in an FJ Holden ute with a caravan on the back to get there. Later Dad had the dairy in town and brought pasteurized milk to Boorowa. I used to go with Dad to make deliveries to the monastery at Galong and to a milk factory at Harden. Dad eventually sold the dairy and went back to work for the Postmaster General's department (PMG), where he had worked for a time before getting the dairy. When we woke on Christmas morning, I remember my brother Ian and I had to sort out who got what toy from under the tree. One year, there was a pair of Tonka toys in yellow, one a grader and the other a bulldozer. It was hard to decide which one you wanted most as a little fella. When I was five years old though, I got a marvellous plastic dog for Christmas, named 'Pluto.' You would drag it with a string, and it would walk behind you.

I must write this about my young childhood. I always felt that I was loved by my Mum and Dad. We may not have had lots of material things, but we always felt loved, appreciated, well fed, and we had a reason to be on this planet. There was always music, especially Mum singing. We all loved that. Sometimes as little kids, if Mum was belting one out, we would cover our ears – she could hit high C. She was in a band when she was younger and had made some vinyl records that we listened to on the record player.

As a kid, I always liked to be working with my father and grandfather (Pa Oxley) and whenever I could, I'd go to the farm with Pa while he tended the sheep. He was always looking out for flies, clipping back the sheep's wool, and putting a white liquid on them to kill maggots. He used to be concerned about 'pinkeye' in sheep too and would always rub the bottom of the bottle of poison around the affected area. I loved getting firewood in the paddocks and helping Dad cut it up on an old saw bench. The engine which ran it was the front half of a T-Model Ford, with a belt off a pulley from the drive to the saw bench. Later, we used Pa's saw, which was a Mobil Co. saw and not run off a pulley from a car engine.

When I was four years old, nearly five, our cat went missing. We could hear him down in the old well, so Dad got a square piece of wood and tied four bits of rope on it, joined to one long rope and lowered it down the well. We were happy to see the cat climbed on the timber and our hero Dad lifted the cat out of the well.

I had a bad experience at five years old, which to this day I haven't forgotten. I knew about Heaven and Hell, God, and the Devil. Somehow, I got my foot stuck down a rabbit burrow and couldn't get it out. I was screaming,

"I've got my foot stuck in the ground, and the Devil's got my foot and won't let me go." I was really scared. I was so bloody happy when my dad got my foot out of that hole. Makes you wonder what little people think sometimes. Dad fixed a lot of things for us kids.

When I was about 10 or 11 years old, my Pa and Nan started paying me a 10-shilling note each week for the work I did for them at their place, which was once a maternity hospital. They called the place 'NIDRI.' I would chop the wood and split chips so the fires could be lit. There were about four fireplaces in that house, so a lot of wood and chips. I would also feed the chooks, collect the eggs, pick the fruit, and pick up fruit from the ground. Another job I would do for my grandmother was making breadcrumbs for her cooking, such as lamb cutlets. She would dry out stale bread in the oven, then I would wash my hands and turn the handle on the mincer to grind the bread down to breadcrumbs.

At home I always did my share of cutting wood and getting the wood in for Mum too. We did this as Dad had to work away on the PMG and would get home most weekends depending how far away, he was. He and his team were working doing pole work and later laying coaxial cable. I remember being with Dad cleaning out dams when young as well. He used a horse, and a scoop called a 'Tumbling Tommy' at Jim Heafy's place. Another job us kids did to earn money was by picking dead wool. This was not a nice job as the sheep would have to be rotten to be able to pull the dead wool out, "a stinking job." I think you could get a pound note from Moses Wool Store for a wheat bag full.

Another job I did for Pa Oxley was to collect the eggs. One day I found a nest with I think about 30 eggs which I had missed in an old shed. Being an enterprising young bloke, I found some egg cartons and made up a stall so I could sell them. My first customer was my Aunty Lola. She bought a dozen as she was out and needed some straightaway to bake a cake. I was stupid and very young, and I didn't know they were that old they were rotten. All I knew was I had to give the money back and copped a good tongue lashing.

Looked like that was the end of starting up my own business. I was destined to always work for someone else.

I would also go and see my Mum's parents, Pop and Nanny Howe and next door to them was my Nan's sister and her husband. I would stop with them sometimes; they never had any children. I loved looking to the skies at night-time with Pop Howe. We would watch for falling stars and wait for SPUTNIK to come over so Pop could point it out to me. Years later I figured out Pop found some peace in the night sky, especially as at that time he had memories only 15 years earlier of being a prisoner to the Japs on the Burma Railway. He also found peace in his vegetable and flower gardens. I can still see him just standing there, watering his gardens, always with a smoke in his hand.

Mum's mother, Nanny Howe, would look after me sometimes too. She had a good sense of humour, like all my family did and she loved playing cards. Nanny Howe always spoke of England and would say she came from there, despite being born in Australia. One time, my uncle showed us all a little movie on 10-millimetre film that he had taken somewhere in England. As he drove along the road in the film, Nanny was watching intently and started telling us what was around the corner and what we would see next, so maybe she had been to England in another life after all.

My old Uncle's father was another favourite of mine, a nice old bloke who died at the age of 102 years old. He was born in about 1860 and had lots to tell me about the old days and what the bushrangers got up to.

Chapter 2

School Years

A t Boorowa school, we wrote with ink. First, it was a wooden pen which you pushed a nib in, then after a while the wooden bit was changed to plastic with a nib which you dipped into the ink well in the desk. I never realised why it was so hard for a left-hander or what we called in those days a 'kacky-hander' to write from left to right with wet ink; how hard it must have been not to smudge their writing. When we were issued with biros, it must have been like heaven for those kids, especially the girls which sat in front of you with long pig tails (which would 'accidentally' dip into the ink well on my desk).

When I was at primary school, I could not read very well, and we had a teacher who would read every so often from the book, Tom Sawyer. I'll never ever forget about the bit when the character of Tom was punished by having to paint the picket fence and how he let his friends 'help' him paint it only if they paid him for being able to do it. I hope I remember that properly, but I loved that character.

All through my primary school, the kids all called me 'Fox' This was because when I started school at age five, my grandmother made me a Davey Crocket hat out of fox skin for the winter, with a foxtail down the back. The kids teased me and called me a fox, and I would cry. Anyway, I must have got over it at some point and to this day some still call me Fox, 61 years later.

When I was five or six years old, I had to be in a school play called 'John Peel' and I had to be dressed in a black coat with tails. Mum made it and, on this day as I am writing, I have that tiny coat in my room. Dad made me a little cropping whip and I had a little plastic trumpet. Despite my fabulous costume, I nearly didn't make it into the play as my teacher, Mrs Clarke, had trouble getting me to gallop like a horse. She said,

"I'll show you one more time," and she started to gallop around the room. We had mats on the floor to sit on, and she slipped on the mat and went face first into the floor. About 45 years after the event, I was having a beer in the club and asked Bugs Riles if he could remember that happening. To my surprise he said,

"Yes I remember, I was the kid who put the pencils under the mat."

Once there was a contest at school where you had to dress up as someone well-known. Mum put me in a white shirt and shorts, tennis shoes and I held a tennis racket. I was supposed to be a great Aussie tennis player of the times, Lew Hoad. I wasn't too impressed about this one.

We frightened a schoolteacher in about fourth class. It all happened down at the wood heap at the school. It was a special place because it had a fire and a copper where the school would heat us up hot chocolate to drink, made on milk. Anyway, I was there at the wood heap when my friends and I found an anteater. Beside her desk, the teacher had a four or five-gallon drum with the top cut out and painted yellow as a wastepaper bin. We thought an anteater in the bin would make a bit of a fun fuss and get the teacher wondering what the noise was. She didn't react too well and for a short while it had worried her. It worried me and my mate a bit too when we had to visit the Headmasters Office.

Thinking of it now, the cuts weren't nice, but the time you spent waiting outside the headmaster's office was scary too. That reminds me, I don't know whether it made the cuts not hurt, but the trick was to pull some leaves cut off a Pepper Tree and rub them on your hands hard, and that was supposed to take the sting out when you got a couple, or six of the best!

Another punishment for me was a stand or cupboard display thing out the front of the class set up for a Punch and Judy puppet show. The teacher had to leave the class for ten minutes and she asked two girls to write the names of anyone who misbehaved on the blackboard. Those girls didn't go much on me and put my name on the board straight away. When the teacher came back, I then had to stand in there like a puppet while the class could laugh at me – not nice.

I completed Primary School in Boorowa and did okay but never passed Maths exams till sixth class. I thank the Deputy Principal Mr Malone, who was also our neighbour, for this. I liked him and he liked me, so we became friends of a sort and because of that, he got into my head and helped me understand Maths well-enough to get my first pass mark ever – 134/200 in sixth class.

We had a Mr Yarham, another next-door neighbour who was also a deputy headmaster at school. At least two, or possibly three of my brothers and me scared the hell out of him one Sunday morning. He was washing his 1962 FB Holden in the driveway before going to church. My brothers and I had got some rifles out of the 'Old House on Wheels' down the back and had the rifles poked through the netting fence. We yelled out "Hey, Mr Yarham," who looked, saw us and the guns, dropped the hose which wriggled on the ground like a snake and hosed him all over. It was funny until Dad got us.

Leading up to the end of 5th class, I ran into trouble with another teacher, Mr Doherty. We had a little Christmas party in our class-room and a classmate, Marguerite McDonald, brought a Xmas cake her mother had made for the class. I knew her mum was not well (she suffered from that thing with the inner ear, and she didn't have good balance), so I decided to yell out loudly "Three cheers for Mrs McDonald!" Next thing, I am out in the playground and Chris Baker comes up to me and tells me that Doherty wants to see me in his room about me yelling in the class next to his. Mr Doherty had a reputation for bashing kids, which I knew all too well, plus I think he suspected me of writing on the walls of the toilet in chalk for all to see "Mr Doherty loves Michelle Chappell," another teacher. I knew if he got me, I would cop-it, so I hatched a plan. I ripped all the buttons off my own shirt and went home from school telling mum that Doherty had grabbed me and ripped my shirt, knowing mum would keep me home the next day. On the last day of term, she confronted Mr Doherty, so for six weeks of holidays I fretted about going back for the new year in 6th class. Mr Doherty never said anything to me though. Cripes, Mum must have given it to him, I thought.

When in years 5 and 6, I had a music teacher named Miss Elizabeth Hurt. In my mind, she was beautiful and looked like Liz Taylor. My mate Doug Riles and me for two years were given the role of locating the record player wherever it was in the school and bringing it to our class for lessons. I told Doug that I loved Miss Hurt and he bloody told her. To me it seemed like for a whole lesson, she sat on my desk and held my hand. I couldn't believe how much I was sweating with fear or whatever it was. I was really embarrassed. I wasn't game to look on the floor under me as I thought I would see a pool of water there. On the last lesson that we would ever have with Miss Hurt, and the last lesson for the year, I told my mate Doug to tell Miss Hurt that I was going to miss her and that I really loved her. I said to Doug to make sure I'd left the room before he told her, so that way I would never see her again. But Doug, well in usual form he told her before I left the room and when I was walking past her to leave and never see her again, she called me over and gave me a big cuddle. There was nothing I could do, but it felt so good and to this day, I still remember Miss Hurt.

Reading, spelling, and writing were not my best subjects or anything else. Sixth class was when I first past maths and I was doing year five reading and spelling in sixth grade. I still can't spell all that well and just couldn't read books. I used to tell people English was my 'bestest' subject. I don't know what I am trying to write my life's story for when I've only read about three books in my life. I received The 'Magic Pudding' as a book award in 1963 and it is still among the many books I have not read. I promised myself when I received this book that when I was old and buggered, I would read it. To this time, I am happy to say I have not read it.

Chapter 3

Larrikin Childhood Memories

had never told anyone, but from about 10 years old I had a bad hernia. I had no idea what it was, but I was embarrassed that my guts seemed to hang out of my groin and then duck back where they should be. I don't know why I kept this my secret because it caused me so much pain! I'll write more about this later when I get to the age of 21 years. At about this same age, I had a large cyst appear on the back of my neck which was very painful. I remember Dad took me to Doctor Kelf and I had to stand between Dad's legs while he sat on a chair and arms around me tight so I couldn't get away, while Doctor Kelf lanced the cyst with what I thought was a razor blade. The doctor worked on this cyst, and I really felt pain that day, screaming quite a bit.

Another time, I got myself badly sunburnt at Wyangla Dam and was in a bad way. I needed a doctor and Mum got him round. Mum told me that when the doctor came round to the house, he was drunk. I needed an injection to put me right, but because the doctor couldn't see what he was doing, Mum had to get the amount out of bottle into the syringe.

When I was about 10 or 11 years old, my mate John Cassidy and I decided to run away from home. Our loose plan was to ride to Yass, jump a goods train to Sydney, stow away on any ship bound for America, then drove cattle down the Chisholm Trail. It was about 100°F, we had no supplies and no water, but took off on pushbikes towards Yass anyway. In those days, this was still a dirt road. By about the Yass side of Kangiara, parched and sweating, we stopped and went down to the creek to get a drink. Right up until we nearly got bitten by a brown snake and decided we weren't that thirsty after all… instead riding to the top of the next hill and eating our fill of fruit at an orchard. Sometime during our rest at the orchard, we had determined we had better go home, even though we had made it about 16 miles so far. Riding back down the hill towards the creek, I saw a PMG ute coming up the hill and said to my mate, John,

"That's Pop Howe, he'll take us home and put the bikes in the back for sure." How wrong was I? He told us off as our mothers were worried sick about us, then he made us get back on those bikes and ride all the way home again in the heat, which we did. We were a long way short of our goal in reaching America. I never knew it at the time, but I would leave home when I was 16 years old and go to 'Wee Waa' NSW…not America.

I also remember 1963, we were sitting around listening to the old Bakelite wireless. They were talking about the naval blockade that JF Kennedy had put out to stop Nikita Khrushchev putting missiles in Cuba. I was very fearful of what was happening as I had heard a lot about war because of my grandfather and uncle being

POWs to the Japs. I followed the news even then, and I knew about Fidel Castro and Russia, and America.

On the wireless there was Dad and Dave in Snake Gully, Blue Hills, and Martin's Corner. A man named Keith Smith had a radio show called 'Keith Smith and the Pied Piper.' He came to Boorowa in about 1962 and recorded one of his shows in the Guild Hall. As part of the show, he asked my younger brother, Paul, to tell him a riddle.

Paul said, "What cot can't you sleep in?"

Keith said, "What?"

Pail said, "Apricot."

Then Keith asked him if he had another riddle, and Paul said, "Is it cruel to stick pins into spiders?"

Paul told Keith "No, it wasn't."

Keith asked "Why?"

Paul said, "It's not, because you sew buttons on flies."

I don't believe that went to air on the show, but it was exciting for my brother.

When I was a kid, I had a crystal set. It amazed me then and still does to this day. How could I hear the wireless station, the music, and the news with no batteries to operate the machine?

We first got a TV in about 1963/64 when I was 11 or 12 years old. We watched shows like 'Whiplash' a story about Cobb and Co. Coaches in the 1800s; Jet Jackson about a flying commando (I think this might have been dubbed because the voice never seemed to match what was on the tv); Rescue Eight; Sea Hunt with Lloyd Bridges; a show called Helicopters...no wait, it was 'Whirlybirds'; Voyage to the Bottom of the Sea; The Beverly Hillbillies ('Jed' was Buddy Ebson, 'Granny' was Irene-something, 'Elly Mae' was Donna Douglas and 'Jethro', I can't remember the actor's name); quiz shows like BP Pick a Box with Bob and Dolly Dyer – Bob would say "call into BP Service Station and tell them Bob sent you." Some of their contestants went on to fame: one was George Black who used to work for PMG, and another was Barry Jones. Whenever he was asked a question, Barry would always rattle on with other information he knew before finally answering the question he had been asked. I used to think he was a bit of a know-it-all, but I still watched.

As a kid I would dress in all black: black boots, black shirt, and black cowboy hat, as did my hero Jess Harper in the western called "Laramie." Like all good cowboys, I would wear that hat in the bath. Once when I did that, I pulled it over my face and Mum found me in the bath like that sound asleep. (That habit of going to sleep with my black cowboy hat over my face strangely saved my life when I was 17 years old, which I will write about later).

I loved western shows, and another show was "Bonanza." There was old Ben Cartwright and his sons, Hoss a big fellow, whose real name was Dan Blocker. Then there was Adam, and of course, the youngest son Little Joe, played by Michael Landon. Of course, the other western was 'Rawhide.' I think the trail boss was Gill Favor, the scout may have been Peter Nolan, the cook was 'Wishbone' who looked after the cooking and the chuck wagon, and of course Rowdy Yates, played by the iconic Clint Eastwood, still alive today. You can see where I got the idea to run away from home and attempt to get to America to drove cattle down the Chisolm Trail.

I could at that time ride a horse, and my mate Johnny Cassidy and I would ride horses for a bloke called Mr Smith. He had horses up past the Red Hill and he would get us to ride them to keep them quiet. One day, one of his horses got out and I caught it and put it in our front yard in town. We had no gate, so my brother Ian got me a length of steel pipe and we tied one side to the fence. As I was tying the other side, the horse nudged the pipe with the bridge of his nose and the pipe flew up, hit me in the forehead and flattened me for a few minutes. The horse bolted. Another time, I was on one of those horses and went down to Skelly's corner. They had a dog, and it barked and chased the horse, which ran down two town blocks to a T-intersection in Campbell Street and threw me. I never got on a horse again till I was 17 years old at Wee Waa...but that's another story. (I was teased at school for a little while because I had to wear jodhpur trousers to school, those stupid 'Pommy' riding duds. The kids gave it to me and said, "Fox's wearing Shit Catchers.")

I remember I think the first time I ever went to the pictures. I saw a movie called 'Smiley' about a bush kid like me. Chips Rafferty was in that; I think he was a policeman. I also saw a movie there called 'Dad and Dave.' I still can see a bit of it in my mind; they drove an old car through a haystack.

My older brother Ian and I watched the wrestling on TV, so we started doing some throws. Unfortunately, my brother had me behind him, got my left arm over his right shoulder and went to throw me and smashed my left arm in three places. I then spent six weeks in hospital with my arm in splints, top half, and bottom half. After four or five weeks, the doctor, who was German, asked me how the exercises were going with my arm? I asked what exercises? He said, "straighten your arm out." I couldn't and had to work on it for some time after that. While I was in hospital, I even learnt to do x-rays. I think we used three or four solutions and would set an alarm clock to take the x-rays out at the right time to develop them.

I always felt a connection to double-wing aeroplanes and I would always draw planes. I did this to a point I got in trouble in scripture when asked to draw Pontius Pilate. I drew a double-winger and another behind it in a dog fight, writing that the dog was Snoopy, and Pontius Pilate was the low-bastard attacking an innocent dog.

When I was 15, Mum brought me a book on double wingers, which I then lost in Wee Waa somewhere. The book was about an Aussie pilot in the First World War in Europe. It turns out it would be one of only three books I've read in my life. The pilot was Sir Gordon Taylor; I think his plane was SOPWITH 74309. Gordon Taylor was amazing to me, as was a man I was told about in primary school, a Douglas Bader known as Tin Legs Bader. He was a real good Englishman and was looked up to and looked after by even the German Luftwaffe.

Some stories my Pa Oxley told me when I was a kid were about the old days when he was working with a few other workers chaff cutting. He said he had an Englishman and an Irishman working with him. I suppose this was in the 1920s or '30s. It was a dusty job, and the Pommy one day was complaining of the heat, with sweat rolling down his face. Pa said the Irishman told the Pom, who hadn't washed for a couple of days, that it wasn't sweat on his face, it was soil erosion.

Another story was that they had made the Irishman the camp cook. When my grandfather asked him,

"How is the job?" the Irishman said in his Irish accent

"Ah tis a greasy job to be sure. I am that greasy the dogs are running along behind me lickin' me shadow." Another time, Paddy had to catch a train in the morning, so he asked the domestic at the Central Hotel to wake him in the morning. That night, Paddy got on the drink big time and a couple of the boys shaved his beard clean off. He caught his train okay, but the domestic servant told all that when she knocked on his door to wake him, he looked in the mirror and yelled

"Hey girly, you've woken up the wrong fella." Old Jim Heafy told me he was a professional fox shooter. He used an old Muzzle Loader. He told me he put powder in then knife blades and nails. He would shoot as the fox ran past a tree and the blades would skin him and the nails would tack the skin to the tree to dry. True story, I think.

My Pa's Uncle Bill used to tell a few tall yarns too. He said he used to break horses and once he was breaking a horse in the house yard that was bucking him that high, he yelled out to his wife and told her the chops she was cooking for lunch were burning. When his wife yelled back,

"How do you know that?" he said he could see them down the chimney. Things you remember when you're a kid - like hearing some stories of your uncles or aunties. One I heard about my Uncle John, one of Mum's brothers was the following. John was caught swearing by my grandmother, and she was going to give him a bit of the switch around the tail, he was only a kid then. John took off and was hiding under the house and Nan said as she couldn't get up to where John was, so she told John his father would sort him out when he got home. Pop went under the house, and John heard him coming. Pop yelled out,

"Are you there John?" as it was dark. John yelled out

"Is that you Dad?" and Pop said

"Yes," to which John replied,

"Is the old bastard after you too Dad?"

While still very young, about 10 or 11 years old, my older sister Marian would pay me two shillings to chop some chips, light the chip heater and run her a bath. This was on Sundays, I think. I would take my tomahawk up to where the old show ground was opposite the hospital because there were old palings hanging off the fence. This went well for quite a time until I ran out of palings and had to source my chips somewhere else. That's when I made a big mistake. I had no idea that Mrs Webb would not look kindly at me tending to her old fence with my tomahawk.

As a kid, I read comics: they were easy to read because of the pictures. I liked the Phantom, and I had both a silver Phantom ring and a rubber one. It was like a stamp that you could press onto the ink pad and if you hit someone, it left the Phantom's skull on their face. We made Bull Roarers out of flat bits of wood from old fruit boxes. We would put a hole near the end of the board and tie a piece of string to it. When we swung it round our heads, it would make a roaring sound, like a crude example of an Aboriginal bull roarer.

Another thing we did in the 60s when frisbees came out (which I don't think Mum and Dad would have liked it), was to make our own frisbees by putting 78 and 45 records in the oven, heating them up and shaping them into our own frisbees. A game by the name of 'Boob Tube' came out then too. Heaps of marbles in a plastic tube with holes through sections – you had to shake all the marbles through to the bottom of the tube. Funny name though.

Once, when I was in hospital with a broken arm, I became friends with a man in the same room as me. His name was Mr Gordon – "Arthur." He was an old man who had a farm called

Langley on the Kenyu Road. I would see him on Friday afternoons over the street, and he would always give me 2/- shillings. When I got out of hospital, I used to ride out to his farm to visit him, and the magpies would swoop me, so I got pegs from mum and cardboard and would secure them to my pushbike so the spokes hit the cardboard and made a noise, and the magpies wouldn't swoop me. At least I thought they didn't...maybe I just couldn't hear them. Mr Gordon lived with his sister, and I called her Miss Gordon. She would always give me cakes and let me play their piano. They were kind and patient with me, and Mr Gordon didn't mind me getting his hat and bending up the sides to make it into a cowboy hat.

When I was 11 years old, I had my appendix taken out by Dr Kelf. On the same night he took my adenoids and tonsils out and took my brother Paul's adenoids and tonsils out at the same time. We were in an open mens' ward, and we were talking so much that night the old blokes said,

"Keep quiet you buggers; you'll be bloody quiet tomorrow after Kelfies finished with you." It made no difference. Next day, we threw up a bit of blood and ate some jelly and ice cream and straight back to annoying those old buggers. One story we heard in the hospital was about a bloke named Ned, who was a patient there. He disappeared, and the nurses couldn't find him for over an hour. One nurse found him sitting on the throne. When she asked,

"What's going on, we've been looking for you?"

He said,

"No paper."

The nurse said, "Haven't you got a tongue?" Ned said, "Yes, but I haven't got a neck like a bloody giraffe."

We had a billy cart that was built from dodgy wheels on a house door. With four of us on board, we roared down garbage tip hill, but it was not exciting enough. We were about 11 years old and should have had more sense, but we lined the centre of the road with empty long neck beer bottles, smashing them with the belly board. The only semblance of sense in this act was we put sunglasses and goggles on to protect our eyes from the broken bottles. I learnt how to answer smart arses when I was a kid on my bike. They used to see me riding past and they would yell out

"Hey mate, your back wheel is going round." I would yell back

"So would you if you had a greased axle stuck up your arse."

On Pa's farm I once got hold of a 22 rifle and near the orchard up a tree, I was shooting rosellas. When I went inside, Nan said

"What have you been shooting?" I thought I was going to cop it, but when I told her what I had shot, Nan said,

"Where are they?" When I said I staked them under the tree she said bring them in you can help pluck them and she made a rosella pie. In the same vein, I had heard the story of Mr Shean when he was asked how many kids him and his missus had; he said,

"Twelve last count, that's the ones the foxes didn't get."

As a kid I heard plenty of stories of Mum's grandfather, Dr Clifford. He was a little bloke, and in the Queens Arms Hotel, he had a run-in with the biggest bloke in Boorowa. The story was he flew up on the big fella's back and left him out to it on the bar-room floor. The doc thought it a fair fight even if the fact was, he had held a handkerchief soaked with chloroform over the big fella's face. It was a technical knockout or TKO.

The doctor's bedside manner was well known. When on a home visit where the father was crook and the mother had passed years before, the kids asked how their dad would be and the doc replied,

"I would be surprised if you kids were not orphans by the morning." On another occasion, he went to the family home of a sick mother and after tending the woman, he noticed a pig in the house lying in a bit of mud under the kitchen table. The husband was told his wife was quite ill and that he should get the pig out of the house. With that, the husband said,

"Cripes doc, do you think the pig could catch it too?" The doc made the local paper by resolving a disagreement with another bloke by setting fire to his abode, which happened to be a tent. When the doc was on his death bed, he went out hearing music as the town band got together outside and played the little doc off on his last journey.

Stories about the Dunny Men in Boorowa were always told to me as a kid. One day as they were emptying the pans in a pit, one bloke dropped 2/- shillings in and straight away opened his wallet and dropped in a one-pound note. When his mate asked,

"Why did you drop that quid in there?" the other bloke said,

"You don't think I am going in there for two-bob do you?" Another bloke was getting a bit hot emptying the pans and tied his coat around his waist, which came undone and fell into the pit. He found a long stick and started getting the coat out, and his mate said,

"You don't want that coat out of that," and the other bloke replied,

"I don't want the coat, I just want my sandwiches out of the pocket."

I don't know why, but old Uncle Jack Riles made this poem up about me as follows:

Steve the reeve
The sick stick Steve
The re-ball, the ribald
The cocktail
Bandy-legged Steve.

What that was all about I still don't know, but that was Jack for ya! After he shot a cat, Jack was told by a concerned lady that he was a cruel, cruel man. Jack told her how his mother was the kindest women God had ever put breath into. The lady said,

"You find that - kind parent cruel son," and Jack just replied,

"Yes, she would always warm the water in the bucket before she drowned the kittens!"

As a kid in Boorowa, I had an Aunty named Diane. She was more like a cousin or sister to me. Diane was a bit of a tomboy, a modern Tom Sawyer. Diane would get us kids together at her home and when Pop wasn't about, she would get us to pick up yellow dead grass. When it was dark, we would help Di roll a big wooden cable drum onto the road in front of our grandparents' house. Us kids would push all the dead grass in the centre holes then Di would light it, get on top and ride or walk on top of it down the dirt street. Us kids loved it, to see Di do her circus act in the dark down that dirt street with flames coming from the holes each side of a cable drum. One day Di was playing golf in an empty block over the road and slogged a ball and yelled out "four." She must have sliced it a bit, and it came across the road towards the house. Her dad, my Pop was there as that ball hit the louvre windows and Pop observed that only two louvres had broken and just yelled out back to Diane,

"No, only two." Pop always had a sense of humour.

As a kid, I always carried a pocketknife. It was just a normal thing to do in those days. Like most kids, we would go to dams to find tadpoles and keep them in jars and watch evolution as those little swimmers turned into frogs. We always had pets like dogs, cats, and rabbits, and at one stage in Boorowa, Dad brought home a little joey kangaroo. Dad hung a cut-down wheat bag on the back of the laundry door to act as a pouch. It was nice to see that joey dive into the bag to sleep after his bottle.

My older brother Ian ran away from home and Mum was very worried for him until our Uncle Brian, who had searched all over town for him, found him in an old water tank we used to stack wood in at the back of the house. At least when I ran away from home, I made it halfway to Yass, while Ian never even got off our house yard. As kids, Ian and I made a boat out of a brand-new sheet of corrugated iron and when Dad found out he thought we were stupid, but we weren't that stupid. We took the boat up to the Red Hill on a billycart and as we knew the dam was full of leeches, we decided to put Leo our Labrador dog in to test the buoyancy of the boat. Leo wasn't a good captain – he swam out and didn't go down with the ship.

When my older sister Marian was being taught to drive the Holden station wagon by Dad with four or five kids in the car (which with us wild buggers, couldn't have been easy), she used to have trouble taking off. We would start to move off and the car would jerk a bit, and sometimes stall. Dad would always tell Marian to "ride the clutch." Ian and I thought it a good idea to try and make Marian a miniature horse saddle to place on the clutch pedal as dad was always telling her to ride it.

One day after Marian got her licence a few of us kids and our Aunty Diane were taken over to Papas' Café. We were about to get out of the car when Basil, a drunk, flew past the side of the car. Brother Lewis was standing in front of the café window when the drunk's car mounted the footpath, hit a veranda post that came down just missing Lou, and went through glass at the front of the café. The drunk got out of his car raving on about his brakes that had failed, and I heard some new language I hadn't heard before. Not from the drunk but from Diane directed at him and he could not have been uncertain of what Di thought of him. As a kid, I always loved having Di about as it seemed that being around her, it was never boring. If nothing was going on, she could always stir up action. This was my childhood in Boorowa, well some of it!

Chapter 4

Gerringong

think we moved to Gerringong in January 1965. I still remember nine of us all in a 1962 Holden station wagon with a trailer behind, loaded to the hilt. Even had the chooks in crates. Going down Macquarie Pass in front of us, there was an accident. We were held up there for a couple of hours. I remember watching people walking past us and looking at all our stuff on the trailer. I remember thinking they probably think we looked like the Beverly Hillbillies.

We moved into a rental house in Campbell Street, Gerringong, up behind Cronin's Pub. My older brother Ian and I started school at Kiama High School. I think we were there for a bit over a year. I find it hard to believe, but I still remember the 'Kiama School Song.'

I loved it at Gerringong – I loved the ocean, Werri Beach, Boat Harbour and Seven Mile Beach at Gerroa, climbing the cliffs and collecting fossils. An old lady Mrs Chittick at the café at Gerringong told me when she was a kid, she saw Kingsford Smith take off the beach at Gerroa and did the first flight across to New Zealand.

At Kiama High School, I had to learn to stand up for myself as I was picked-on a bit. Once I showed them, I would fight and not take it, it all stopped and then I made some great friends, and all was okay. It could be a bit dangerous at times at school. At that time there was a show on TV about Japanese Ninjas and the kids were making star knives in the metalwork room. Sometimes you might walk past the wooden classroom and next thing star knives would come from nowhere and stick in the wall beside you...bit scary.

On one occasion, the boys were sticking pins out the front of their shoes and would kick you in the back of the leg. This happened to me and when I made it to Maths class, I pulled the pin out of my leg to find my sock and shoe filling up with blood. Mr Manwaring took me to the First Aid lady, Mrs Cameron and then to the Headmaster Mr McFaull, who was related to us. He gave me a cuppa and biscuits and asked who did it. I said I didn't know. At lunchtime, I punched the bastard out in the playground...so back into the Principal's Office. Again, Mr McFaull asked why I did it and again I said I didn't know. All my mates thought I copped it from the principal, but Mr McFaull told me not to say he just gave me another cup of tea and biscuits. Mr McFaull then called a general assembly and put a stop to the 'pin thing' and the 'star knives.'

The rest of my time at Kiama High School, I just loved every day of school, learning and cricket. We played cricket near the Kiama pool near the harbour, where once we watched a fishing boat come into the harbour and sink. They tried to teach me to swim at that rock pool. I was a bad learner at that too and I still can't swim to save my life. I loved body surfing and I'll never forget getting dumped three times. Every time I went to get a breath in, I thought this is it, another wave and I am going to die. Next thing a wave got me and put me on the beach. I just laid there. My friends raced up thinking I was dead, but I was just stuffed with no breath and no energy. Someone was looking after me that day.

We hadn't been in Gerringong all that long when I was down at the Boat Harbour on my pushbike watching some fishermen cleaning their catch and one had a 4ft shark. I asked about it and the fishermen asked me if I wanted it. I said I'd have to go home and ask mum. Mum said bring it home, and I wrapped it in my towel and tied it on my bike and pushed it home about 2 kms. Dad cut it into steaks, and it was nice to eat. Being a kid from the bush, I thought shark was no good to eat.

On Sundays, Dad would load us all in the old station wagon to do the bottle run from Kiama to Gerroa. We would pick up empty drink bottles in caravan parks and even along Mount Pleasant between Kiama and Gerringong. We would cash the bottles in at Mrs Chittick's at Gerringong and go down to Pyke's fish shop and buy our fish and chips and a brick of ice cream for Sunday night tea. On another outing, I remember seeing the Elvis Presley movie 'Blue Hawaii' at the Gerringong pictures.

Our neighbours over the road in Campbell Street were a lovely family, the Stuarts. I can remember their kids; one boy who they called Roy Boy and one girl called Leila. Roy Stuart, the father, worked for the Gerringong Council and I believe he did so for many years. I remember as a 13-year-old watching Roy play football for Gerringong, and I saw him get a try from one end of the field to the other. I thought how good he was, especially to be able to run like he could at that age. He was probably about 40. When Roy and his wife had another baby in

1965, mum made them some paddy cakes and stew a few times, which they really appreciated. I know after we left 22 Campbell Street, Roy had won some money in the lottery and bought the house we used to rent. I think the person Dad rented that house from was a P.J. Noble.

One of our friends, David Fielding's brother, I think his name was Richard, rode a skateboard down the hill from shops at Gerringong all the way down towards Kiama or Omega Railway Station. What bravery we all thought in 1965. I was once with my brother and Kevin Friend from Boorowa, who was working with Dad on the PMG. Kevin caught a shark off Werri Beach, and we put it in the boot of his FC Holden to take home and put on the footpath of Gerringong's Main Street, at the top of the hill. It was alive and the Main Street being steep, it took itself down the footpath, past the shops and caused a bit of a stir, with people coming out of the café to see a shark heading down the footpath.

At Kiama School and in Gerringong it was good to know all the different nationalities. We all got along; it didn't matter where you came from on the planet.

I had a pushbike that had no brakes, so I saved up some money, and for my bike I bought a Speedo. There were good steep hills and the one going down to Boat Harbour at Gerringong would be great to race down there. I couldn't stop, couldn't get my foot on back wheel and straight down the slipway and into the Pacific Ocean. One day at Werri Beach, I was chasing my friend Richard Carr on a track near the cliff at the pool. We were on our bikes and Richard hit the brakes. I had no brakes and swerved to miss him and went over the cliff. It was like riding off the roof of a house. As I was heading headfirst to the flat grey rocks, I put both my hands out to break the fall and sprained both my wrists.

One teacher at Kiama, Miss Hicks in science, got a kid from Fox Ground to bring in a rabbit for dissection. First, she tried to wring its neck, didn't work, so she tried a rabbit chop to the back of its neck. That didn't work, so she drowned it. With all the stress that rabbit went through, it had quite a bit of urine in it so as she nailed it to a wooden board to dissect it, she squeezed its belly, and it squirted urine over her. We thought it was good, from death the rabbit got its revenge. The same teacher got a hydraulic jack to teach us about hydraulics. She pumped the jack up and tried to push it back down. It would not go down and she explained you had to loosen a hydraulic release valve and could even take it all the way out. Then she pressed down on the jack... and the girls in the front got sprayed with oil!!

Chapter 5

15 Hogarth Avenue, Warilla (Railway Work)

We moved to Warilla at the end of 2nd Semester in high school. I never told anyone, but I was so sad to leave Gerringong and my friends there. The house we moved into was a brand-new housing commission home (I've just realised that in my life, I've never lived in a brand-new home besides that one. The house I now live in back in Boorowa I built myself in 1986 as an owner builder).

I didn't like the new school and I didn't like the fact that there were drugs in the school and good-looking girls trying to get you to try them. I believe I only travelled on the school bus a couple of times because I didn't like kids pushing drugs on the bus. I decided I would ride my pushbike to school over the hill from Mount Warrigal Primary School and down through paddocks to Lake Illawarra. I could be wrong, but I think I rode onto the road that ran along the lake then to Oak Flats High. So, as if I wasn't getting enough exercise riding to Oak Flats and back each day, I got myself a job as a paperboy in a paper shop at Windang. I would ride the bike to Oak Flats High, ride home, then ride to Windang the other side of the bridge from Lake South, over Lake Illawarra. I would roll up papers and put them in my bags on the bike rack which dad had made for me, delivering to customers' homes. I would then go back to the paper shop, pick up loose papers and go to the caravan parks on the lake's edge around Windang and on the way to Port Kembla, selling papers at Primbee Caravan Park. I must have been fit in those days riding from Mount Warrigal to Oak Flats, all-around Windang delivering papers, then to all the caravan parks selling papers before riding back to Warilla, which I did for over a year. It just hit me that when I was doing my paper run, I was attacked on the northern side of Lake Illawarra on sand by two blokes on motorbikes. I thought I would die. One bloke sat on my chest filling my mouth with sand, while the other one was jumping on my bike. When the bastard pushing sand in my mouth got up from me a bit, I kneed the mongrel where it hurt and got away. I still sometimes dream about those bastards.

At the age of 15, I left school. Even though it was my last year, the English teacher had written on my report that I should apply myself more next year! For the first time in my life, I took notice and as my father had always said I should always get a good safe government job, I applied for a job on the railway (even though I always wanted to be a builder or carpenter.) To my delight, I got that job, and I must say now, my twelve months working for them, it was the first time I had ever been on a train.

The hours we worked on the railway were funny times. One time, a man from the old blue weatherboard station house near the crossing came over. It was dark and he was trying to annoy me in the office. He wouldn't leave so I hit him, and he hit me back, knocking me over the parcels in the office. I punched him again and he wound up on the platform outside the door. To this day I don't know how I managed this as he was a big man. Thinking things were over I went out the door, but he punched me again, knocking me onto the platform and when I got up, he hit me again, driving my head into the chrome water bubbler. The next thing I knew I was riding my bike down the Princess Highway towards Kiama – I turned and went back to the station, but it was already all locked-up. To this day, I do not recall locking-up or leaving. I told my Mum about this incident, and she told me years later when I was working in Wee Waa on cotton farms that the bastard was dead; had blown his brains out in a picture theatre in Wollongong.

Another time I thought I was going to die, I raced my pushbike flat out for a good distance and when I got off the bike, it felt like my temples were going to explode, my heart was racing that quick. Everything in my vision turned to a bright white light and I couldn't see anything but the light. I sort of resigned myself that this was the end, and I would die, then my heart started slowing down until it seemed a long time between beats, and I thought 'where is the next beat?' Then the beats became steady, and I could see again. I don't remember being scared to die, but I was happy to know I would not be dying that day either.

One night while working on the railway I had a dream. I was walking along the track with the kerosene lights to swap them over in the 'home and distant' signals towards Oak Flats from Albian Park Rail. I dreamt I saw smoke coming up through the tracks and rock ballast. The next day, I was walking along the track with the kerosene lamp not far from the distant signal (sometimes called the Distant Stick) when I saw smoke just as I'd dreamt of it, rising from the tracks. I put the signal light down and walked down the bank to inspect a small wooden bridge under the tracks, where it looked like the timbers had been burning for some time. I ran back to tell the Station Master, Mr Albert Rivers Vickers. The signals were put back and a train crawled up to the home signal then they let it into station. The gangers were informed, and they put the bridge on safe working – trains could only cross it at a slow pace until the work was done on the bridge repairs.

I was talking to my dad one day at the station when we saw a woman in a mini skirt, and he said if it were any shorter, she would need fur lining on the bottom to keep her neck warm. At the station in those days, there was an 'honour tin' with change in it. People could put money in the tin and take out their change to buy the Sydney papers. I never remember the tin being short on 'different days.' One day at Albion Park Station, the Station Master and I had to help and stay with a girl who raced a horse across the track, it slipped on the tracks and fell on the girl. She was knocked out with head injuries. I stayed with her while the Station Master raced back to the station to ring for an ambulance. We checked up on the girl and after a few weeks she regained her memory, and she was AOK.

I also worked at Oak Flats Station. It was a one-man station with no safe working required for signals and such, and there were lights on the crossing. One day I was on a platform near the office, and a train was pulling up. Just about stopped when a girl stepped off the train in the wrong direction. She lost her footing and as the train was still moving, the lower part of her legs went down between the carriage and the platform. I pulled her out of there and we were so happy she suffered no injuries. The platform was made of very rough timber. At Oak Flats Station you would put a remittance bag on the train with the mail bags at 7-16 pm at night and travel in the guard's van to Albion Park for an hour and then go back to Oak Flats till 10.44 pm before knock-off and a ride home to Mount Warrigal.

One cold and dark winter's night, I got into the guard's van for the trip to Albion Park. I noticed when we got going, the guard wasn't present, and his coal fire was nearly out. Then I saw a coffin, which frightened me no-end. I climbed down the side of the van and jumped to the back of the carriage on front of the guard's van. The train was an old red rattler. The back door was locked, so I took out my biro pen and used it as a key. Don't know why I would fear a coffin, but I was and made my get away while the train travelled from Oak Flats to Albion Park Rail.

One Monday morning at Albion Park Rail about 5:30 am an old bloke had brought his weekly ticket for the worker's train to the steelworks before buying the paper. I asked him how he was going, and he said,

"Never felt better." He went out, sat on the seat near the door of the office to read his paper, had a massive heart attack and died. The Station Master got me to help him get him on the canvas stretcher which hung on the wall, and we put him in the ladies waiting room and locked the door till the ambulance arrived. That was not a nice experience at 15 years old.

One morning when riding to work, I still hadn't received my railway uniform and I was stopped by the milkman. He grabbed me by the throat and said

"Got you, you little bastard. You are the one been pinching milk money." I had to convince him it wasn't me and I worked on the railway. I was 15 years old, and the Station Master slowly got me to change, pull off signals, cross trains, changing points, taping trains in and out, getting staffs out, putting them back in instruments, passing the staff to moving trains. I could even do that one-handed with a light engine and they were fast just a single engine alone. I watched everything the Station Master and the ASM did. I would write trains details in and out, put staff numbers on scrap paper for the Station Master to later enter into the Train Register Book in his own hand.

One day while riding my bike home from Albion Park Station, I was on the Warilla side of Millers Hotel, which was open country with cattle in paddocks at that time. A truck came up behind me, hitting me with the front left guard. I was lucky I never went under the truck, but instead was thrown up in the air, the mirror and side of the truck hit me in the backside and the top of my legs before throwing me into a barbed-wire fence. A nurse in a VW Beetle came to my side and another car pulled the truck up. The nurse got me his name, licence number and address. Everyone was happy I was okay, and I told them I was good. I had to push my bike home about 3 kms and when I got home, I told Mum what happened. Next morning, Mum woke me early to go to work and I couldn't get out of bed. The muscles in the top of both my legs were nearly twice their normal size. Off to the doctor and a few days off.

On the railways, once a year, the Commissioner for Railways, Mr Kusker, I believe his name was, would inspect the stations. This was 1968. He would check out stations, and you would get an award if your station was the nicest, tidiest station. Station Master Mr Vickers got all of us Junior Station Assistants to bring stag horns and pot plants over from the Station Masters house. The station, gardens and toilets were hosed down and cleaned. The place looked good. The Commissioner came down from Sydney checking out the South Coast Line. I think the train number was '99' and it was called the 'Flyer.' The station was inspected, and he got back on the 'Flyer' and went on down to Nowra. The flyer arrived back about 1.15pm. The Station Master told me to make sure the Commissioner was on the train. I don't even think the train was past the starter signal before we started taking the Stag Horns and plants back to the residence. The station won an award that year for its lovely, if temporary, presentation.

Another thing that happened while working, we had trucks on the main line late at night when the station would normally be unmanned. There was a shortage of empty railway trucks because of a strike in Darling Harbour. It was customary to pull the home signal off for a late workers train from Port Kembla to give a green go signal, but the distant signal would be red. This meant the driver was to proceed with caution to be able to stop at the home signal. This night, there were no signals-off and the Assistant Station Master heard the train coming fast and said get under the goods shed. The train crashed into the empty wagons on the mainline and carriages tipped over. Luckily no one was killed. During the enquiry it was found the driver was so used to coming in with a green light on the home signal, he never slowed down. It was discovered the driver thought he had seen a green light, but it turned out just down the other side of the station was a pub called the Oaks Hotel, and the neon sign had a green Oak Tree on the sign, which had tricked the driver. The next day me and my mate stuck signs 'GO RAILWAY THE SAFE WAY' on the carriages laying on their sides in the loop.

One day I asked the Station Master if there were any trains coming from Shell Harbour. He said no, so I asked if I could take the pump trike to change the kerosene lamps in the distant and home signals. He said yes. On the trike, I was pumping away up a slight hill towards Oak Flats when I saw a light engine fly down the hill towards me. A light engine is an engine only. I had to quickly throw the trike off the track. The old bastard could have got me killed.

When I was working at Shell Harbour Station at Dunmore Quarry, I had to put up red lights on the Highway to stop traffic for the trains going into and out of Dunmore Quarry, closing and opening gates on the railway crossing at the station. Thinking of it now, that was a big responsibility for someone at 15 years of age. We had people's lives in our hands. I didn't work much at Shell Harbour, but I remember the station was a long way from Shell Harbour through open dairy country. People coming to pick up parcels now and again complained the station was a long way. The Station Master, Maurice Gun, told me if the customers said that I was to tell them that if they built the station in Shell Harbour, it would be too far from the tracks.

I remember a guard who worried me a bit. I think he was mainly on goods trains and his name was Jack. He may have been trying to scare all the young juniors on the South Coastline, but we all spoke to each other about him. If he had occasion to speak to me, he would say in a weird voice.

"Here's a nice little boy, would you like to ride in my van with me to Dapto?" He could have been joking, or in my mind he could have been old paedophile.

The railway phones linking all stations were magneto phones. Each station was rung by winding the handle and tapping the button to give a short or long ring. I am sure Oak Flats was four shorts and Albian Park was three shorts and a long – I could be wrong but after all this was 1968, but I would nearly bet on it.

All that year I worked all public holidays as I realised you not only got paid for them, but I also thought they got added to your annual leave. I think I was earning about $22.00 a fortnight. Like my friends on the railway, other Junior Station Assistants, we used our free railway pass tickets not to Sydney, but to the City Circle. We could go anywhere for nothing on the City Circle. We went to see the AMP building, which was Australia's tallest building at the time, going right to the top of it. It freaked me out a bit.

Other things I remember in my work on the railway were how hard it was to swing up the S truck doors and lock them into position and emptying K trucks. They had hay on them during the strike at Darling Harbour. We would roll the sheets (tarpaulins) and ropes up in the yard after trucks were unloaded. Sometimes, we would have empty trucks in the loop. We would use a crowbar-type thing, maybe called a pinch-bar, bent at the bottom, and you would jam it under the truck wheels and push down so you could move railway trucks weighing tons. Once a week, you would take a bucket of oil, a paint scraper, a brush, and a key to change, open or close the points. I would scrape the points and then paint fresh oil on them. You could only take the key out once the points were set back to normal and you couldn't pull signals off if the key was out.

Another job was to take a bucket with a stick that had a metal point and get down on the tracks in front of the station picking up rubbish paper and sometimes toilet paper (even though people were not supposed to use those toilets on those trains whilst in the station). Shit job, literally. All brass taps were to be cleaned and polished with Brasso[1], the wooden toilet seats

---

[1] A brand of cleaner to polish brass

hosed down and scrubbed with large blocks of sand soap and hosed off. We also had to put phenol disinfectant in the toilet pans. All the signal leavers had to be shined-up and cleaned. The Station Master or I would hang on to pull levers to operate the signals and when you had them cleaned properly, even though they were plain steel, they would shine that much they looked like chrome.

When I was selling tickets from the ticket office, if a young girl asked for a ticket to say Wollongong, if I thought I could get away with it I would ask 'Is that pensioners?' Monday mornings early before the first train, a worker's train to Port Kembla was always the busiest selling ticket as that was when you sold most of your worker's weekly tickets. I remember I played a trick with another JSA, Steve White. We nicknamed him White Ants. I was riding home from morning shift at Albion Park, past Oak Flats station one Thursday, when I thought I would jump on the phone at the end of the platform. I rang the four shorts for Oak Flats and White Ants answered the phone. I changed my voice and when Steve answered, I told him I was 'D.S. Daily,' the District Superintendent of Wollongong. I told him he was in trouble as a couple of women had reported to me that he'd been heard swearing and been seen spitting on the platform. Poor Steve was worried, then I asked him,

"Do you know where my office is at Wollongong Station?" He said,

"Yes, Sir." I then said,

"I see you are on afternoon shift next week – be at my Wollongong office at 9am Monday."

He said, "Yes Sir." I didn't let him worry for long as I called in on the Friday at Oak Flats Station when he told me what had happened to him the day before and what DS Daily had said to him. Then I said did he ask you to be in his office at Wollongong Station at 9am Monday? He said,

"How did you know that?" Then he called me a "Bloody bastard."

About two weeks later, I was on the shift at Oak Flats Station. I think it was about 8.30 pm at night. I came back from the hour on the train at Albion Park and there were some young girls there who helped me bring parcels up from the end of the platform where the guard had left them. The girls and I were in the office, a couple sitting on some parcels, when a man came to pick up parcels. A little later, the phone called with four shorts. I picked it up and said Oak Flats Station. The person on the other end said, "This is SM Albert Rivers Vickers, I believe you have some young women in the office and that's not on." I immediately said,

"Get stuffed you stupid old bastard" and hung up. I told the girls about it and said that was Steve White getting me back for how I fooled him. I sure got a shock when Mr Vickers walked in and blew the bloody hell out of me and told those girls to get out of the office and go home. I had stooged myself!!

Whilst living at Warilla in the housing commission area, I had a few occasions to witness some bad goings on. There was a fire in a Valiant car in the driveway in the house behind ours. I climbed up on our shed and could see it going up. I found out later that a young man was in the car, he had poured petrol through the car and over himself and set it on fire. He had been going with the lady from the house. She was an older woman and had called an end to their relationship, and because of that the young man killed himself in that terrible way. Another incident I saw in my time at Warilla, which I never wanted to see, was a grown man in another house down behind ours, who threw his 2-year-old daughter through the back-screen door. This was the same bastard who built a wooden dog kennel and when the dog wouldn't come out, he smashed the kennel with an axe. It seemed I would witness this stuff from the top of Dad's shed.

When I had to catch the train to Albion Park at 7.15pm from Oak Flats for an hour and do a handover, a man would wait till I had the office shut and locked and standing on the platform with mail bags and leather locked remittance bag ready to put in the guard's van before he showed up. I would ask him where he was going, and he'd say Wollongong. I had no time to open the office so one night I had a single ticket to Wollongong in my pocket and made him pay for his ticket, which was 42c. Incidentally, I smoked Marlboro cigarettes and they cost 42c. When you pulled a ticket out of the ticket rack that meant the next ticket didn't stick out so when you did your handover, you would see that and account for that sale in your handover. The tickets were all numbered in sequence so that was how you would account for the number of tickets sold. When I did my hand over the next ticket somehow was sticking out that bit, so it was not accounted for in handover and I forgot and the 42c was in my pocket, so the handover balanced. Was I in for a shock when I arrived at Oak Flats next day to start work and take over from Mr Harold Goodwin. There were two blokes there to greet me from the Investigation Branch. Bloody Goodwin never gave me a chance to explain what happened and as his handover didn't balance and was short 42c, he checked the numbers against 42c tickets to Wollongong and they didn't add up. He was making out I got him for the 42c so I could buy a packet of Marlboro. It scared me a bit with these investigation fellows, but when I explained it to them, they believed me, and all was well in the world again. I wasn't too impressed with bloody old Goodwin after that!

While working on the railway, the Assistant Station Master A.S.M. Ray Fittness got me a second job sawing timber at South Coast Timer Supplies, which I did part time. Interesting work but could be dangerous unless you were careful. Another JSA worked there too, and I don't know how he got his nickname, but it was Buttercup; could have been because of Buttercup Bread. All the JSAs I worked with from that time had nicknames of some kind or other: Steve White 'White Ant,' Phillip Atkinson 'Pom,' Lester Crane 'Aussie' and Peter Stanford 'Aussie.'

I had another job there while on the railway. I would help Fitto out on a milk run around Jamberoo. The run was great to do as we would take a truck, drive out to Jamberoo, pick up the papers from the newsagency, pick up bread from the bakery and then pull up to the wooden stands at the gateways to the properties, wheeling the drums of milk onto the back of the truck. We would leave the papers and bread for the dairy farmers in a wooden box on the platform then take the milk to the Milk Factory at Albion Park rail. In the factory, there were big round tanks or vats of milk and sometimes when I was rolling sheets on a hot day, I would dip my mug in for a cold drink of milk. We had an electric jug in the office at Oak Flats station, so I could have a cup of coffee and milk. One night in Oak Flats station, I was sick of eating my sandwiches, so I laid the bar heater on its back and found I could toast my sandwiches.

One day while working the morning shift at Albion Park some kids came and told me there was a funny man down the Oak

Flats end of platform and he was talking to the little kids, wearing a dress. I sneaked down the platform and he couldn't see me for the toilets. He was bloody weird, so I went back to the office and told the SM who rang the police. I'll never forget that day, it was a public holiday and the traffic going past the station was very slow. Between the station and the Princess Highway was a park. The police came, this weirdo in a dress took off running through the park and a copper did a great tackle on him. I still wonder if the people in the cars seen this and thought 'Police brutality, smashing an old woman to the ground.' It did look funny to me.

One day after a shift at Albion Park, I was riding my bike towards Oak Flats. I was just before the Oaks Hotel when I nearly got hit by a VW Beetle. There were four young fellows in it, but I still abused them. They made their intentions clear, so I raced into the car park at the pub while they chased me in that Beetle. I went in and out of cars and got to the fence and threw my bike over, getting onto the railway track and away. Further up the track, I came out and back on the Princess Highway. I was just on the turn-off from the Highway at Oak Flats station when there they were onto me again and yelling out at me. I raced the bike straight under the Oak Flats station which was high above the ground about 6 to 8 feet. I flew straight out from under the platform onto railway tracks and jumped up onto the platform. JSAs Peter Standford and Lester Crane were there. They went out and gave a bit of mouth to those creeps, jumping on their motorbikes and calling for me to look after the station. It was an hour at least when they got back on their bikes. They said they chased them mongrels all the way to Kiama then came back.

Another night I was working at Oak Flats when I saw some bikies park at the station. I shut the office door and heard them go into the waiting room next to the office. I could hear them smashing things, and one said,

"Let's set fire to this." I yelled out and said I had called the police and they better get going. As they went past the office door, which opened onto the platform, they slid the bolt across and said,

"Get out of there if you can, mongrel." I then rang Albion Park Station and my ASM Ray Fittness came up to let me out. There wasn't much damage to the waiting room, but they had started tearing the timetables off the black painted boards they were stuck to and had set them on fire.

There was a young German bloke named Ziggy who loved making me give him one of my smokes after he'd get off the 8.30pm train into Oak Flats. He must have also loved Marlboro smokes. Anyway, I got sick of him pushing me around for a smoke, so I scraped a heap of red stuff off the packet of red head matches and carefully unpacked the tobacco out of a cigarette and packed about two thirds down in smoke stuff off match heads then repacked the rest of the tobacco. Ziggy, I thought, I'm ready for you. He got a smoke out of me, and I watched him across the other side of the track. It was dark and next thing that smoke flared up. He wasn't impressed, but I didn't get the flogging I expected, and Ziggy never asked for another smoke from me.

There was a young fella Jorge Jeske I went to school with at Oak Flats High. He was also from Germany. He gave me a big talk at the station at Oak Flats about the world going to end in two years' time. He was a Seventh Day Adventist or something like that and really believed the crap he was telling me. Then he asked for an apprentice ticket to Port Kembla. When I sold it to him, I asked him how long his apprenticeship was for. He said four years, so I just took a bit of time explaining to him he was wasting his time doing a four-year apprenticeship when the world was ending in two years.

When I turned sixteen, Dad and Mum put me on a plane for my first flight for my birthday. We took off from Albion Park Airport in an underwing plane and flew over Lake Illawarra. At some stage, I was looking at instruments and the pilot said to look at the wing tip. He banked the plane and then I was looking down the wing straight into Lake Illawarra. That was a great, memorable birthday present. Mum gave me a book as well that birthday. It was written by Sir Gordon Taylor, a WW1 pilot in France. He was an Aussie who flew a Sopwith Camel or Pup; I think the engine was a ninety horsepower Le Rhone motor and I think the plane was Sopwith 74309. That book is one of three books I've read (and I lost it while at Wee Waa).

One mate I had in Warilla was Patrick Slater. He was a Pom, and he told me his mum was one of the people in England who tracked and plotted the course of German aircraft and ours by radar to help the war effort. She was a lovely lady. Patrick had that Pommy sense of humour. He was quick. One day at school someone yelled when they threw a ball "Catch it!" Patrick stepped back looking round the ground and yelled out,

"Where? Did I walk in it?" He and I went into a corner store in Warilla, and he asked the Italian owner if he had any hundred and thousands, when the owner said,

"Yes," Patrick said,

"Give us a thousand black ones."

One day we wanted to get the attention of a few good-looking girls. We were on our bikes, and I said why don't we race flat out at each other and at the last second, I go left, and you go right. It worked, we got their attention and nearly needed the attention of the ambulance. What a stupid thing to do eh!

Chapter 6

Wee Waa Cotton Farms

'll start off this way – I was just 16 when I caught the Northwest Mail train to find out just what could be in life for me. I always remember that at the time I didn't know I wasn't just going up there to Wee Waa on holidays from the railway. I thought I would return to the railway and was only just using up my free railway pass. I had originally organised to go to Melbourne on a train but changed my mind, which turned out to be a good decision as I could have been on a train that crashed. I think it was in past Albury in Victoria; it was the Southern Aurora Feb 1969. Anyway, I caught the Northwest Mail, and I don't know why but I have always remembered stopping in very early sunlight in a place called Werris Creek. There was a lot of big grain silos there. I got off at Narrabri Station and caught a two-car diesel train to Wee Waa.

At Narrabri Station, I remember thinking to myself that was the first time in my life that I was disoriented to the point I did not know the directions of North or South; it didn't feel good to me. Anyway, I made it to Wee Waa and stayed with my sister Marian, her husband and baby daughter. My brother-in-law told me of a job going in Mack Dickinson's Golden Fleece Service Station serving petrol and cars. I thought this could be different for me, so I saw Mack and the pay was a lot better than $22.00 a fortnight and Mack said he'd put me on and teach me to do the car services. I caught the train back to Sydney and then down to Warilla or Oak Flats, all the way home worried what my Mum and Dad would say, especially as it had only been a year since my dad told me I could only leave school if I got a real secure Government job.

When I got home from Wee Waa, Mum was there as she always was, so I thought I would run it by Mum about going back to Wee Waa. Dad was not back home from work at the time, and when I told Mum what I wanted to do, Mum said,

"I don't want you doing that but anyway your father will sort you out when he gets home!" When Dad got home, I told him what I wanted to do. I was really worried how Dad would take it, and I have never been so surprised when Dad said,

"It's your life, I can't stop you from doing what you want to do, but I only ask you this. Don't ever hurt anyone in your life and always do the right thing by everyone." To that, I promised my father I would do as he had asked of me. So back to Wee Waa in the Northwest of NSW to take up my next job as what they called Service Station Attendant and as the ad on TV said at the time, I was a 'Stanley.' I think the ad said, "If you want your oil, water or tyres checked, just ask Stanley."

While at what would be my first stint at the Service Station, I also took on some other work on farms as second jobs. I went out hay racking and putting hay that was cut into wind rows and then we would bale it. I remember working with two old blokes hay carting. One day I drove the tray-top truck while the other bloke stacked the hay. On my first day throwing bales, it nearly killed me. I had to throw them up on a cleared spot on back of the truck for the stacker as the truck was driven around the paddock. I don't know why we didn't have a mechanical loader, but I suppose that was why I was employed. The truck had a big hole in the exhaust, and it popped and burbled along, which attracted emus to follow us as they thought the sound was like an emu. After the first day, I was really worn out and the heat, and the hard work had knocked me about. The next day, I was back at the hay carting, and I think the two old blokes were surprised to see me. They asked how I felt and after I told them, the old buggers taught me how to rest the bale on my right knee and knee the bale up with my leg. This made the work a lot easier as I was not a big lad and never was more than nine stone ringing wet.

I found the Monday work at the Service Station much easier. At other times, I would go out part-time marking on cotton. This was when they sprayed the cotton from aeroplanes such as Pornee Grumman Ag-Cats Double Wingers and Ag Wagons. I was told that as the planes come towards you with sometimes wheels clipping the cotton, that you had to do 22 rows at a time. You would wave a flag in daylight and a torch at night for the pilot to line up on you so they would know what they had sprayed with the chemical. Some of the chemicals I remember were Herkafein, Atrazine, DDT defoliants and at one stage it was said they had some defoliant from Africa, which was Agent Orange. They used to say if you took eight steps as the plane got close, the wheels and the prop would miss you: advice worth taking.

I would also go out cotton checking at times with my brother-in-law. He was a bug checker for chemical companies such as Lanes Chemicals, Amalgamated Chemicals, and Bayer Chemicals. After a bug check and bug count in the cotton, he would advise the growers of what chemical to use and the rate with which to use it. I remember some of the bugs we looked for were looper, rough bollworm, heliothids, red spider, thrip, Rutherglen bug, and tip borers. Two or three days after the spraying - I only did this a few times with my brother-in-law - you would walk through the paddock and do what they called spot checking to see what sort of kill you got. As my brother-in-law did this for a living, he was more exposed to the chemicals, as they have what they call a residual time to stay active. I specifically remember I was marking on a property called Widgeewaa one day and was told to tell some people in a house on the property to close all their windows, so any drift from the spray didn't get into the house. I thought later what about the water tanks on the house for their drinking water. It was apparent to me how deadly the chemicals could be, when I noticed tiny dead fish floating on the surface in the main channel. My brother-in-law ended up with oesophageal cancer which went to his brain, and he died at the age of 48 years. My sister, his wife, also died 10 years later after trying to tell doctors she had cancer of the oesophagus, as she was operated on for cancer as well. Many people involved in the cotton industry and with chemicals have passed away with cancer.

At some stage in my time in Wee Waa working on farms, I got a job with a bloke named Geoff Mann. I was employed to do a bit of fencing and then driving a dozer. It was a Komatsu. I would start work at 6pm and drive all night till six in the morning when I would refuel the dozer and hand it over to the next driver to do his shift. I remember seeing things in the night skies and I used to think am I imagining things or is it my mind playing up just to keep me awake. One night, I was driving and towing I think about six ton of ripper – a three-tyne ripper stick picking and pulling up roots of old trees off a dozer and unloading into a tractor trailer at the end of the paddock. One night, I felt the dozer grab and spin the left-hand track, then a big jerk and it let go. There were correction levers or clutch to keep the dozer straight as you were ripping. The outside tyne on the ripper had caught on a good root and tipped the ripper over. I had travelled about 15 metres further, so the hydraulic ram on top of the ripper was now in the deck and hydraulic hoses were broken off, with oil going everywhere. I left the dozer as it was about 8pm and I could see the lights on at the homestead and walked to the house to inform the boss. When I got to the house and knocked on the door, the boss yelled come in. The boss and his wife were just about to have tea or dinner. When I told him what happened, he went off his head and grabbed a stock whip off the wall. I thought I was going to cop it. He screamed,

"Come with me you stupid bastard; I told you if you turn too sharp at the end of the run the draw bar on the rippers is long and it will catch on the tracks, and you'll tip the rippers over." I tried to tell him that's not what happened as I was back to ripping and about 50 metres back into paddock and caught on a stick that didn't move and that's what tipped the ripper over. The mongrel once he saw it had to agree with me. To this day he has never paid me for my last two weeks work slashing down a crop of corn which he couldn't sell, as he only had a verbal agreement with Kellogg's for the crop and they reneged on buying it. I still think he was a low-down mongrel.

Another job I had was working on a property for JVH Cotton where it was that you had to work for 6 weeks before they made you permanent. After only three weeks, I remember they made me permanent. Why? I remember it because several the other blokes employed there had the shits with me for that. The real thing was I would work any overtime, especially weekends. I could calibrate the spray rigs on the Lilliston Roller Cultivator to spray for bugs in the cotton whilst knocking weeds out. Some of the blokes I worked with helped me out when I did a stupid thing whilst driving that tractor. I decided I should get myself a tan and took my shirt off. All I can remember, I got burnt bad, and I only know just before I went out to it, I knocked the tractor into neutral at about 2800 revs. The next thing I could hear people whistling out loud. This was in the background of the engine revving on the tractor. They got me off the tractor and dragged me into a concrete pipe which was under the built-up roads. It was cooler there, and I slowly come round with water they gave me and the water they put on me from the channel. I guess I owe them fellows. I may have died if they hadn't found me.

So, as it was another stint I did in the Golden Fleece Service station for Mack Dickinson, I have to say what happened one very hot day. An American cotton grower's wife, a Mrs Freer, came into the station to get fuel and as I was a Stanley, she asked me to check the tyres, battery, oil, and water and clean the windscreen. The car was a big V8 Holden Brougham silver blue and vinyl top. I did all she asked, but the car engine was very hot as she had driven from Narrabri, and I suggested to her that I park it for a while to let it cool down. I gave her a chair in the shop and made her a coffee. Then things went wrong. Mrs Freer asked me in her Yankee accent,

"Did I come from Wee Waa?" I said,

"No, I originally came from a place called Boorowa." When she said,

"Where's that?" I said,

"Down near Yass." With that she was not happy at all and never spoke to me again. I checked the water in her car, and she was off.

That evening as would happen, the servo was like a pub. The boss would have beers in the fridges and his best customers would come in for a few drinks. One of the customers was another American named Ken Frisck; he had land planes and Wabco Scrapers. Ken asked how I was going, what sort of a day I had. I told him about Mrs Freer and that she seemed upset with me. Then he told me why, in his Yankee accent, that when she asked me where I was from and I had said Boorowa was down near Yass, that she thought I said, 'Down near y' arse.'

Another job I did was burr cutting. I remember out in a real big paddock towards Burren Junction. Out there was so flat as far as you can see in any direction. I had a water bag hanging in the only tree in that paddock and you could see the dust rising from a car all the way from one horizon to the next. The dust reminded me of the vapour trail behind a jet plane. I would take my hoe at the tree and walk chipping burrs out to the fence and then chip burrs all the way back to the tree. It would take about 50 minutes and it was very hot. When back at the tree, I would lie down against the tree with my back against it and drink a little water. It never bothered me that I was half lying down in sheep shit there in the shade of that tree. I have spoken many times to people who have done burr-cutting and one thing everyone agrees on, anyone who claimed they had done burr-cutting and says they've never missed any had never actually done burr-cutting. After you've been at it for a while, you go burr blind, so you miss some.

I tried another part-time job picking onions. I think they were dug out and you had to top-and-tail them, with your own wooden box to fill. The box was about 5-foot square and about 3-foot-high from memory. I do know for sure, you got $10.00 a box to fill it up. I didn't do much of this as the hernia I was carrying was not good. I remember there was an old Aboriginal man, probably about 60 years old and he could fill four boxes a day. Earning $40 a day, 7 days a week, he was making $280.00 a week. This was big money as when I was on cotton pickers working at least 84 hours a week I would earn $110.00. Anyway, as I said, I only lasted a week at this job and I made more money on my motorbike riding into Wee Waa for the other pickers buying drinks and food for them, than I was paid for picking the onions. That's all I can say about onion picking.

I got a job with a fencing contractor for about four weeks. His last name was McKosker, and we were tacking down old fencing wire netting, replacing posts, running some new wires, and putting up new ring lock fence. On one of those days, I had a close call on a Fergie tractor which I was never to forget. We would put the bar down through the end of the ring lock which we had rolled out and secured or tied off one end. We would wire the bar at the end of the ring lock to the back of the tractor and use it to strain the fence up. My foot slipped from that stupid clutch pedal, and the tractor rose on the back wheels at about 65' when I got the clutch in. I was very careful about doing that in the future.

The boss was a funny bloke and would hardly say anything while we had our lunch and every day when it was time to get back to work at 1pm, he would say this,

"Ahh, so that's what he said, eh." That was the sign he was about to tell us some yarns. To this day, I could tell and remember a few of those yarns and jokes he told us. This would often go on for an hour. It suited us as he was the boss, and we were getting paid to be entertained. Anyway, that was short-term work and didn't last, so I left to look for another job.

I went cotton chipping for an Australian named Bobby Wilson. I did this job for a short time and worked alongside Aboriginals and old white itinerant workers and university students. My last day on chipping cotton (hoeing out the weeds between the cotton rows), I got a bit of heat and a real severe nosebleed. The boss and owner Bob Wilson saw me and took me back to the homestead and gave me a job in the garden under the big shady trees. He was a real nice bloke, but I left there and looked for easier work. The easier work was stomping cotton for a yank named Johnny Lusceretta, aka 'Not.' It was on a property owned by another yank and Johnny was a picking contractor. I stomped cotton for 42 days straight and it was a tough job after all. We were in very long paddocks and a double row cotton picker would have to be emptied at the end of each run as the basket on the picker would be full. Because of this, we had empty cotton trailers at each end of the paddock. My job was to be at and in the trailer when the picker arrived. I would help to pull the cotton out of the basket especially as the trailer was filling up. When the picker went back into the crop, I would stomp cotton down in this big cotton trailer, keep an eye on the picker and when he was not too far from the other end, I would climb over the top of the trailer, climb down, jump in a ute, race up to the other end and get up into the trailer before the picker pulled up and repeat the same old procedure all day. As I said, I did this for 42 days straight. I asked Johnny if I could have a go at driving the picker. He said it would be a long time before you drive a picker. He was wrong.

I left Johnny's and ran into a bloke named Bob Margah and guess what, he was looking for a picker driver. This was a much easier job and I loved it. From memory, first thing in the morning you checked all your cotton spindles and there were hundreds of them. They had a rough serrated edge which spun and went round in circles that would pluck the cotton from the plants. In the morning and during the day picking, you would check all spindles now and then as sometimes the cotton stuck to the spindle and set hard, and you had to use a sharp knife to run down the side of the spindle to remove it. This was necessary as if it got too hot and ignited due to spontaneous combustion, you could catch cotton on fire as it is highly flammable. For that reason, I couldn't smoke on the job. We had to make sure our water tanks always had water in them on the pickers. The water was bloody important to making sure your picker didn't have a cotton fire. The tanks were up high to create for a gravity feed. They had water trickle down on rubber pads that had soft ripples on them, and they cooled the spindles as they came in contract with them. They were called moisture pads. Also, in the head gear on a picker were these round hard rubber things that as the spindle hit them, they would rip up cotton from the spindles. These from memory were called doffers. You would pick as soon as the moisture was gone from the cotton from a night-time dew and pick until it settled again at night. It was nothing to work a twelve-hour day and would often be a lot more. I have done 14 hours and even 16 hours straight if there was rain coming and no dew had settled on the crop.

I used to take my lunch, and most days I would keep picking until about 3pm in the arvo so as I knew I would most times only have to do three or four hours after lunch. One day in the morning, I was picking, and as you sit up high on the picker, I saw ahead an emu egg in the row between the cotton. I stopped the picker, climbed down, and grabbed the egg and put it in my tucker box which was sitting near where I was driving. That picker was a single row picker, a McCormack International Tractor converted into a cotton picker which you were driving backwards. Anyway, when I stopped for lunch, I noticed the emu hanging about and as I always did, I used to have my lunch sitting on the ground half under the picker in the shade. Anyway, I decided to eat lunch up on the picker in the sun as that emu was acting up, coming up close and making what I would call 'glug-glug' sounds. I thought it was after the egg or after me. It was agitated and worried me a bit.

One of those days, we were picking late as it had been a warm day and soft dark clouds filled the sky out to the west so no dew would settle on the cotton. The boss Bob Margah told me to keep picking and when the basket on the picker was full, not to tip it out into the trailer as it was better off in the picker when it rained. At that stage, I had been working for about fifteen hours and I was stuffed. I asked Bob if this instruction went for all the pickers, and he said yes. I said,

"So no more cotton is to be emptied into the cotton trailers," and he said

"Correct." My picker was full first. I shut it down and I knew the others as they were bigger pickers would take a while to fill up their baskets. I climbed up into the cotton trailer, three parts full and laid down in the cotton and as it was cooling off, dragged a heap of cotton over myself and pulled my black cowboy hot over my face and covered that with cotton as well and I went into a bloody good sleep. The next thing I know is someone yelling

"He is under the cotton, he moved." Yes, one of the drivers dumped a load on me. The other blokes with Bob, the boss, were looking for me in the water in the channel in case I had fallen in there and drowned as to them it was a mystery I had completely disappeared, and they just wanted to go home. There had been a couple of kids died in the cotton, suffocated while I worked in Wee Waa, so I have to say, I was lucky I didn't step on a rainbow that night.

I also worked on a property that was sheep and crop farm where I started off working in the workshop servicing and looking after the machinery, tractors, dozers and implements such as ploughs and scarifiers with a mechanic. Now and then I went out into the paddocks loading sheep into stock floats, hay racking, bailing, sorghum fence repairs and all other work I was asked to. By the way sorghum is itchier than oats. I was always annoying the boss to let me drive the dozer and he would always say we have a dozer driver, and the driver knows what he's doing. Well, one morning I asked the boss again, and he said the same thing. That's when I told him I had had to repair fences when he went to sleep at night, but I didn't think I could fix his last stuff up. The boss said, "What was that", I said to the boss,

"You know that windmill and water trough in the north paddock?" He said,

"Yes." I said,

"Well the dozer driver had a gap between the windmill and the water trough of fourteen feet, and the scarifier he was towing was 16 feet wide, and he tried to go through." The boss said,

"So I suppose he got the water trough?" I said,

"No, he pulled your bloody windmill down." The boss wasn't too happy about things, and with me, he said,

"See that axe there in the workshop, you take it and that tree that came down go and chop it into firewood at the homestead."

I started chopping and after an hour or so I had had enough, and I let that axe fly back over my shoulder, went to the workers quarters, and packed my swag. Then I went down to the homestead to get my pay. I decided I wasn't working for a mongrel like him any bloody more. I knocked on the door. The boss's wife answered, and she said the boss wasn't there. I told her I was quitting, and I'd like my pay. She gave me a cheque and I started the long dusty, hot walk to the main track past the property. I thumbed down a long old back Jaguar car an old bloke was driving. I remember the seats in the car were covered in black and white spots like leopard skins. He preached to me all the way to Wee Waa even if I didn't agree with some stuff he was saying, I agreed with the lot. It was too hot and dusty to get out and walk. I got a job at Cudgewa station again and was picking cotton and we had an old army blitz truck for the water tanker to supply water for the cotton pickers. I remember getting a few scares with that truck. It had what they called around there Armstrong steering, especially so as it had no engine – you needed a lot of strength to steer the damn thing.

Another bloke I was working with would tow me with a bench seat chamberlain tractor around the place up on channel banks. It would scare me a bit as no engine, no brakes, no power steering, and those chamberlain tractors could get up to 30 miles an hour. He also freaked me out of a morning for about a week. The batteries were stuffed in my picker which was McCormack International turned into a one row picker. I'd have to hit the picker with an aero start; I think it had ether in it. Then he would tow me to start the picker, but you had to be towed backwards to clutch start them and not forward, as if you did you would drive the head gear (the picking part of the picker) into the ground and cause untold damage to the machine.

Another time I went back to work at the Golden Fleece Service Station. I remember an old drover there. He had a big white tobacco-stained moustache and we called him the Marshall as he looked like the Marshall on Marshall Battery ads (Sid). Anyway, he came in one day for me to service his '59 Holden sedan and there was another young bloke working there then who loved to drive the cars in to go on the hoist and back out. Well, I drove it in to put on hoist. When I stopped, I could smell something in the car. When I looked on the back seat there was a big sheep's rear leg rotting and sinking into the seat and crawling with maggots. I serviced the car and let the apprentice drive it out and park it. He was often not impressed with me.

One day I serviced the police bull wagon and was asked to take it back to the station, where one of the officers would drop me back. I took the first left from the service station and there was a left-hand bend just covered with loose gravel. I think the devil made me do it, but I chucked half a donut in the bull wagon. Someone saw it and the police weren't happy, letting me know in no uncertain terms. This was the second last time I worked at the servo. I got another job driving a picker with a mate of mine we called Banjo. We both took on picking 420 acres of cotton at Merah North for a Mr Bill Ingram. He had come up to Wee Waa to try cotton farming. He was a sheep farmer from down south at Wagga. He had come to an agreement with my mate Banjo and me to pay us $110.00 a week which turned out he would pay us $10.00 less, which I'll explain later.

I was picking there one day, and Bill came out, pulled up in his ute and was watching me for a while. Bill got out of the ute and was waiting for me and called me over to have a go at me for leaving a couple of plants not picked at the ends of the rows. I tried to explain to him it was easier to leave them and get them on the second pick as if I picked all the way to the ends of the rows of cotton then tried to turn to go into the crop again that the rear wheel on the picker would go up the channel bank. This would, in turn, drive the picking gear or the headgear on the front of the picker into the ground. I had already bent up some stalk guides. Anyway, old Bill went into a bit of a spin and decided to have a heart turn on me. He was a big man. He had got in his ute behind the wheel and started to collapse. I pushed him into the middle of the Ute, and he started talking,

"Get me home to my wife, she has my tablets there, I need them urgently, I am having an angina attack." I raced him into Wee Waa, down the Main Street and he was leaning on me, and I got him to his house blowing the horn. His wife came out, raced back into the house, and put a tablet under his tongue. He came good. She took him to hospital. After all that, I was in the pub having a beer or two and a couple of my mates who had seen me driving Bill down the Main Street give it to me. Reckoned it looked like me and the boss were getting on well and never seen anyone crawl up to the boss like that before. Even after looking after the boss and working about three weeks and going into four, he was still paying Banjo and I $100 a week. Understand this was still a lot of money in about March of 1971 even though you were working at least 84 hours a week. Banjo and I decided to stage what may have been the first strike in Wee Waa. Never went to work and went to the pub about 11am, having a few beers when Bill the boss walked in and said,

"Are you two fellows coming to work to pick my cotton or not?" We both said,

"We were promised $110.00 a week and were only getting $100.00". The boss said for us to think about it, he would go away and come back after lunch and see what we had decided. We kept drinking and waited for the boss Bill to come back. When he came back, he said,

"What have you boys decided?" We said $110 is what he had said, and he said okay $110.00, be at work in the morning and start picking. I think I had consumed a few drinks and said,

"Bill, I wouldn't work for you for less than $150.00 a week." He said, "Does that go for you too Banjo?" Banjo said yes, and Bill said,

"Righto you two, consider yourselves both sacked." So, I had to find another job, back to my old mate Mack Dickinson at the Golden Fleece. He always took me back when I was in trouble; he was a nice bloke Macky.

I must say, there over my time in Wee Waa, I also worked at JVH Cotton doing irrigating, planting, rotor bucking, so I will say a bit about those jobs now. Rotor bucking is when you drag a three-blade plough behind the tractor. You do this from the end of a cotton row from the hill, four rows or so, to make an extension of the row to the channel bank. When you reached them, you pulled a rope which allowed the blade to roll over. Once the cotton bed is extended, you use the aluminium syphon pipes to the channel, starting by pushing one end of the syphon pipe into the water in the channel and keeping your hand away from the end of the pipe, then cover the end of the pipe with your hand as you pull away from the bank with the pipe still in the water. You repeat these three or four times until you feel the pipe is full, then drop it onto ground and water starts running into the rotor bucked area until it runs the length of the rows in the crop.

One time I was irrigating at Cudgewa, and there was heavy, torrential rain. We had the pumps running water from the main channels to the irrigation channels and all syphon pipes running. We were in the shed and asking the boss can we go and shut the pumps off and pull the syphon pipes out. He said we could do this when we had two inches of rain. Well, we got that and into the Haflingers (a light vehicle that was hard to bog) and we shut everything down. Back at the shed and still raining, I watched the workers leave one at a time and a distance between them try to drive out on that black soil track. You could see how far they go when they left the track. I left last and did what the others were doing, driving in the tracks of the one before you in the mud. It was pure luck, but I drove all the way out to the Buren Junction Road. I forgot to say before when I was driving the dozer all night, how tough that was because it was hot weather, and I was living in a tent. I could hardly get any sleep during the day for the heat plus I could hear that dozer in my head all day even though I used wax ear plugs. Whilst I was living in the tent, I was bashed in the back of my head by a big man visiting my sister and brother-in-law. This was the second time in my life that I got that heart race which I had at Oak Flats where I thought I might die.

Not too long after that incident I was unlucky to run into a mob of blokes I called the Kelly gang. I was in the little entry to the cafe when one of the Kelly gang decided to pick on me. There was a girl with them who was a sister to another bum in the gang. One Kelly was eating a sandwich and asked me if I like sandwiches. I said yes, and he rubbed it in my face. I took a swing at him and hit the girl by mistake. Next thing they pounded me. They let me go as there were people about, so I started walking home and when I was around the corner from the Post Office, I saw a white Falcon pull up, and they got out and give it to me. I hit the deck in a ball, arms and hands over my head and those bastards kicked the hell out of me, then left. They were a pack of low bastards.

When I was 17 or nearly 18, I went into the pub to cash a pay cheque. One of the gang grabbed my cheque off me. I tried to get it back and he just kept stirring me up. When I had had enough, I did a stupid thing. He was sitting on a bar stool; I was standing to his right side, I put my right arm across his chest under his chin and threw him backwards to the floor and grabbed my cheque, had one beer and was leaving by the front door of the pub. I did not see it coming. He bashed me in the back of the head, and I fell to the foot path and bashed my head on the pub step and was just about knocked out. Got up in my ute and got out of there.

Other jobs I did whilst working at the servo was helping a bloke repossess cars for Esanda, a part of loans through the ANZ Bank. Mostly you would go to pick up the cars with the repossession man and I would follow him in the car to Narrabri where we would lock the car in the Holden Garage. One car we picked up; the owner gave us the keys very easily. We soon found out why when a wheel fell off and the nuts were loosened off the other wheels. Another one was an EH Holden sedan, which the repossessor got the keys to by plying the owner with free beer in the pub. I drove the EH to Narrabri and the repossessor followed me. When we got back to the service station, we looked through the car and found the owners tucker box and a spear gun. He came to the servo, and we gave him his stuff. He was now agitated and drunk and wasn't too impressed with me and loaded the spear gun. I got behind the little tree and the spear went into that. I was now getting a bit worried about doing this job and wondered was the money I got for doing this worth it. The last straw was when the

Esanda man needed help to repossess a television set. We took that set when little kids were sitting on the floor and watching it. I felt bloody sick doing that and never can forget it. With that, I told the Esanda man that was it, I would never help with a repossession again.

One time in Wee Waa, I had a run in with the Crown Sergeant. He would always pick on a friend of mine and had booked him falsely so he would lose his bike license. One Sunday, he checked my ute out and was going to put a defect sticker on it and nearly blew the motor up with his number 10 on the accelerator. I had extractors and copper pipe coming out the left side in front of the back wheel; it would make a racket. He run out of stickers of the defect type and told me to drive it to the station which we called the opera house. Because of the carbies on the motor, it would not start unless I had foot flat, so I wound it till the battery was flat and he said bring car to station in the morning and he would defect it. I run into the young policeman in Wee Waa who had become friends with me and told him. He said,

"You still at the servo?" I said,

"Yes," he said.

"Quiet the ute down and when you come to station ask me to come out and listen to the ute." Well, that happened and Ray, my mate, told the Crown Sargent you can't defect that ute and I got away with that one. Then one day I pushed the Crown Sargent again when I was sitting with a mate in the gutter in front of the café with our bikes, and the Crown Sargent drove past and dropped off two young girls and gestured for us to move on and he drove off. Well, I spoke to those girls and said what are you doing with the Crown Sargent, and they said they were there from Curlewis, and he was their uncle. What could

I do, I was riding a 450 Honda and asked the girls if they would like to go on the bike? Naturally, one at a time, I rode past the police station. I can say he never ever booked me for one thing, I felt a bit like the Road Runner it was a game for me.

Now, my stories to do with the flood, which was very hard to take, and I never want to go through again. I was working in the servo, and we would keep a watch on the flood coming in from the Namoi River out on the Narrabri Road. In one day, I was serving petrol to cars, four-wheel drives and then tractors. As the water came in closer, I said to my boss Mack, I knew where I was putting my ute and that's on the hoist in the lube bay. Mack said he was putting his VC Valiant Regal on that hoist, so I had to think quick and as Wee Waa is so flat, I thought the railway platform would do, so before anyone else would think of it, I raced up, drove my ute on the platform, locked it and left it there. I went back to work and the boss had his Valiant car up on the hoist. By the end of that day, I had got up to serving tractors fuel and then a couple of boats. So, now starts three weeks of walking in flood waters and getting bloody sick of it. The boss got a cotton trailer we cut the side out of and went around the town dropping off forty-four-gallon drums for people to put their furniture on in their houses to keep above the water. We carried bits of dog chain to kill the snakes that would get up on the porches or at the front doors of houses we were delivering the forty-four-gallon drums to. I killed many snakes and an old black fellow told me that the snakes can't strike you in water. To this day, I've never found out if that was a fact. A sad thing about people putting the stuff up on drums in their houses was several of them never put water in the drums and so the drums floated, tipped over in the water and they still lost their belongings.

I was always trying to help people out during the flood and met up with people who I became friends with, one being a young girl. The food came into Wee Waa from out of town on a small airstrip in a Caribou aircraft from the Air Force, then was brought in by railway and helicopter to the town. All flood supplies were taken to the ANZ bank and the Post Office in the Main Street as those were built up several feet above the flood level. I would walk about a kilometre and a half one way to the Police Station twice a week to pick up a $3.00 food voucher and then walk through the water to the ANZ bank to get my supplies, and back home again. It really takes it out of you doing that. One day, I thought I would walk to the railway station straight up the Main Street to see how my EH Holden ute was going. I was walking up the centre of the Main Street as the water was a bit shallower there and I was in front of the western end pub. I heard a woman scream and a dog barking up on the top veranda of the pub built out over the footpath. The woman screamed out

"For Christ's sake do something with that bloody dog before it kills Joey." They had saved a little roo[2] and the dog was having a go at it. Next thing, I hear a dog screech. I look up and over the balcony flew a dog down into the water, splash, not far from me. That sorted that dog out. Anyway, my ute was different to that dog as it was high and dry.

A few days later, I splashed and trudged my way down to the service station to see how Mack the boss was going, and he took me into the lube bay. There was about three foot of water in there

---

[2] A baby kangaroo, which is called a 'Joey'

and sitting in the water was Mack's Valiant Regal. I felt bad, but Mack hadn't lowered the hoist down on drums. What happened was I had told Mack several times that the Outlet Valve on the hoist was leaking so when I serviced cars, I always left the inlet valve slightly on to keep the hoist up. There was no safety bar to drop down to keep the hoist up as it was broken off. Anyway, in the peak of the flood the power goes off, so the compressor doesn't cut in and the car comes down in the drink. I felt so bad for Mack, but it wasn't my fault.

Something that annoyed me during the flood, and I told a couple off that there were some houses like my sister and brother in laws that were built up off the ground a few feet that the flood waters had not quite reached. Bloody idiots driving tractors down the streets and instead of crawling along, they were travelling fast, and the wheels were pushing up waves of water that would then enter houses that were inches above the water, brain dead idiots. Two stockmen died moving cattle to higher ground. I don't know where you could find it, as, at some time, I climbed up on the house and for as far as I could see 360° I could only see muddy brown water. The stockmen were found stuck in a fence, both drowned. A girl fell over the front veranda and washed under the house and caught at the netting across the back of the house. She was only about 2 or 3 years old. There was also a man went down in the cellar at Narrabri, I think to get a keg of beer, and he drowned as well. Mack had a boat and we used it a bit in searches for people and brought a few to town.

Well finally, I remember another thing in that flood, and I ran into an old Englishman in the pub. The town was still flooded, and I'd been out helping people, and I had just walked into town on the Narrabri Road, just out past the servo. I told the Pom when he asked me how I was going that, that day, I nearly drowned. I had been that exhausted walking in the flood waters, I fell over and if there wasn't a guidepost there for me to hang onto, I was stuffed. I never forget the next question, which was strange. He asked me if I was Australian. I've thought about it, and it must have been he thought that all Australians could swim. Finally, the waters went down and went away, and I could not figure out how all that water could just go away. Where could it all go?

Well, I'd had enough and all I wanted to do was get out of Wee Waa for one weekend, so I went to the railway station to get my ute and get out of town. Unless you've been in that situation, you don't know how that bloody water affects you. I felt that my nerves were shot, and that water had even made me that cranky with it, to the point I found myself punching into the flood waters and screaming for it to piss off. Well, when I got to the railway platform to get my ute, I never expected the Station Master to get stuck into me. Not for leaving my ute on the platform, but because when I left the ute there, I had pulled the handbrake on and for some reason I couldn't get it off, so I revved that engine up and dropped the clutch and ripped up a bit of the platform. Anyway, I packed my gear, filled the ute up with fuel and found out the Narrabri Road was still closed. I then found out you could get out via Yarrie Lake Road, and I got out and on my way to Wollongong. Don't remember why Narrabri Road was closed; it could have been something at Yanco Channel Dip.

I had a good catchup with family and in a way, I didn't really feel like going back to Wee Waa, but I was the one who had decided to go there, so I felt I had to return. When I was near a bridge over a railway track near Gunnedah or Narrabri, I came across a car broken down I thought. When I stopped to help, it was just a flat battery in the car and it was the girl I had got to know in Wee Waa in the floods, with a bloke I didn't know. Anyway, I jumped started the car and they were off. At the time, I didn't think anything of this encounter.

I drove on and got back to Wee Waa, ready to get back to work at the garage for old Macky. I ran into a few mates at the café, and they asked if I know what had happened to the young girl I had befriended in the floods. I said for a joke; I've got her in an old shack out at a place called Cubbaroo where there's an old wine shanty. Because I'd seen her, I just thought she's alright and my mates were just mucking around with me. I found out the next day at work at the garage how it was not a laughing matter. I was at work and Mack came to me to tell me the girl's father and the police were at the back office, and I had to go and see them. The girl's father was very wild and looked like he could kill me. He asked me where his daughter was. The policeman then asked me what's this story you've told your mates? It was then that I realised this was a very serious matter and I told them about getting the car going and described the bloke she was with. About a week later they found her somewhere in Queensland and she had run away with that bloke. Not a good idea to make that story for a joke, but at the time I didn't know what had happened with her; a bloody stupid thing for me to do.

Well, I was now the busiest I had ever been servicing cars that had gone under in the flood. I lost count how many I serviced, changing transmission fluid, gear box oil and diff oils and engine oils. I think we ran some sort of oil in them like it was called running oil which was used in dozers. We took door trims off and floor coverings and sprayed fish oil through the cars, changing all oils the second time. I remember I felt like asking everyone, 'How did the flood treat you?' I asked two ladies together in one car and felt so bad and sad when they answered that they were the wives of the two stockmen they had found dead in a fence.

My Marian and brother-in-law Michael Hume's yard in James Hibens Avenue was taken by Marian when they were taking an elderly lady to visit the doctor as she had a severe nosebleed, so she was put in a boat and towed by a John Deere tractor. From the roof of the house as far as you could see was brown dirty water.

I couldn't understand how cotton was virtually planted to the backyards of houses in Wee Waa. That land was owned by growers, and I would see that land sprayed with poison and how dangerous that must have been to the town folk. When I had planted cotton, I think it was a six-row planter, and after cotton had come up, you would check for bits that never came up and drive around with a single sow planter and do what was called a spot plant.

One thing which a couple of my friends and I saw whilst sitting on the Post Office steps opposite the pub was so bloody funny. The Bull Wagon pulled up and apparently there had been two black fellows fighting with each other in the pub. The police came to pick them up for being drunk and fighting with each other, both police entering the pub together, catching one of them and putting him in the back of the Bull Wagon before both going back in the pub to get the other one. We watched the other fellow come up the footpath beside the pub, sneak over to the Bull Wagon, let his mate out and they both took off. Well, we just sat there watching and after a while the two police officers came out and one said to the other,

"Oh well, we got one of them, we'll take him to the lockup for a while." We just sat there laughing after they left and said we would like to see their faces when they got to the station and found after all their efforts, they hadn't caught anyone. Those two buggers had put it over the cops that day.

Now a funny thing that happened one day just to the west of the café in the Main Street of Wee Waa. I happened upon a bit of a gathering on the footpath near a pepper tree. This was to be something I would never forget seeing my first soap box preacher. Standing on a box, this preacher telling all who would listen about God and Jesus and sinners! An old Aboriginal fella was there and as the preacher was telling all that God had made the world and everything in it, the old Aboriginal said,

"Did God make the kerb, and guttering Bud?" The preacher said,

"Yes." The old codger asked,

"Did he make the footpath and the road Bud?" The preacher said,

"Yes, God had made them." Then the old fella said,

"That's bullshit Bud, the bloody Wee Waa Council had built all that stuff Bud, they made them." We got a bit of a laugh out of that old bugger.

Well, I put in a good effort at the servo and got itchy feet to get out on farms again, leaving with Mack's blessing. I found out after the floods that it was a bit harder for me to get work, then I heard there were some places that had tractors wrecked and needed cotton hauled into Wee Waa cotton jinn. I knew Mack's brother had an old Oliver 1800 tractor and asked him if I could use it to haul cotton trailers in. Chris said yes and we worked out how much I would get to haul in each trailer and how much for each empty one I took back, then how much Chris would get for hire of his tractor. I put the word out and a very weird thing happened. Bill Ingram, the bloke who sacked Banjo and me from picking his cotton, hired me to haul his cotton in. It was a long haul from Merah North to the Wee Waa Cotton Jinn. I had done a bit of cotton hauling before, a Cudgewa with a 50/20 turbo diesel with an eight-speed power shift. The older Oliver 1800 was not as good a tractor, but she would do the job even though a bit slower than the John Deere 50/20. To do the job, you would join up to four trailers on by joining the draw bar to the back of the next trailer and would haul them in along the stock routes all the way to an area on Burren side of the river about a mile out of Wee Waa. You would then leave the other full trailers and take one full one in at a time, bringing one empty out and so on. You would drive the trailer to a weigh bridge. The police never worried you if you did that this way, one trailer at a time. You could have multiple trailers on the stock route, and I had towed more than four at times.

One day I ran into a bloke hauling cotton from Cudgewa and he was driving the chamberlain which was bloody quicker than the old Oliver and I knew it. I was heading off and saw him coming over the bridge. He only had to join his trailer onto the others he'd joined-up as you bring each empty out. Anyway, I bet him I could beat him to the turn off to Cudgewa. The next day I saw him, and he was pissed off with me and wouldn't pay the bet. I had done something before I headed off in the bet and he didn't appreciate it. I went to his line of empty trailers before I left and pulled all the draw bar pins out and dropped them on the ground. He'd join the trailer he brought out onto the first one and go to leave with two trailers and leave the others behind then he would have to re-join the trailers. He wasn't impressed, but I thought it was a top stir.

Well, I got that job done and decided I would leave Wee Waa, but for the first time in my life, I found it hard to get a job. It was mid-1971 and there were lots of people unemployed. I drove many miles looking for work and was unsuccessful. It was a worry to me but even though I was out of work for about six weeks, I did not apply for assistance from the Government in any way. I would drive into properties offering to work for fed and found (I offered to work just for food and a place to sleep.) I found that I could not even do any good at that and when I got to Dubbo, I was told there was big trouble with unemployment as a flour mill or something in the town had just closed. It had employed many people, so there were many more than just me seeking a job.

So, with my quest for work, I headed down to Boorowa, my hometown. I went to a shearing contractor, and he was going to give me a job and teach me to be a roustabout in the sheds. Sadly, this job didn't come about as the contractor let me know he had not been paid for the shed a year before, the shed he intended to start me in. Apparently, the cocky was a bit of a bugger for not paying. I happened to tell an old uncle of mine about this. My uncle was a real old worker who had made a living most of or part of his life ploughing with his beloved horses. He told me that the bloke who hadn't paid the shearing contractor was as mean as cat shit. The story was, he was that mean that at some stage, his kids had become bound up and couldn't crap! Instead of going to the chemist and buying some medicine to free them up, he sat them on the outside dunny on a stormy night and told them ghost stories – 'True' I think. That was the end of me ever going to work in a shearing shed. I left Boorowa and was heading towards Wollongong and called in to see Dad at Gunning. Dad was working along the railway track between Goulburn to Wagga with the No 3 Primary Works PMG.

It seemed my life had made a 180° turn and once again there I was with Dad telling me I should have a good safe government job. As they were putting men on to dismantle the Sydney to Melbourne trunk route that used to take all phone traffic and had been made redundant due to the coaxial cable network. I must explain this was a pole route beside the railway tracks and Dad talked me into putting my name in at the PMG Line Depot at Gunning for a job as a Linesman, Exempt Linesman Grade One. Not knowing if I would get a start, I then continued onto Warilla at the Gong to see if I could get work there. I put my name down for the steel works, asked around Wollongong, but no jobs so I left Warilla, drivin-up as close as I was game towards Sydney, then Southern Highlands and even down the South Coast as far as Eden, calling in on dairy farms looking mainly for farm work.

One more funny thing I heard in Wee Waa was at my sister's house. I was out in the yard and her neighbours were having a big fight in their housing commission house. She screamed out,

"I am going to throttle you now." I heard him run down the hall in the house and she was after him. Next thing I heard her scream,

"Come out from under that bed." He yelled back,

"I am the boss of this house and I'll come out when I want to." That didn't sound to me like he was the boss of that house.

Chapter 7

Dismantling Goulburn to Wagga, Gunning to Cootamundra

Having done no good looking for work, it was a good lesson for me, as I really hadn't known till then how hard it could be to find work. I had been like a cat thrown into the air as I always landed on my feet. I was down the South Coast a fair way and I rang our next-door neighbour to talk to Mum. Mum asked where I was and said you better come home; the PMG want you to do an entrance exam in Wollongong for a linesman's position on the dismantling job Dad was on. I went back to the Gong and sat the exam, thinking I had no real school certificates, not even the intermediate certificate. It was a state-wide exam and as it turned out, I passed with high marks and was put on as exempt linesman on the same job as Dad. This job was not a permanent job straight away and I was only guaranteed twelve months of work. Just before I started, I was back at Boorowa at my Mum's parent's place when Mum rang and said there was a telegram there from JVH Cotton from Wee Waa asking me to accept a permanent job back there with them.

I asked Mum what she thought I should do. I decided I would stick with the PMG job and made a start. It was the middle of winter and I started work at Jerrawa, off the highway between Yass and Gunning. Boy, was it cold that winter of 1971 – down to minus 8 degrees. We were living in a PMG camp of aluminium caravans in a paddock on the edge of Jerrawa on the western side. We had a couple of 44-gallon drums outside in the camp which we would burn untreated bits of the poles we pulled down. Sometimes those drums would get that hot and glow red. You would feel like you could see through them, and they sure threw the heat out. Many a beer and yarns were had around those drums.

In that camp, we had a wet canteen, which was our own pub run by Noel Lickers, as there was no pub in Jerrawa, only a small number of houses, a showground, a church and hall, a railway station, and a bit of a shop. The weather was that cold we had antifreeze in the trucks, wheat bags over the radiators and wheat bags on the ground under the radiators. Still, it was that cold you would get up in the morning, have breakfast, pack the lunch box for work out in the paddocks along the railway track and several mornings you would only get about one mile from the camp on dirt roads and the trucks would boil as they were frozen. Even when you did make it to the pole route, you would often light a fire, and only start work after smoko. We weren't bludging, it was a real safety thing for myself and my workmates, that's the ones who would climb the telephone poles, who could not walk on the cross arms as you could slip on the frost and ice on the arms and come a gutser and end up back on the deck. We were supposed to wear safety belts while up a pole, but I never wore them for two reasons. The main reason for me not to use a belt was that in your right hand, you would carry a pair of 'Diags'[3] and have a pair of lineman pliers on a strap in a pouch around your waist. As you had to climb all over the pole cutting the ties of the often-copper wires to the insulators away to free the wires you just couldn't or wouldn't bother to strap yourself to the pole with a safety belt. The other reason I wouldn't strap myself to a pole was I had heard that sometimes as you cut the wires from the pole or the longitudinal stays (or the side stays) on a bend, the pole could come down and if your weight strapped to the pole determined the way it came down, you could be trapped under the pole. This was possible!! The only time this nearly happened to me, I had gone up a pole and one bright spark was cutting side stays on a bend. I looked down and saw him about to cut the side stay, screamed out don't cut it and he cut it straight away with his bolt cutters. I felt the pole move; it lent over on a good angle. I hung on till it stopped, held up on an angle by all those beautiful copper wires on which I had been cutting the ties off the insulators. When I got down, the drop kick and his bolt cutters were gone. That shook me up a bit. Whenever I was cutting ties after that, I would always cut from the top of the pole to the bottom and to equal amounts left to right.

Even doing this, sometimes you would feel a creak or twist in the pole, you would never clip all the ties on one side and then the other. The job had two gangs and two-party leaders. Dad was one party leader and for a week or two I was in his gang. Our job in Dads' gang was to follow the wire gang. After all, wire gone, we

---

[3]Diagonal pliers used for snipping the ties on insulators

would cut the poles down or mostly use a big four-wheel drive rubber-tyre tractor with a side boom on it and winch the poles up whole out of the ground and lay them down. Then we would strip the poles of all insulators, spindles and throw them down the pole holes and fill holes in. We would strip all arm braces and steel angle iron off poles, plus crossarms. We would saw up poles for posts and sell poles to cockies and use any money we got for our food in our mess van. We also had an ex-butcher with us, and we were now and then given jumbucks from the cockie's "sheep" for some poles. Poles that weren't treated were cut to firewood and in the towns, we worked through, Dad would find old-aged pensioners and deliver the wood to them for free. Pubs, on the other hand, had open fires and beer in them, so go figure what we did for the pubs. Anyway, for that part of the job in Dad's gang, he probably had me working as hard as anyone else, but a few blokes kicked up a stink reckoned the old man was looking after me, so that's how I ended up on the wire gang climbing poles, which I enjoyed anyway, very much.

The camp and all its vans and mess vans, shower vans and cook's vans had not long been set up before I started on that job at Jerrawa, but there was a couple of complaints put into the union and one day we were told not to leave the camp as a couple of engineers from Sydney were coming to talk to us. 'Ginger beers' as old Kanga in our gang called them; he loved that rhyming slang did Kanga. The engineers did their speech to us, and Dad raised most of the complaints about the camp. One thing he wanted was a cover over and between the two mess vans up to where you got your food from the cook's van and duck boards to make up a floor in the dirt. The engineers from the city got the cranks with all of what was asked and said to us,

"Most of you blokes have been put on this job because there's not a lot of work around and you couldn't find work. So do you want us to take six weeks to fix up these requests and you can all go home with no pay till it's to your satisfaction?" That's when Dad yelled out,

"You're nothing but a bunch of Blackmailing Bastards!" I thought my career on the PMG was done, and that day I would be walking out the gate with Dad. Then the Union Rep stepped up, and it was calmed down, and the engineers agreed to get it done quickly, without sending anyone home. They then asked if there were any other problems with the camp and Jimmy McKenzie from Cootamundra spoke up and said this,

"My complaint is that living in these aluminium vans being so cold. I have a problem sleeping because while I am breathing the moisture builds up on the ceiling, and the 'constipation' keeps dripping off the ceiling on my pillow." That brought a bit of a laugh around the camp and ended up the engineers gave us red chicken incubation lights in the ceiling to stop the condensation dripping off the ceiling. After that, the joke around Jerrawa and the area was that the PMG camp was known as the red-light area of Jerrawa.

There was something to me about the railway line which seemed to amaze me, and that was the railway bridges. The brick work in building those bridges and how the archways in those bridges and I wondered who and how they were built, what ability all those years back the builders had and how they created in my mind such art. One day a few miles towards Yass from Jerrawa, was a day I thought could be the last for a few workmates and me, all because of Kanga's rhyming slang. I was driving the small bus taking us to work through paddocks along the railway track when we came to railway gates in a deep cutting on a bend in the railway line. I drove parallel to the tracks and stopped. Kanga got out and opened the gates; I had to drive on a slope turn right onto tracks up a slope onto the tracks. I started this when Kanga waved me on to go. Next thing, he's screaming out,

"A shower of rain!" I yelled out.

"What?" He yelled out.

"A lover's lane!" I yelled.

"What?" He yelled.

"A bloody train!" The front of the bus was on the track and because of frost and ice it wouldn't move. I put bus in reverse, backed off track and slid down the paddock slope till we stopped and watched the train go through. BLOODY CLOSE. So, I had to learn a bit more about Kanga and his way of talking.

Kanga, 'Tom Beresford,' kept on with his slang. One day, he had a crack at our party leader Hank Polsen, who was always standing with one foot up high on a fence with his right elbow on his knee, holding a smoke in his mouth with hand on his face and mumbling his orders to us. Kanga said he was nothing, but a side stay for the fence who does nothing else and while the boss does nothing, that he, Kanga, is jiggy-jogging up and down the track, up and down poles, Julius Marlo transport wearing holes in his boots. Kanga then said after all his work there's his boots with the soles in them worn through and he didn't know whether to half-sole them or arse-ole them. Every morning, once we were out on the job, Kanga had things to do before he started any work for the PMG. You would see him in his blue overalls and slim dusty hat set off on foot over the hills, over his shoulders were rabbit traps to set and check. I asked him one morning what plant account he booked that down to as we had XWR was one which meant Exchange Wire Recover.

He said he had a plant account which was R&M. I asked what's that mean, and he said 'Rabbits and Mushrooms.' Kanga hitchhiked always and was a professional at it. He had a five-gallon drum cut in half with hinges on it and a latch. In this he carried his clothes and stuff in a swag. The trick was people would see him trudging along the road and think to give him a lift, poor buggers out of petrol. The best story about Kanga's hitchhiking involved his patter to get to his hometown of Temora. He would get a lift to Cootamundra and once there, stop the traffic. He told me when there was no traffic about, he would close the railway gates across the road and go and hide out of sight until he had a few cars stopped heading his way. Then he'd go down and ask each driver where they are going. The story he would tell them was that he had got there off a train travelling in the dog box and the Station Master had asked him to open the railway gates on the crossing. He would always get a lift this way. How goods that? Stop the traffic to get a lift. Only Kanga would have thought of that.

I worked with a Greek fellow too. We called him Mick the Greek or Black Mick. He was dark, a solid man, barrel chest and bull neck, could have been a wrestler. On a wet day out in the bush, we would sit in the bus and Mick would teach me a bit of Greek. 'Kalimera' for good morning and 'Kalinychta' for good night. Along that track, we would yell out "Paper!" real loud to the guards on the Riverina Express and it didn't take long for the guards to throw us out a paper as they went past.

We would drop all the wires on the poles without cutting outside the angle iron to the cross arms, then cut all the others between the pole and the angle iron and then join them up again back on the ground. When we had them, all joined, we would put together at the end and tied them on the two drums on the back of the winch truck. I'd always get a laugh when the Party Leader, Hank Polsen, would yell out through a loudhailer "all clear," then to let the operator know to throw the rollers in gear to start rolling in the wire, would yell out through the hailer, "Right o, roll them." I used to think he thought he was a movie director/producer. One Monday in the camp, I was talking to Kanga, and I asked how his weekend was at Temora.

"I went to the Temora Joe Blow, had a great day, consumed a fair few amber liquids after the show with a few china plates in the devil house, got home too late, his trouble and strife wasn't too impressed, so he hit the sack, laid the bit of lead down on the weeping willow and had a real big Bo Peep."

Chapter 8

Dismantling 1971 – Trunk Aerial Route Gunning to Cootamundra

n about October 1971, it was time to move camp from Jerrawa as we had pulled the line down as far as Yass. We moved the PMG camp to Binalong, just out from the Boorowa Road about a mile from town. Our PMG gang was in the area and at the same time there was another gang of workers from the railway who were replacing sleepers along the track. Between Yass and Jerrawa, I did a bit of operating the Abbey Basket. This was the bucket on the booms on the back of a truck to work on the poles. I didn't like it too much as one day I was travelling standing up in the bucket along a dirt road which I should not have been doing. I had my back to the direction the truck was travelling and one of the boys on the track yelled out to me to duck, which I did straight away as a low limb on a tree we were passing under crashed across the top of the bucket. I felt blessed!

Near Yass we got a real lot of rain, and we came across a place where alongside the track it was very boggy. We told old Hank the Party Leader we shouldn't go through there with the trucks, that we should cut a fence further along and come back on the other side of the bog. Hank always knew better and ordered the winch truck and the Abbey truck through first as they were four-wheel drive. So, we decided bugger him, he'll pay for not listening to us, so the boys in the four-wheel drives were told to gun them as far as they could. The rest of us would stay close and we bogged the winch truck, two Abbey trucks, the Tip truck, and the double cabin. You just couldn't tell Hank so we were bogged for two days until Dad could walk the dozer miles behind us to pull us out. Sometimes bosses should listen to the workers!

At Binalong camp, Jumbo, one of my workmates from Wollongong, a big overweight fella, offered me a lift on his 450 Honda from the pub back to camp. That day we went through the two bends under the rail overpass, and I saw sparks off the footrests on the bike. I decided I would never be doubled on a motorbike ever again. Jumbo was bloody crazy. Anyway, all along that job to now all the same up to about three weeks before Xmas 1971 when we were to move camp again to Wallendbeen, between Harden and Cootamundra, just working as usual. Dutchy Lee, the publican and owner of the Binalong Pub, said between the PMG gang and the railway gang, we had really helped his pub and appreciated the way both gangs got along and there was never one fight in his pub. For that reason, he put on a Xmas party early and told our cooks not to cook one night and he put on a party, free grog, and food for the night before we moved to Wallendbeen.

By the way, now I was 19 years old as in November past, it had been my birthday. The line inspector had a PMG motorbike which he could ride out on the job and inspect the gangs at work. The motorbike was broken down and I asked Ernie Pavel, the line inspector, if could I ride it from Binalong to Wallendbeen. He said I could if I got it going, which I did. I pulled into Galong and did something I should not have done; had a few beers and then a few more at Harden Murrumburrah. By the time I got to Wallendbeen, I should not have been riding that bike and there was a bloke digging trenches for the drains for our camp from the cook's van and shower and toilet vans. I decided I would jump the trenches on the motorbike and got away with it without breaking my neck. Then I went to talk to the backhoe operator whose name was Pat Allen and realised he was drunk. He told me he had driven the backhoe from Canberra and only had a few beers in each town starting with 'B.' I said not many starting with 'B,' he said there was Burrambateman, Bass, Bowning, Binalong, Balong, Barden, Burrumburrah and Bolendbeen. He was pissed, so I asked if I could have a go on the backhoe and he let me. I'd never told anyone I had operated one a bit on cotton farms at Wee Waa.

The next day we all went to set up the camp and we were all stopping in the pub on TA allowance which was a lot more than camping allowance. Old Hank was at it again, wouldn't listen to us boys. Pat was digging the drains for the camp and old Hank the boss was checking for the fall in the trenches with a spirit level in the bottom of the trench. We couldn't believe it to get the spirit level to show a fall he would stick a clod of dirt under one end of the spirit level. We just let him go and when the pipes were put in Hank found out that water doesn't run up hill. Didn't worry us, we got a week and a half stopping in the pub on big money till the camp was fixed and passed okay to live in.

We were in Wallendbeen about three weeks before Xmas and Jumbo, the big boy from Wollongong was going to make some extra money hay carting. I was thinking of my early days hay carting in Wee Waa and told him it could be a tough job and he said he'd done it before. He did the weekend and when I got back to camp Sunday night, he was a wreck, completely stuffed. I said you knew what you were in for, so it was too much for you. Then I said how much hay carting had you done before then? He said he used to cart hay to his sister's horse!!

One day out on the job, there was four of us in the double cab truck including Kanga when we came to a gate and the strainer post on the latch side of the gate was completely covered with bees. We weren't going near the post and old Kanga talked us into getting up close to the post saying they don't attack when they're like that. When we were close to the post, Kanga took his hat off and shoved it straight down the post. We all took off and Kanga couldn't stop laughing. He did later when three of those bees were in his hat and bit the old bastard on the head. Justice, we thought.

Another time, we all had lunch in the Wallendbeen Pub as we were dismantling close to town. It was a real hot day and there was a couple of young fellows there having lunch and a few beers. They had been hay-carting after starting work early that day and were settling in for the day having a few amber liquids as Kanga would say. That's when Kanga comes out with a bottle full of ants and bet a few schooners each with those boys that he could put those ants in a milk bottle full of water and after work he would kick them over again. When we came in from work, the boys were still there and had been watching the ants at the bottom of the bottle on the top shelf. They were dead, not moving. Kanga took them out to my ute out the front, drained the water off in a newspaper, opened out the paper on the bonnet of my ute and the ants all came around and started walking and Kanga had free beer for the night. The ants on the hot bonnet just walked. I think you can't drown ants. I think he put salt on them.

While working at Wallendbeen, we were getting close to Cootamundra and on 20-12-1971, I went into Cootamundra with Kanga to get some tyres on the old Austin Tip truck which we carted the roles of copper wire to Port Kembla with. First thing we had to go to the police station so I could get my truck (or Class 3) licence. The policeman got me to take him for a drive around Coota and suddenly, he yelled "Left here" which I didn't. He asked me why and I said look out your window – a bloke was going past on a pushbike. The cop said "that will do you, straight back to the station and I'll give you your truck licence." Next point of call, Kanga and I dropped the truck off for some new tyres to be fitted. Kanga looks around and said that's a devil house there, we will have a few amber liquids while they fit the tyres. Well, we had quite a few then Kanga said,

"You're driving back to camp young rooster" and I said,

"No way I just got my licence today and I am not losing it today." He drove us back to camp, but he wasn't too happy with me. The next day, 21st of December, I got a job with the tipper to take a load of angle iron to a property near Stockinbingal. Old Mick George, the Greek and John Cassidy went with me and after we had dropped it off, the cocky said there was beer paid for us at the pub in Stock, a Tooths beer. We had a few and Mick the

Greek drove us back to camp. Back at camp, I was clearing some gear off the back of the truck and tore my left arm open on sharp tin on the aerial toolbox. Never got stiches, still have the scar.

Out on the job at Wallendbeen or Nubba, I saw a young fox about half grown. I could run and said I would catch him. The boys bet I couldn't. I chased that fox up hills and down for half an hour and then the fox did something that surprised me. He ran back down to the boys on the railway track with me on his hammer and stopped in front of me. I took my chance and grabbed his tail. He swung his head around and latched onto the finger on my right hand next to my thumb. Naturally, I quickly pulled my hand back and those little sharp teeth ripped my finger open, but I won the bet. I caught the fox and the fox caught me.

Ernie Pavell, one of our line inspectors, we nicknamed him ENOs for two reasons; 'e knows everything, plus he could give you the tom tits. One day old Hank the party leader was doing his old trick, one foot up on the fence wire impersonating a side stay for a fence and old Kanga counted the wire he had his foot on and pulled out his lineman pliers and cut that wire and Hank went arse overhead.

Chapter 9

Training School, Kenmore, Goulburn – Lineman in Training 1972

D ear old Dad was at me to get my permanency so I could start paying into superannuation. I could either do an exam that seemed you nearly had to be a Rhodes scholar to pass, or I could do a six-month PMG Postmaster General School as a linesman, training at Kenmore in Goulburn. Dad got his way and I started at the school. At 19 years and two months, I did something I thought I would never do...went back to school.

On the first day, our instructor was laying down the rules and said to raise our hand during lessons if we needed to go to the toilet. I was 19 and the other blokes in the class were about 40 and 50 years old (old to me at the time), so we thought that rule was bloody stupid. One bloke, Michael Kelly, had only asked to be excused twice with the hand-raising rule before the instructor decided if we needed to go on a toilet break, just go, as we're grown men. The second time Michael asked, he said

"May I be excused Sir, to go and give birth to an instructor." That was the end of that rule.

We had to learn how to climb poles and build a pole route – aerial route with copper wires. The instructor knew I had come from dismantling the Sydney-Melbourne trunk route or part thereof, so he chose me to show the boys how to use a safety belt. I left a tag inside the buckle which was a no-no and could let the belt slip while up the pole. He decided to make a fool of me, especially when I told him I had never worn a safety belt and why. What he did next was bloody crazy and I let him know what a smart arse he was and bloody dangerous. We put two ladders up either side of an ITP Pole. This is just an isolated terminal pole, no cross arms, about 25 feet up. What the mongrel did next was bloody dangerous: both him and me put our belts around the pole and clipped to the belt. As he was on the other side of the pole, I didn't see him take a hand full of my belt on his side of the pole. He said to lean back in the belt, when I did, he let the belt go. I would have only fell back about four inches, but I thought I was falling all the way to the ground. I needed a way to beat that mongrel and on the next day, I got the bastard off my back.

Out in the yard at the school, we were learning how to stand on the ladder up an isolated terminal pole with the safety belt on, leaning back in the belt using both hands and drilling a hole in the pole with a brace and bit drill. After being spooked a couple of times up the poles at the school, the instructor thought I should go first at this task. When I leant out in the belt and tried to use the drill, my legs went to jelly and I couldn't do it, so the instructor said my ladder wasn't out far enough. He said to stay up the ladder, laid across the top of the pole, while he moved it. Bloody dangerous manoeuvre. I set myself up again to drill and just couldn't do it. My legs felt weak, my nerves were shot, and I'd had enough of that bastard. I climbed down the ladder to the ground, undid my safety belt, let it drop to the ground around my feet, picked it up and threw it to the ground in front of the instructor. With that, the instructor said, if you don't get back up that pole and do as you're told, I will put you on paper for refusing duty. I said, well there are twenty witnesses here who saw you take my ladder from the pole, and I am sure with their witness statements, I could put you on paper! With that the instructor laid off me and not another problem with him I had.

While building our pole route, I was up a pole and noticed an Aboriginal bloke in our class mumbling, walking under the pole I was up. His name was Neville Foster, I think he came from Windang, near Wollongong. He had a bag of white insulators in the canvas work bag and said he was taking them back to the instructor for some different insulators. I said,

"What's wrong with the ones you have?" Neville said,

"They're all white." He would only put coloured insulators on his pole. Neville was a bit of a character!

We had two mates in our class, they had both been together in Vietnam and now they were given a job on the PMG. They worked well together as a team and really proved that in paddocks. We were having a bit of a battle with a couple of magpies swooping us in the yard whilst trying to build our aerial pole route. One of the boys got clipped by a magpie and they decided to get even. One went out in the open carrying a banjo 'shovel' when the magpie was coming into attack his mate yelled out "Incoming at 3 o'clock," and he took him out mid-air.

Another instructor was Arthur Franks, who we nicknamed H.B., because every time we asked him a question, he would say 'just look it up in your handbook.' Other instructors were Don Catlin, Jim Whiley, and George Bowden, the one who gave me a hard time up the poles. The Boss of the school was a real nice old bloke named Vin Ashton. Maurice Kerr was another instructor who was a real character. He was also a mechanic and re-tensioned the head of the engine in my EH Holden Ute after I had a new head fitted by Freddy Addison at Kiama. Anyway, we never knew where Maurie got stuff from, but you could buy just about anything from him. He even sold ladies stockings. Our lunches were made by nurses and workers at Kenmore Mental Home. We would put in our order daily and Maurice Kerr would take them down the road to Kenmore. Now and then, you might get a letter in your lunch and one day I got a lovely letter from Nancy. I met her; she was a nice girl. I think the local girls in Goulburn would keep an eye out on the new fellows in the PMG school and a few would end up marrying these girls.

Enough of that, back to the school where we also had to learn manhole building. We would have to go to the tool store and get our shovels and crowbars. Anything we got out of the store, the instructor would book out and book back in at the end of the day, he would never lose a thing all the way down to a drill or even a drill bit. We built the manholes out of concrete, but we mixed pot ash in the concrete so when we had them built, we could smash up the concrete to be carted away and fill the holes back in with the soil we had dug out. One lot of manhole building, we were filling in the hole and the instructor had to go into the school to see old Vin Ashton for ten minutes, which was all we needed. In went a wheelbarrow and we worked double-time shovelling like mad filling the hole back in over the top of it. That afternoon, the man who never loses anything was checking all the tools back in and couldn't account for...a wheelbarrow. He searched and searched and even kept us back looking for that wheelbarrow. It may well still be buried in the yard to this day. He must have wondered for a long time how such a large item could have disappeared from his store.

For the whole time I was at the school, I stopped in a boarding house at 248 Sloane Street, Goulburn. It was two-story dump, which we used to call 248 Slum Street. We were three to a room and I was in with John McWhirter from Katoomba, and Peter Wallace from Tamworth. Those boys would get sick of me coming in late from the Hibernian Hotel every night waking them up. I just drank and helped at the pub setting up kegs in the cellar. Tapping new kegs was a dangerous thing to do with a few whiskies under your belt, but that was me and never had time to study for exams. I was doing the same as school, thought you should do all your learning at school, not after it.

One fellow who was in the school with me was Paul Smith from Bargo. He could be a bit of an embarrassment to be seen out with in Auburn Street, Goulburn. When he could see a bit of an audience, he would sit on the footpath begging for money, bending his wrists over and twisting his arms to look like he was half deformed. As people walked past, he would say in a weird voice,

"Money, money, need money. War damaged, hit on head with Napalm bomb." People walking past never knew how to take that poor bastard.

In the school, we had to do first aid class and pole top rescue, climbing a pole with a cross arm at the top where a bloody heavy dummy that had a 'heart attack' or was 'electrocuted' was hanging in the safety belt. You would have to throw a safety line over the cross arm twice and tie it under the arms of the dummy, take up the slack, all the while leaning back in your safety belt, take out a sharp pocketknife, cut the belt of the patient and lower them to the ground. Likewise, we had to do manhole rescue for a dummy who was 'electrocuted" or was "out to it from gas.' The thing reinforced to us was not to make yourself a victim like the one you were trying to save. I really took all that safety training, heart massage and artificial respiration very seriously.

I did give Vietnam a bit of a thought at times as I knew I had to register for National Service and a few friends of mine at Wee Waa that I knew ended up in Vietnam. This was my year to register. I was prepared to go if my number came out in the ballot but with some of the stories I'd been told, it wouldn't be so good.

At that time of white feathers and conscientious objectors, university students, mothers objecting in street rallies against their sons being taken to be killed, it was natural to have Vietnam on your mind. I was talking once to my brother Ian about it and about people getting killed over there yet how some of our blokes were treated by our own people for going to Vietnam. Ian said what's the difference to us going to Vietnam or the old diggers in WW1 or WW2 or Korea – if you cop a bullet in the head, you're just as dead no matter which bloody war you're in. We were pissed off with the treatment of our blokes by our own people. It was a bastard of a time.

Well, I learnt a bit in the school and Jim Whiley was an instructor who could get through to me. I really liked his teaching about Applied Electricity, protons, neutrons, electrons and magnetism, electronic fields, sacrificial anodes. I loved learning about current flow and that where you had a potential difference, current must flow. With current flow, as Mr Whiley put it, the thicker a real copper wire was the less resistance you get to the flow of current so it would travel over a longer distance easier.so he likened it to pumping water through a large pipe compared to a small pipe. Through a large pipe less resistance so more water would flow. Through a small pipe, more resistance so less water would flow. If you had a cable running along with a high voltage power cable, because of the difference in voltage, the current from the high voltage through the electric field would be induced into another cable. So, even if a cable was ploughed into the ground along a high voltage line and the cable was open each end of the length before it was jointed-in, just the static electricity in that cable would allow current to flow into that length of cable. This meant you had to earth an end of the cable to discharge the build-up of power before joining cables, as you would get a good kick out of it otherwise. The length of cable had, with the induced power, became a capacitor, which until earthed-out, stored electricity. This would go to earth through you. All this makes you think of Tesla and his theories.

A thing we learnt about the old telephones and how they worked amazed me. Magnetism and current flow to send voice over a pair of wires by the mouthpiece on the phone, being compressed carbon granules, which when your voice hit them jumped around and sent your voice through the wires and the receiving end with magnets. A thin tin plate vibrated, and you heard a voice you could recognise, if you knew the caller that was.

Next, we would learn about mechanical advantages in how pulleys work. Advantages from say wheels, levers, and fulcrum. To figure out what mechanical advantage you could gain to lift or move a load, we learnt about efficiency percent, drag, co-efficiencies of friction, drag on slopes and friction equations.

Mr Jim Whiley had a way of making you see what he was trying to teach you. I made a lot of friends there at the school and one was Bob Marmonte from Dapto. I would give him a lift home on weekends when he was going home. I think his family originated from Captains Flat. His old man worked in Appin Mines and ended up with what they called 'dust on the lungs' in those days. Another bloke in my class was Charlie Mitchell from Wellington. We came from all NSW.

It was late in the time at school when I found out that there were positions all over NSW for us to be sent to after the six months of school was completed and sadly for me, most were in Sydney. Then an instructor told me something that had me worried and that was that the choice of where you would like to go was figured out on your exam results. Straightaway I knew I was in trouble. I had passed all exams without studying but was behind all the other blokes' marks. Mr Jim Whiley told me I'd best do better in the last six months exam to try and get a country position which would probably not be the case! Off to Sydney I feared!

So, for about the third time in my life, I set about studying for the last exam. I tried studying the books and written schoolwork and got a cassette player and taped myself reading and would go to sleep listening to my own words to make me remember and lock in all I needed to know for the big exam. I really studied applied electricity and natural science, and when I sat the exam, Mr Whiley was in charge. When I completed the exam, I handed my paper to him and he said,

"You can't be finished, have you?" I said,

"Yes" and he said,

"Okay, you can leave but the only thing you would have studied would be the barmaid in the Hibernian Hotel." Once it was all marked, Mr Whiley could not believe I got a mark over 90%. When he told me, he also said he knew what I was doing, trying to get a bush-placement, but I was too late trying. The station in Mosman, Sydney needed a trainee, so that was to be my Head Station to complete my field training.

One more thing to do and that was to say goodbye to Goulburn. We did that in a big way which should have made front page in the Goulburn paper. A farewell party was organised at the RSL Club for the Friday night and the next day we would leave Goulburn. At the party something happened I would never forget, and it was to be with those two tough Vietnam veterans. I would think of those two buggers with M16s in the Vietnam jungle, but next thing one goes over, lifts the lid on a piano and starts playing like a pro while his mate pulls a piano accordion from somewhere and the whole mob is singing and putting on a show.

We all had a great night, with more to come from these Vietnam Vets at midnight. They had got hold of about eight army distress flares and came up with a plan for us to split into groups of two or three men around town. The Vets went up to the top of the hill where the War Memorial was, with the idea to set-off a green flare and signal the rest of us to let-off flares all over Goulburn. I was with a couple of blokes at the showground – our flare went past me and luckily missed Graham Stephenson, or it could have killed us. Apparently, you must hold a flare with the back of your hand pointing to you so when you hit the detonator on the bottom, it doesn't kick back into you. Might have been good to know these things both before letting one off...and sober. Don't know if it was ever reported in the Goulburn paper or not, but that was the end of my six-month school stint with PMG – 'Farewell Goulburn.'

Chapter 10

Sydney – Balgowlah & Mosman – July 1972- Mid 1973

As the result of not studying, I found myself sent to Mosman on the North Shore to do my field training and it was made my Head Station. I was far from the bush I longed-for. To make me feel worse, when I walked into the Line Depot at Mosman, I was asked who I was and what I wanted. When I told them I was their new linesman in training from the LIT School at Goulburn, they said I was not expected and that they had their staff numbers already sorted. They made some phone calls and sent me out with a gang down a leafy street past the Strata Hotel on Military Road off to the right well before the Spit Bridge. They decided I should have a go on the pneumatic-spader, like a jack hammer, only with a steel spade on it. I was digging along listening to the machine and the compressor running and thinking about where I was and not the bush and I shouldn't be where I was. Then I hit something and an Italian bloke in the gang that was watching me pushed me over and yelled out,

"One bash and your ash." I had hit and smashed an electric brick which they would lay along in a trench to warn over high voltage power cables.

I had moved into my accommodation at Wallaringa Mansion in Neutral Bay. It was up the hill from Neutral Bay wharf about 500 metres, to the left going towards the wharf down a long road from Sydney Road and close to the Oaks Hotel. The manager of the boarding house was an ex-boxer and didn't take anyone playing up in the mansion. Our board was setup for us by the PMG. I spent a fair bit of my time sitting on the Neutral Bay wharf watching ships and big white passenger liners going to and from Circular Quay. That pastime, even though I was surrounded by the city, always gave me a certain peace, probably like Gordon Chater's 'My Name's McGooley, What's Yours?' because he spent a lot of the time on the wharf just thinking and fishing.

After a few days working at Mosman, I was called into the office and the line inspector said that there's no position for me in Mosman. For a minute I allowed myself to dream I might be sent out into the bush, but I was quickly stopped with that thought when I was told I was being sent to Balgowlah and that would be my Head Station. I was given some paperwork and directions, which began my time for twelve months working in Balgowlah, Manly, Manley Vale area. One good thing about that was I would have to drive past Mosman to get to my new station, as the PMG had found my accommodation at Neutral Bay, I was entitled to ETT – excess travelling time, paid daily on top of my normal wage and non-taxable.

There were a few blokes getting ETT money and it always came on a Wednesday and the fellas would always put a bit on the TAB. One Wednesday, I told them I would put my money on the daily double and backed on 'Western Yarn and Stormy Seas' and I won a nice bit of money. I chose Western Yarn only because I always thought of heading west and that day the seas were rough and stormy.

I was working in a gang doing pit and pip, and the Party Leader was big Steve Moxham. I found I enjoyed working in that gang. As I found in Sydney, in gangs doing that type of work, the Italians loved operating the jackhammers and the Greeks loved concreting. One day we were on top of last hill going down to Manly in Military Road (on the right looking down to Manly) and we were in amongst a rabbit warren of tall blocks of units, creamy brick buildings. We were laying pit and pipes for the cables; it was a bit rocky and looked like railway or tram lines had been there once. Steve, the Party Leader, told me to go over the road on the corner where we had a work caravan and a good dump of sand, fill the wheelbarrow with sand to put around the asbestos pipes and pits we were laying. Just down a bit from that corner where the sand and caravan were, there was a house with a house name on it called the Shiralee. At the time, I had been to Gosford for the weekend to visit my dad's parents Pa and Nan Oxley and that weekend on TV was that great movie the Shiralee with, I think Chips Rafferty, then on the Monday noticed that house and thought what a coincidence, same name 'Shiralee.'

Anyway, back to the wheelbarrow full of sand, I'd filled the barrow and had pushed it across Military Road and got it onto the footpath. I was about to push it through the rabbit warren as I called it and an old bloke pulled up in a white HT Holden

Kingswood. He got out of his car slowly as I watched him, and I said G'day. He said G'day back and asked me if I could carry a heavy parcel for him as he had the gout and lived on the top story. I said no worries and went to the boot to get out his heavy parcel, which happened to be a box of longneck beers. We got them up to his place and he said,

"You better have a beer," I said,

"No thanks, better get back to that barrow." Then he told me he had been a shearer who turned out to have shorn with my uncle Hilton Morgan, and he said on the strength of that I'd have to have a beer with him. So, we had a few, talked about the bush and Brewarrina, then I left to get back to work. When I got back down the barrow was gone and I had to go front big Steve Moxham. Steve said where the bloody hell have you been, so I told him my story, all of it. Steve said,

"I suppose you had a few beers?" I thought bugger it, you can sack me, and I'll be back off to the bush and said,

"Yes, I had a few." Then Steve said,

"That's good, if you hadn't had any I'd have sacked you."

I was put to work with an Irish cable jointer, his name was Bobby Burns and we worked on fault repairs. Bobby was a bit of a rogue and he knew where every fruit tree and unattended vegetable garden was in the area. One day, he said we better go down to Manly and see how his choco farm was going. There was a vacant block and a great choco vine growing on the neighbour's fence and he said he always gets his chocoes there. There was a house in Manly Vale that had a big orange tree to the front and left side of the house, so we pulled up out the front in the PMG Ute and I went in with him. He said to the lady we had just cut over a cable round the corner and were making sure the phones were all working. He checked the phone and told her all's okay. When we were out the door, he remarked how lovely those oranges were, she told us to help ourselves to some which we did. Back in the Ute, I said Bobby that was all bullshit we're not even working in the area, he said, "Just shut up and learn."

After work I would drive back over the Spit, go down to the wharf, sit and watch the harbour for a while then go back to the mansion in Neutral Bay and have dinner. Often, I would go out with Bob Marmont who I met at the school in Goulburn to have a few beers at the Oaks Hotel and almost as often we would run into John Mellion, a real drinker, but a bloody nice bloke. I ran into John and his mate in wine bars along the Sydney Road too, most memorable in the Strata Hotel at Mosman where a loud-mouthed Yank was screaming that he was going to go into the bush and bag a few roos. John was having a bit of fun with the bloke that night, so I joined in, all with a bit to drink and taking the mickey out of this Yank. I made out I was really pissed-off with him, saying it gave me the shits how the Yanks come out here and shoot our pets. The poor Yank must have thought I was fair dinkum, so he changed tack and said he was thinking about corralling them. We all laughed and told him he'd want to build a high fence. That night, John Mellion and his mate were broke, and I brought a sterling silver ring off them for $10.00, rough holes in it with purple stone. I still have that ring.

Next thing at work, I was put with another jointer known as Blinky Bill because he had a constant blink. I thought working with him he'd get me sacked and, on my way back to the bush. He wasn't very far off retirement and did not give much care about things, along with no fear of the bosses. We worked out of a Red VW Combi Van with the gold lettered PMG on the doors and

I was the driver. We had a job one day in Condamine Street that wasn't far from the depot so the bosses could keep an eye on old Blinky. We had to open-up one of the big main cables, about 1000 pair cable, lead sheath cable paper insulted wire conductors. As was required, you would have to ring and get a sequence number to be able to open the cable and you could open the cable by plumbing off the seam on the joint with a flame and a hook shave. Well old Blinky didn't seem too interested in doing that job and said to me,

"I don't think we should open this cable; you know. The rules say we can't open it if there's rain about." What I noticed about Blinky for a city bloke was he spoke really slow with a bit of a drawl. I said,

"Blinky, it's not going to rain and there are no clouds. We better get into it." He then tells me,

"There's a heap big storm coming" and he rubbed his hands together and said clouds could just be lurking. I asked him where they were lurking, and he said just over the horizon. Then he asked me to drive him to some lookout, high ground to check all directions for clouds lurking over the land's horizon and the ocean's horizon. Blinky told me where to drive looking for these non-existent clouds and we ended up way out of our area at Mona Vale. It was while parked in Mona Vale that I noticed a boss's car pull up and bugger me, it was Les Smith our Line Inspector, and I knew we were in big trouble. Told Blinky and said to him,

"For Christ's sake don't tell Les know we are up here looking for clouds." Les said,

"What are you two buggers doing up here in Mona Vale when you're supposed to be in Cordamine Street, Balgowlah?" With that, Blinky told him,

"As you know we had to get a flamethrower to open the cable and we came up here to buy a box of matches." Once again, I thought this was going to get me out of Sydney, but instead they just put a ban on the two of us from any overtime for six weeks.

Another thing about Blinky is when we had a vehicle, he would get up people, if he seen an old bugger on a pedestrian crossing, he'd say 'keep going run over the old bastard, he's had his time.' Once, it was 100 degrees and we saw a Priest on a crossing. Blinky said,

"Look at that mad bastard, black coat, black shirt, black duds, even carrying a black bloody bible. He deserves to get heat stroke the mad bastard." I do not know why but old mate was often not too happy with the world and its inhabitants. One day, we were both in a manhole and there must have been a big soccer game in England the night before. A pommy came up and of all the people in Sydney, he picked Blinky to ask,

"Who won soccer last night?" Blinky answered by saying he didn't know and that's all you poms know is soccer and soap dodging.

Blinky told me of a story when he and another bloke were at some Japanese people's home around Cremorne and the Japanese had to leave and said to them to help themselves to drink while they wired the house. They were running a cable through cupboards under the sink and Blinky seen an earthenware bottle with Japanese writing on it. His mate asked what it was and Blinky told him SAKI. His mate grabbed it and took a good swig. It turned out to be washing up detergent. Blinky and me were then to work out of a cart, joining-in and cutting-over the cable in that rabbit warren, Military Road where I worked in the gang with Steve Moxham. We had no vehicle to get away into places like Mona Vale. Couple of days in on that job, about 10.45am, Blinky said we are walking down to the pub in Manly. I thought bloody hell we will get in trouble again, but we never did get found out. A couple of days later, after being told our foreman, Bill Scarlet, had been looking for us and couldn't find us at the work cart, we were instructed that we had to stick a note on the lid with insulation tape letting him know where we were always that we were not working at the cart. So, at 10.45am, Blinky said we are going for a walk down to Manly pub. I said what about a note on the cart to say where we are. Blinky said he did. I went over to the cart and sure enough he had written where we were as 'IN UNITS.' We could have been anywhere in that rabbit warren of a place.

After that job with Blinky, I was to work with Johnny Hall and he was a terrific teacher and the most conscientious cable jointer and worker in Balgowlah, and we did big cable jobs, a cut-over of pillars, the works. John would share the crap jobs with me and wouldn't ask you to do anything, or work under a house, that he would not do himself. I went under a house on a real steep two-story, Arnott's house at 40 Baskets Beach, and coming out the same way I went in, I got stuck under a beam. It scared me a bit and I had to be dug out. I don't know if it's true, but one of the boys told me when you get scared you swell up a bit. I don't know but it sure wouldn't surprise me. I worked with John for a few months, and I will be honest, the only thing I ever saw John do slightly wrong was when we were cutting over a new pillar in Military Road, Balgowlah. It was on the southwest corner, east of the Post Office. John said to me to do and finish a 50 pair joint while he was gone. I asked where he was going and he said,

"Just around the corner to get a haircut." I said,

"You can't do that in working hours," and John said,

"I am only getting the stuff cut off that grew in working hours." You couldn't find a bloke more honest than John. Johnny and I were doing a big cut-over, replacing a whole street from old cable to new cable at Manly Vale. I was left in a six pit to do some dead jointing on a 50 pair plastic joint. I had the guards up around me and the tent over the top listening to my transistor, jointing away, quite relaxed you might say. Next thing I heard an engine rev, then brakes, then bang into guards and tent, which somehow rolled, and I went rolled in it, upside down. One front wheel of an EH Holden was in the six-pit on the footpath where I'd been working. An old woman got out, hair looking freshly permed and coloured, screaming,

"Oh my god, what have I done," plumb in the mouth and all. I untangled myself, raced over to her and gave her a cuddle, saying,

"Don't worry, lady. I'm alright!" She immediately said she wasn't worried about me, what on earth had she done to the car. Old bitch, I thought! When we finished that job, John stayed in the Depot upgrading the plans and I would go and pull out all the old cable. I had the back of that jointer's ute covered in cable going back to the depot when I got pulled up by a bloke on a Stop-Go sign. He said,

"G'day OX." I couldn't believe it a few million people in Sydney and a bloke I grew up with as a kid pulls me up in Sydney road-works. Talk about a small world.

Every payday, I would give the blokes on the pay car a letter to take back addressed to the Divisional Engineer at Chatswood. Another application for a transfer to all these different places in the bush. I met the engineer one day and he told me that they were extending an office at Head Quarters at Chatswood and were putting another girl on just to process my applications for 'transfer anywhere in the bush.'

Every Wednesday night at the Oaks Hotel at Neutral Bay, there would be a talent quest and the talent there was really very good. I used to think about their ability and one night I was asked to help judge them. That night an aboriginal man about 60 years old got up and sang Al Jolson songs. He got my vote and won that night. One night three of my mates and me decided to go into Kings Cross and it was a night I'll never forget. First, we went to a bar called the Beef and Burger where I ran into some of the low life in Sydney. We had a couple of rounds of drinks and then it was my shout which I ordered and paid for. We were sitting there, having the drinks, when a big overgrown goon came up to me and said,

"When are you going to pay for the drinks." I stood up and said I've already paid. He grabbed me by the shirt front and a girl who worked there came over and said to me, you better pay him, or he'll take you out the back. I paid up and we all left that dump never to return. We walked up to the El Alamein fountain and there was one bloke bashing another fellow backwards down the centre of the street. We decided to walk down to the Ned Kelly Tavern and after being in there we would walk to Circular Quay and catch a ferry back to Neutral Bay. While walking along one of my mates said look over the road at four skinheads walking along the footpath on the other side of the road. My mate said watch them, we're all long hairs and they may attack us. If they do, you fellows run, and I'll try sort them out. The skinheads ran across the road towards us, and my mate said run. We got about thirty yards away, stopped and looked back. One skinhead had our mate. We were going back when we heard a crack like something broke and a scream from a skinhead. They stayed together and we took off to the Quay when our mate showed us what he did. The skinhead grabbed his hair, and our mate locked his own hands together over the skinhead's hand, pulled down on his hand, ducked down, turned away and with a sharp jerk away from the skinhead, snapped his wrist. After that night, if we went into Sydney, we would just go to the snooker parlours in the main drag over the road from Central Station. That was enough adventure for us.

One night we were late getting to the Quay and missed the last ferry and so we walked over the Harbour Bridge to Millson's Point and onto the mansion at Neutral Bay. A lot of boys who were sent to Sydney from Goulburn school decided we would have a reunion at the Oaks at Neutral Bay six months after leaving the Goulburn school. We started off well with about ten of us going to Millson's Point to a restaurant called the Dinosaurus Inn. I asked for a glass of wine and was told they only serve by the bottle. I said don't worry about it. That's when two snobs in suits said where you blokes from, so I told them we were part of a football team from Cootamundra. They said to the waitress, give these boys a bottle of wine and it just kept coming. We all had a meal and when it was time to pay and go, these two city slickers were gone, and we were stuck with the wine bill! I was arguing about the bill and the restaurant was threatening to call the police on us. There were two levels in the floor where we were eating, so they went back to get their smokes and put together the money to pay for the wine. We paid the bill and when we got outside, they said to run to the cars, they had knicked all the cutlery from the tables as payback.

Neville Foster, our aboriginal mate, suggested we go into Redfern to a pub called the Princes Palace. We weren't there long as some black fellas were trying to get money off us and Neville told them to do what he was doing and get a job. There were thongs all around the walls and chairs, with the jukebox playing Lionel Rose singing when a 'BOY BECOMES A MAN' over and over. A couple of women started fighting and the natives were getting restless, so we got out of there. It wasn't long after that, I was at the Oaks Hotel and a bloke named Denis who lived at the mansion too, left the pub, walked out into traffic in Sydney Road and was skittled and killed.

Johnny Hall tried to get me paid an allowance for jointing money. He had taught me to joint all cables including plumbing of lead cables, which you needed to have a bit more ability to achieve. He had me doing all types of jointing and taught me all the colour codes as well. He was a good teacher, conscientious, honest and a respected man on the job. Anyway, when he put it to the engineers, they said I could keep jointing all cables, but I was not to do any plumbing of lead cables. In that way, they could still use me as a cable jointer, but I wouldn't need to be paid a jointer's allowance.

I still spent a fair bit of time just sitting at Neutral Bay wharf, looking at the harbour. Being there in the guts of Sydney it somehow, for me, was a place of peace. I must say that my twelve months in Sydney was made easier because of the North Shore, and I have a lot of good memories of that time.

At last, the day I had been waiting for arrived. The line inspector, Les Smith, called me into his office to tell me I had annoyed the Chatswood office enough that I had been given a transfer to Jerilderie. Johnny had however been pushing a bit for more school for me and I only spent one week in Jerilderie before starting a ten-week cable jointing school at North Strathfield. I was paid Capital City living away from home allowance, which was worth a packet, non-taxable and I never lost my room at the mansion.

I did the school at North Strathfield for the ten weeks, but I had a little trouble with the supervising instructor there. The school was easy as I knew jointing cable after six months with John Hall, but I hadn't counted on clashing with the supervising instructor. Half our school was a written exam and the other half we were assessed on our practical skills. I was opening a cable and slipped with a pocketknife and cut my left hand. There was no instructor in the room, so I went over the hall into the first aid room, put some Dettol on the wound and a couple of band aids. The supervising instructor walked in and asked what happened and made me complete a P400 accident report. I had to mark the cause as one of three:

1: Lack of instruction, I said no.
2: Unsafe workplace, I said no.
3: Unsafe work practices, I said no.

He then wrote on the report that I was a careless worker and that I was unsafe to work with. He made me sign it and I went back to class. In a German Gestapo accent, I warned the boys. I said,

"Ve have certain vays of finding out za infamation vich ve vont to know das is known as za P400." I turned around and guess who was at the door listening to me put the bastard down. Didn't know at the time, but I was to hear more about this incident two years later.

Chapter 11

Off to Barham and Jerilderie 1973 Part 1A

I completed jointing school and then it was off from the big smoke and out to Jerilderie. My first job in Jerilderie was fixing a 200lb copper wire on the J route (that's a pole route open wire telephone line between Narrandera and Jerilderie). The country was wide and flat, and I was up the top of a pole just looking at the openness, remembering the buildings, tar, and cement of the city and then I was thinking of the Harbour, Opera House, and Neutral Bay wharf.

The next job in Jerilderie was to pump out a manhole on the corner in the Main Street outside the Royal Hotel. I put the centrifugal pump on the back of the ute and Jerry, the boss, said he'd walk up the back lane and direct me where to park on the footpath. When he told me to stop, I said I needed to go further as the pump ran off a pully under the bonnet and it wouldn't reach the manhole. The boss insisted I set it up where he said...that's when I realised, we were pumping out the beer cellar on the pub. We left the ute running with a brick partially holding the accelerator down, while we sat in the bar drinking free beer. How could I forget that being one of my first jobs out there? After very little time re-making all the cable joints in the Main Street business centre of Jerilderie, the boss came to me with news that the Divisional Office in Narrandera wanted me to go and work at a place called Barham. I said to the boss, where the bloody hell is that? Jerry said it was 60-mile upriver from Swan Hill, on the Murray River and 60 mile the other side of Deniliquin. I said for how long? He said could be six weeks, you'll be paid TA and you will be getting paid jointer in charge or JIC allowance as well. So, I took it on and off I went to Barham wondering at the time how I landed that. Did Lionel Chapman, the Divisional Engineer at Narrandera have anything to do with it. Lionel had been my engineer on the Primary Works job on the dismantling of part of the Sydney-Melbourne trunk route.

My first day at Barham, I made a bit of a fool of myself. I went to the Barham Hotel for a counter lunch and while having lunch noticed a great big fish up on the wall. It was bloody near as big as me and I asked a local,

"Who put that together is that real?" He said,

"Bloody oath," that's when I told him I had no idea that a freshwater fish could be that big. We had a laugh and he introduced himself to me. I told him I was looking for a place to stay and he told me the PMG blokes always stopped at Matesy's Pub over the river in Koondrook, VIC. I crossed the border into Mexico and booked into the pub at Koondrook. I got a room to the front of the pub, furthest room from the bar, next to the kitchen and opposite the bathroom. One of the first jobs I got was with Mick Lewis. He had a bit of a reputation for catching snakes. We were doing a joint one day in a bank by the road where there was a bit of a creek, Cow Creek. We heard a vehicle pull up on the road at the top of the bank. Mick said,

"That's Lofty Howard our line inspector from Balranald. We don't want him to see the way we are doing this joint." Mick got up and walked towards Lofty and said,

"I've seen a couple of red belly blacks down there," then I heard Lofty say,

"Jesus bloody Christ did you get the bastards?" Mick said,

"No they're still down there somewhere." With that Lofty said,

"Alright I've got to go I'll leave you two fellas with it I will catch you boys later." That's when Mick said,

"That's how you get rid of Lofty. He's shit scared of snakes."

We had a good bit of open aerial work and lots of faults in duck season as the rice attracted the ducks and you would hear gas scare guns going off a bit, to scare the ducks. You learn quick if you had a short circuit on an aerial fault. Instead of testing in spots, you would drive the pole route and look for a duck, especially near water. They would hit the wires in flight and the wires crossed over each other and the duck would be hung there by the neck. Mick told me he did a lot of duck shooting with his dog 'Ripper.' He met an Italian shooter from Melbourne who told him all birds are good to eat, even pigeons. Mick said he meant Kookaburras. I went out shooting with Mick one time and he lent me a side-by-side shotgun. I managed to miss everything until I had only one shot left. I saw a duck going over, stood up from where we were sitting on a track, and I fired nearly from the hip and got the duck. Mick reckoned that duck was the unluckiest duck that ever flew.

One weekend in Matesy's Pub in duck shooting season, the place was full of Mexican duck shooters sprawling out of the pub, under the verandas and onto the footpath. It was a hot day and anyone who had just pulled up at the pub would wonder what all the laughing was about. What had happened, a bloody great praying mantis had come along into the bar, and he had a thirst. He had a bit of a drink out of the tray near the beer taps and was staggering down the bar slurping up any spills. I have never seen a praying mantis drunk and I don't think anyone else had. He had his work cut out for him trying to control those long spindly legs. If only I could have filmed him.

There was a bloke who drank at that pub who had a real bad fear of snakes but had another problem he could not knock back a bet. One bloke bet him he couldn't have his green Queensland tree snake around his neck for half an hour. He took and won the bet but threw up for about half hour once they got the snake off him.

Billy Street was a dairy farmer there and he always used to have a go at me by calling me a government-bludging bastard. We were having trouble in the cooler times with fogs and dew in the air with lots of phones on the aerial pole route going off the air of a night-time. The problem was caused by what they called honey spiders who send their young off in the breeze on cobwebs. The webs would hit the phone lines and stick across the two wires needed for the phone circuit. When the dew got on the web, the sheer number of them would put a short circuit on the line and kill the phones. We even hired water pumps from the Forestry Commission and tried to hose the webs off the trunk lines, but it never worked. If you looked up to the sky, you could literally see billions of these white webs floating across a bright blue sky. Bill Street, true to his shit-stirring form, got me in the pub and was going on about the phones being off, saying that bloody excuse about spiders was bullshit. So, I told him, there were two types of people that didn't believe it. Arrogant bastards and brain-dead pricks, he just had a way about him that got to me. One day, Billy drove in behind the pub to get some grog out of pub hours. I had split a heap of wood for the kitchen and for old Chooky Bell, who used to keep the fires going at the pub. I had a big load on the barrow and Bill says,

"What's a government-bludger doing putting such a load on the barrow." That's when some stuff I had learned in Goulburn came to me and I said,

"I have a wheelbarrow to take the load. I have a wheel to assist me. I have the assistance of levers and a fulcrum and by doing it in one load instead of two with just a little more effort I only have to overcome the effects of coefficient of friction once, so I gain a little efficiency percent doing the job moving the load in one movement." He said,

"Oh" and went into the pub to get his supplies for the day.

Another time Bill was winging in the pub about the government, I'd had enough of him and told him you can't blame the government for everything. Told him if he would help his wife milk the cows, he could have more cows and make more money, but instead I've seen of him scratching the front door of the pub before 10 o'clock in the morning like a mongrel dog looking for grog. He could do better to stop blaming the government. Above the bar was a big wooden spoon which had engraved or burnt into it 'Bill Street Shit Stirrer of the Year' and the blokes in the bar said my name was going on it the next year.

Stopping in the pub was a nice old Italian bloke named Angelo. Once a year, he would get on the grog on his birthday and bring out an old squeeze box, playing and singing his Italian songs. He was entertaining and he'd worked forever at the Arbanought's Sawmill on the Murray River. Locals told me as he was still working, that some could remember that was about the tenth time he'd had his 70th birthday.

It happened one day in the pub; you haven't been in a bush pub unless someone rides in on a horse for a beer. Never know what you might see in an outback pub really.

I run into a bloke named Snowy Freeman at the RSL Club in Barham, playing snooker and billiards. He was about 70 and he told me he had been a Victorian Boxing Champion. He said he'd give me a game of billiards with a start of 80 to 100. Then he told me, this bloke saw him playing once and asked for a game. He said to that bloke,

"I'll give you 80-start to 100." The bloke says,

"Do you know who I am?" Snowy said,

"No." The bloke says,

"I am Eddie Charlton" so Snowy said,

"Alright, I'll only give you 50-start." I talked to other fellows around Barham, and they said they thought it was true about his boxing and that he had played in demonstrations against Eddie Charlton. I found out he could box. He showed me. He hit me or should I say clipped both my ears with his fists and punched me in the heart. I thought I was going to die but I found out why even the young fellas in town would not cross Snowy Freeman.

There was a solicitor from Cohuna. His name was McKenzie. He used to stop in the pub in Koondrook one night a week to see clients in Koondrook and Barham. I had a few drinks with him one night and he talked me into making my first will. He told me about how his wife was not happy with him always drinking and enjoying himself, so he sorted that problem out. He took her out with him the Saturday afternoon and then into the night trying to keep her drinking with him. Then on the Sunday morning, she was complaining to him how bad she felt looking for some sympathy, so he said to her, "See and you reckon I am enjoying myself all the time!"

One day we were a bit mean to one workmate from Balranald. We suspected damage to a cable which was run between two poles across the Wakool River north of Barham, we thought the cable had been chewed by cockatoos. We talked Dicky Barber alias Ali, to let us put two pullies over the cable and two safety belts on him and tied ropes to him to run him out to check the aerial cable over the river. When Ali was over the middle of river, we tied the ropes to the poles and told Ali we were going to lunch. We only left him there for ten minutes and then let him down.

I learnt for myself firsthand the problem caused by irrigating rice in Barham. One very hot day I took a drink from a bore pumping up water and running it down a table drain. It was full of salt and where that water would run could only cause harm. I was told because of irrigating rice; the water table was rising. I thought then that was related to trees dying from 'die back.'

John Davis was a barman at the pub I lived in at Koondrook and I found out he didn't have much of a sense of humour when he dropped me in the lady's lounge. All I did was write on the blackboard in the bar 'John Davies Chef; today's special unborn kittens cooked in beer batter.' No sense of humour.

I'd heard about those bloody European carp fish how they travelled all over our waterways and I saw firsthand how. I was heading to Balranald from Moulamein and to my left the Edwards River was in flood and expanded across the flat paddocks to and across the road, about eight or ten inches deep. Then in the water across the road, I see carp splashing about, so I don't know how many I killed but I was fish tailing for a while.

I had an occasion to go to fix a fault at an area call Niemur and as usual you would go straight to the little bush exchange and test the line. There was a lot of PPE lines out there, they were where the PMG would only go so far with cable, or open wire pole routes and the subscriber would be responsible for building and up keeping of their own line past that point. Some of those lines were not anything to write home about and how they worked I didn't know. Some weren't too far from the ground especially if a pole fell from white ant attack. Anyway, I tested the line at the exchange and the line tested okay, so I rang and said,

"PMG linesman here, just tested the line, it's testing okay now." The women who answered said,

"The men had been out in the morning on horseback and had fixed the line, it was those blasted kangaroos jumping into the wires again." Some lines were a bit rough!!

Working with Mick was always exciting in snake season as I always had a job holding the wheat bag open for Mick to drop the snakes in when he caught them. I would sometimes have to get down on my haunches and watch those snakes swinging past my eyes. No one would flog tools in the back of our fault truck in summer times. One day we were coming back to Barham from Moulamein, and I opened my big mouth and said to Mick that as Cow Creek was flooded, the dirt track through the forest would have plenty of red bellied blacks. We went in and Mick caught half a dozen snakes. He did this as he would take them down to a reptile park in Kerang in Victoria to be milked of their venom to save people who got bitten.

Micky and I worked together just about all the time and when we cleared a fault, we would ring the tech in the exchange and get him to test the line and then ring the subscriber while we sat across the line with our phone and listened. Sometimes we wouldn't have the line put right through and when the technician rang, Mick might answer it with an accent or talk like a woman and get stuck into the tech like an irate customer. The tech never knew how to take us, whether he was talking to us, or the subscriber.

One day we were working on a line towards Kerang in Victoria, for a Miss West 532580 and asked the tech to ring the old bird to test the line. This time we listened across the line. He rang and said,

"PMG tech testing the line," and then said,

"Is that Mrs West?" she said,

"No Miss" then tech asked the phone number. She said in a stutter,

"Five th-th-th three t-t-two f-f-five eight aught." Next thing the tech says,

"Listen Mick, why don't you get Steve to grab you by the balls and make it sound a bit more convincing." We cut the wires straight away so he couldn't say anymore to Miss West, and we never ever heard anything about it. The way she said, 'No Miss' reminded me of Dick Emery the Pommy Comedian.

A call came in for a fault at Mallen, so Mick and I went out. It was a short circuit fault with no earth on it. Mick said we'd check the house out first and then the wire across the river. We tested into the homestead, and it was S/C inside the house. We walked around the veranda looking inside and saw the phone off the hook hanging down to the floor and near it a big dead possum. There was no one home. We found a window which was not locked, went in, removed the dead possum, and hung it on a fence behind the shed. Then we left a note on the phone which said we had entered the premises, put the phone back on hook and removed a dead possum, which may have died trying to call triple 000. Turned out the customer had two more weeks away on holiday and dropped in a carton of beer to our line foreman, Herb Klein, for our good work.

There was a good story we got to know about a gang working at Balranald in the street putting in some cable, where an old lady came out of her house screaming the house was on fire and she had to get her piano out. Two of the boys went to help move the piano and one jammed his hand and swore his head off badly. The third bloke put a ladder up the chimney and soaked a wheat bag and put it over the chimney as he figured out the chimney was on fire. One of the fellows moving the piano told Lofty, the line inspector, about the other bloke swearing in front of the old lady. Lofty then made a mistake. He took the swearing bloke round to apologise to the old lady. Lofty said,

"What do you have to say to Mrs Smith" Lofty said and the fella says,

"I've come around to apologise for making such a f'ing bastard out of myself for f'ing swearing in front of you yesterday."

I was sent up to Balranald to help Brum Walker cut-over some new cable in the Main Street near Elders. I would have one night on travelling allowance to pay for a hotel or motel room. When Brum and I knocked off, we went to the Shamrock Hotel and boy, he could drink. I hadn't booked in anywhere and Brum suggested I camp in the pole inspectors caravan in the yard. This was not a good idea; the van was full of bloody mosquitos and that's when I found the line inspector's office was unlocked. It had an air conditioner, and it was bloody hot that night. I dragged the mattress out of the van and while getting paid an allowance for accommodation went to sleep on that mattress on the boss's floor. Next thing I know is bloody Lofty standing over me blowing the bloody hell out of me. I thought that's all I need as if I wasn't feeling bad enough anyway with the hangover I had. Anyway, Lofty forgave me and life moved on.

Stopping in the pub at Koondrook was a relief policeman named Des Purdin and he gave it to me over my doing a few demos in my ute near Arbanought's Mill. I was going past the pub and saw him out the front. He must have heard me I thought, so I parked the ute up behind the pub under the pepper trees and was at the back of the pub when Des grabbed me. He said,

"Was that you making all that noise?" I said yes and Des said,

"Do you realise you could not only be heard over all Victoria but also half of New South Wales." I said,

"I am sorry about that." He said,

"Never again, you need your licence for your job!"

At work Mick and I would sometimes do a bit of circus tricks to fix private phone lines. The GI wires between poles would sometimes be tangled together in the span and you could throw a stick at them till the cows came home and you couldn't knock the short out. We would put a ladder up in the middle of the span, one would hold it straight up nearly and the other would climb up the ladder and untwist the wires. Another trick we did was to get onto the paddle steamer the 'Pevensy' from the bridge. The Murray was running a banker, and Herb, Mick and I got on board and on the front of the Pevensy was a tall pole which I thought was used to lower bales of wool onto the ship. We put two exten-sion ladders either side of the pole and climbed up and strapped on as the steamer sneaked up stream slowly against the flow of the river, where we had to lift the aerial cable that crossed the Murray over that boom, the cable being strung between poles either side of the river. We chugged around the bend at Arbanought's Mill, lowered the two extension ladders onto the bank while the Pevensy chugged slowly against the river. To keep it still, the three of us walked the plank on those ladders off the Pevensy. Herb, the boss, and I went out in the boat with a double extension ladder to fix a broken line on a pole route and the pole we had to get up was in a flood water. When we put the ladder in the water, we couldn't get it high enough up the pole. Herb asked me if I wanted to try the stirrups to climb the pole, but I hadn't used them and had heard of a bloke up in Queensland killing himself with them. Old Herb said he would use them. They were like ordinary horse stirrups on two ropes. You moved one at a time up the pole and you had your safety belt around the pole. I thought lumberjacks might use them. Herb did it and I was his ground sparrow sending gear up the pole on a rope and putting a rope like a snotter[4] on the wires, using the boat to send up to Herb. Only time I was what they called a ground sparrow, in a boat, in the water.

The hernia I had was getting hard to handle. I went and saw a specialist in Wollongong, Dr Michael Rosen and he told me that I had to have an operation soon as I could die very painfully within ten minutes of a strangulated hernia. I asked him when he could operate, and he said he could do it on the twentieth day of November. I said,

---

[4]A rope that you open-up enough to thread a wire through the middle, which when tightened grips the wire, allowing the wire to be pulled up the pole

"Great, let's do it – that day is my twenty-first birthday." I went back to Barham for six weeks and returned to Wollongong for the surgery. So, on the 20-11-1973 I was on the chopping block for the hernia repair which I had put up with since I was a little kid. The day of the op, I woke up and smoked about twenty smokes and was in some pain. They gave me three morphine needles over a couple of days, which made me feel great, out of this world, but when I asked for the fourth needle, they said,

"No, you're getting to like that needle too much."

It was the day after surgery when an ambulance man came to the hospital, which was just a big old house up the hill from the Leagues Club or Workers Club Wollongong. The ambulance man explained to the Sister that he had an old bloke with severe thrombosis in his leg and warned her that he might be a bit drunk. They brought him into my room, and he was singing, with the ambulance blokes' hat on backwards: he was out of it. Later on that day, I got to know a nurse in hospital who was a Pommy and looked like Doris Day, wearing a white top and pink mini skirt. When she came on duty first thing, she said to me in her accent like that Blond on the Rag Trade,

"You still in here, love?" I said,

"What?" She said,

"They're usually only in here for a day love." I said,

"What!" She said,

"Yeah, one day for vasectomy." I yelled out,

"They better not have," she said,

"No, sorry love, my mistake." Later that night she came back, her name was Ann. She asked the drunk (who had settled down a bit) if he had sleeping tablets to sleep, to which he replied "Mogadons." She gave him sleeping tablets and me a needle of morphine. A little while later, the old bloke and I started singing, making a bit of a ruckus and I was so intrigued with the amazing way that the wall joined the ceiling, we were both smashed. After two weeks in hospital, I was put in a wheelchair out the front door along the path to I think Paul, one of my brothers, to drive me home, where I had another four weeks to heal before I would return to work at Barham. I ran into my nurse friend a lot and went out a bit, but it was time for me to head back to the bush and back to work on three months light duties. Back to floods, carrying double extension ladders sometimes in water, or in a boat, or on a tractor, to get to where we had to get to fix the phones.

Hardly back in Koondrook and I get a smack in the face from a girl I knew there. I went to visit her at her parent's place, but while I was away, the poor thing had got some gum disease or something and had all her teeth pulled. She still was a good-looking sort but waiting on some new teeth. I didn't mean to be cruel, but we were sitting talking in the lounge room when she was looking at her hands and said,

"Look how good my fingernails are growing." I said, "You must have stopped biting them," with that she slapped my face and that was an end to the friendship. You can't make this stuff up.

Back at work, Mick and I had to take our flood boat up the Gunbower River to fix a fault. The boat was a fourteen-foot orange-coloured aluminium boat, with a twenty horsepower Johnson outboard motor on it. Mick was the captain, and we were heading upstream in the Gunbower which was flowing strong into the Murray, and it was a banker. I sat at the bow and when we got to an old wooden bridge Mick called me back to the motor and I had to push under the bridge to push the motor lower to get under the bridge. We went and fixed the fault upriver and, on the way, back, Mick didn't allow for the fact we were travelling with the strong flow of the river when he backed off the motor. I raced to the front of the boat to grab the bridge to try and stop the boat going under and wrecking the motor. All I succeeded in was getting knocked arse-over-head in the boat. We got away without damaging the motor. Back at the pub, as it was so wet, I saw something I've never seen before. The road beside the pub which went down to Dick Mates house was dirt and there where cars would park was a big mud puddle. I saw Dick trying to navigate his way from the pub to go home and he was as drunk as six men. Dicky fell over in the mud and was mumbling, singing and on his side but sure enough, he was still walking but getting no closer to home.

One day I got to work early which was amazing. I waited for Herb the Foreman to open the gates. When I had parked, I walked to the veranda steps in front of Herb's office. Herb was just standing there, so I stopped. He put his hand on my forehead and asked if I was alright. Was I sick? It was the first and last day I was on time for work. I could always manage to be late for work though they knew I would work when I got there.

After some time back at Barham, it was time for me to go jump onto one of those big white cruise liners which I had not long back used to watch from the wharf at Neutral Bay. The cruise was nearly two weeks and we hit big seas the second night out and the Oronsay was being battered. Some pursers gave me a key to cabins to help them. You would knock on doors, then go in and shut the steel covers over the port holes and bolt them closed. The sea was breaking over the bows, it was like being on a bloody big surfboard. That night was for passengers to meet the Commodore for cocktails. His name was Captain Woolley and not many people made it to the party. All sick! I was met by a lovely woman in an elegant evening gown. She asked my name, held my arm, and presented me to the Captain. While we had cocktails, I asked the Captain if he'd had experience pulling these ships out of tight spots and told him about some girls, I'd met whose friends took them to see the Poseidon Adventure the night before we left. Wondered if the 'boat' could roll over. He explained about the ballast in the bottom of the ship and baffles to stop water splashing around. Anyways, as there were not many at this party, I grabbed a pocket full of loose cigarettes that were out and went to find my cabin, which I had trouble finding for two weeks. One night, I had won a lot of money on the ship, and I decided to go to the upper-class area out of steerage. There was a dance going and music. I ordered a bottle of expensive wine and I had met up with a few girls and I was trying to impress them. An old toff said,

"I say old chap what are you celebrating?" and I said in a laid-back way,

"Nothing mate, I just like the taste of the stuff." I must have had a bit of the stuff because I got up to a slow dance with a girl from Perth, her name was Gail Toranto, I think she had Italian blood. Anyway, I didn't realise the band had stopped and we were in each other's arms on the floor by ourselves kissing, when some big bloke taps me on the shoulder. I turned round, seen the size of this bloke, and thought Christ, hope she's not his girlfriend and he says so the whole bloody place could hear,

"Excuse me mate have you two been introduced yet?"

On the cruise, first stop was Noumea and after all the rough seas I had been through, I couldn't wait to get my feet back on the land, but then found out I couldn't wait to get back on the ship. Then to Suva, Tonga, Auckland, and home to Sydney. One night I was leaning on the rail of the ship watching the moon above the horizon looking at how the moon seemed to light up a track across the ocean to the ship, waves moving out away from the side of the ship. I was on my own just having a smoke. Then a girl was near me and climbing up the fence, said she was going over. I grabbed her and got her down, took her into her friends, told them what happened. I also met two girls on the ship, they both said they worked at Dorians Cake shop in Broken Hill, both named Robyn. Got back to Circular Quay and back through customs into a taxi to Central to catch a train to Wollongong. After two weeks of everything being so slow, the taxi ride scared the hell out of me. Rush tare bust – Sydney taxi drivers. So back to the bush out to Barham and to the pub in Koondrook and back to work. No longer was I living the life of the idle rich.

I was in the kitchen in the pub one Sunday morning, eating some toast and honey and enjoying a cup of tea when two young blokes who were booked in for the weekend came in. They came from Melbourne, and I believe this was their first time away from their mother's apron strings. They were there for a golf tournament. I'd said good morning to them, they answered back, then I noticed them looking around in cupboards and on bench tops. I said,

"You blokes, right?" They said,

"Where's the toaster and the jug?" I showed them the big black kettle on the wood stove, then I pointed to the coals in the fire and said,

"Toaster there." Then that's when they got me, one said,

"What happened to the toaster, did it blow up?" Poor buggers, I had to grab the toasting fork that was hanging off the mantlepiece, slice some bread and cook them some toast.

I don't know how many times Mick and me were bogged at work. We always carried a turfer[5], six steel posts, a roll of fencing wire, a block buster and naturally, a shovel. We carried guns and had Ripper the duck dog with us. He was always keen to go. One day we saw some ducks while driving, Mick put the gun out the window and the bloody dog jumped out the window over the rifle. He was bloody lucky not to get himself shot for being so keen to get to work. Might have been why I was always slow to get to work. Good old Herb, the boss, always amazed me how he could roll a cigarette while driving. He would sit on the seat, screwed round to the right, left elbow into the steering wheel that would free both hands to roll a smoke. The way he sat like that while driving, I always used to think he looked like he was riding side-saddle.

One day, Mick and I were chasing an aerial pole route fault towards a place called Dilpurra, towards Swan Hill. We drove the route so far along in bush, I said let's leave the ute and walk before we get bogged. So, we grabbed a ladder and an axe to cut the tree limbs which were touching the wires and putting an earth on the line. We walked so far, and Mick said for me to go back to the ute, back it out and meet him down the road at a bend where the pole route came back to the road. I thought as I walked all the way back to the ute, at least this time we are not bogged. Then I saw the ute we had left it high and dry - now she was down to the belly boards. It had sunk just sitting there. Out

---

[5]A clod-breaker

with the turfer again and shovels, I hated getting bogged, but we had plenty of practice getting out. Mick once told me of a Liney who got bogged along the railway track towards Swan Hill. He didn't panic, tied a rope on the ute, waited for the train...and the train pulled him out.

Could never forget Barham and the people I met there like Saucy South and Dicky Mates. They were always drunk, really drunk, leaving Koondrook, and going to Queensland in their dreams. They wrote off a HR Holden at Deniliquin and the police didn't know who to book because neither of them knew who was driving.

It was in the pub in Koondrook where I bought a gold signet ring off a bloke down on his luck. If I was driving the boys from Balranald, they would always make me look like a queer, like the one on the passenger door would get down on the floor in the ute. If I was in the main drag so it looked like two queens driving down the street. That was their stir.

One of the last things I did in Barham was to help a jointer from Balranald do a big cable-out overall, because the blokes along the Murray were keen fishermen. They had picked up some old lead cable before and used it for sinkers and that was okay but this time they were doing a big job and found some buried lead cable. They saw Herb, the boss about it. Herb looked at plans and said to pull it out, which they did, but Herb didn't look at the main cable plans, so Jack and I had a big job in a hurry. Not long after that job, old Jack was taking a ladder off his truck and bumped it into his hip. About six weeks later he was dead of cancer, which had started in his hip.

I went to Mick and Barb's wedding, and I have always been happy to have known them.

After 22 months working at Barham, I was told by my old mate Herb, the boss, that I was being sent back to Jerilderie. He said he was sad to see me go and for that matter, I was too. Before I left Barham, Herb told me I was in a bit of trouble as I had been paid a big travel allowance and a jointer's allowance, but it had come through that I should not have been paid any of that because they just realised, I had failed my cable jointing school. I went off my head and told Herb I had passed all the exams. When Herb said they failed me on my practical work, it hit me. That bastard supervising instructor got me. It couldn't be my written exams, so he failed my practical work. I told Herb to stuff the PMG and Herb told me to calm down. He knew I was a capable cable jointer and he made me promise to just sort it out without losing the plot. He told me I also was a good fault man and bloody capable at whatever he had asked me to do.

So, in 1975, I left Barham and moved back to Ned Kelly Country. I returned to Jerilderie and found board with a family, Nancy, and Norm Lock, in 48 Mahonga Street. It was like being in a family again as they still had a couple of their kids at home.

Chapter 12
Back to Jerilderie Part 1

My first job back in Jerilderie was to sort out my situation. Someone in the Narrandera Office inferred I might have to pay back all my cable jointing allowance. I was a bit worried about the situation I found myself in. When it hit me that the engineer or manager of Narrandera Division was my old engineer when I was on the dismantling job with Country Primary Works No 3. So, when I had a chance, I rang Lionel Chapman, the Divisional Engineer in Narrandera and told Lionel what was going on. He asked me how I had failed the jointing school, so I told him all and left nothing out, not even the bastard supervising instructor story. He said he didn't understand why it took nearly two years for it to come up that I was failed on the Jointing School and told me to leave the situation with him. A few days later I got a message to ring Lionel. When I did, he told me he had spoken to Bill Scarlett my old Foreman in Balgowlah and Johnny Hall who had tried to get me paid for cable jointing, as well as my old boss in Barham, Herb. Lionel said because of the way they spoke of me, that firstly I must stop worrying about having to pay any allowances back, secondly, he had organised for me to do the last four weeks at a jointing school to be assessed on my practical abilities, at a different school to the one in Strathfield where I had supposedly failed.

I thanked Lionel very much for what he had done for me and for giving me a chance to prove myself. Lionel was one of what I considered one of the real honest fair dinkum people that you are lucky enough to run into through your life. I rang Herb, my old boss at Barham and he said,

"That's great news. Now Steve, make sure you pass that school for me." I told Herb I would and thanked him for his words to Lionel. I thought to myself how ironic that the instructor at the North Strathfield School had tried to get back at me. Instead, I get paid jointing money for nearly two years, the same with travelling allowance, when I was apparently not even qualified. Then I got four weeks living away from home allowance in Goulburn while being assessed on what I've been doing for three years. It felt good to beat that bastard and make about twelve thousand bucks while I was doing it.

I worked a couple of weeks at Jerilderie and that's when I first met an old bloke named Bill who lived alone at Cooree South, in an old shed. Bill had no power, cooked on an old wood stove, tank water, a battery radio, kerosene fridge, a bed, a kitchen table, and chairs. He was about 85 years old. Bill had the phone on with open aerial line ran into his place and he had an arrangement with Jerry, the boss, that when he ran out of supplies, he would ring us to see if we were going out that way and we always said yes, even if we weren't. Then he'd ring Birchit's Store in Jerilderie and we would pick his groceries up and drop them out to him. Good public relations for the PMG. I used to run into another old bloke and have a good yarn and three beers. After that, I would have to leave him as he could only repeat the same thing over and over. The poor bugger was like that. I was told because he'd been gassed in the trenches in France during the first world war.

I had a run in with a technician at work. Not unusual for me, my opinion of him was he was just an arrogant know-all German. He put an illegal phone on at his place and I used to get in the cable and cut it off. For my efforts, he threw me on the bonnet of my ute in the Line Depot and tried to choke me to death, and he was a big strong bloke. The boss saw this and informed Tommy Dowdle, our Line Inspector from Lochart and Tom told him one more act like that, and he was gone.

I went to Goulburn to do my four-week jointing school assessment on my practical work at the Linesman in Training School at Goulburn. This was good except for something that had happened in Jerilderie before I left. Three of us, Pat Commins, who was the Aerial Fault man, Jerry and I were having a couple of beers in the Royal Hotel when the barman disappeared. Pat was eager for another beer, so he went round behind the bar to pull a beer and he disappeared. In one minute I was looking at Pat, then next thing, like you might see on a cartoon, Pat straight down, out of sight. The cellar door was open behind the bar. I looked down the cellar, and I thought he was dead. The boss told me to get out of there and they got an ambulance. Pat survived but because he was such an alcoholic, they had to send him to ward 11 at Kenmore to dry him out.

Anyway, this is when it got interesting for me. I was at the PMG School at Goulburn, which is just up the road from Kenmore Mental Home where old Pat was. So, I am in class and Don Catalan who is now the boss of the school gets me to come to the phone. It was Jerry ringing and he asked me to buy old Pat a packet of Phillip Morris cigarettes, a writing pad, envelopes, stamps, and a biro, and take them to him so he could write to his old girlfriend Dulcie in Jerilderie. After I had delivered the things to Pat at Kenmore and had a good yarn to him, I went to leave but as it was after a certain time, all was locked. It was in lockdown, and I really had to do a bit of talking to get let out of there. I never went back again in case.

Well, I did the school and Don Catalan said to me I didn't have to do the last big cable jointing job it as he knew I could do it and I would get a pass on it. He then said Steve, you just walk around the class, help the other boys out and tell them if they're doing something wrong. So, for a week and a half I pretended I was an instructor. Back to Jerilderie to work and a day of drama whilst chasing a cable fault along the railway track towards Berrigan with Denis Skates and Ray Sykes. I opened a pit to test a cable joint and in that pit was a brown snake. I yelled out to Sykes who was keeping up with us in the ute over the railway track on the side of the road to bring my rifle over to me. I stirred the snake up a bit and shot it in the head. That's when big Skatesy grabbed the snake, cracked it like a whip and its head went flying. From then on, each pit I opened, I was expecting to see another snake. When I got down on my knees about the third pit, I hadn't realised that bastard Skates still had that snake and he wrapped it around my neck about four times. So, I yelled out to Sykes to bring my rifle over again. He said,

"Another snake?" I said,

"Yes and the bastards wearing blue overalls."

One day I was out in the bush with Skatesy, and he saw a blue crane bird, grabbed my rifle, shot it, plucked it, cut its long neck and legs off and when we knocked off, gave it to the boss. The boss after having a few beers cooked it and said he ate it. Skates told him it was a duck. Not long after that Skates went to Urana. The boss one day was telling me that a Linesman Grade Two position was in the Commonwealth Gazette for Jerilderie, and I should put in for it. Sykes had put in for it and the boss thought I could do it because I had a lot of experience as a jointer in both Sydney and Barham and had now qualified at Goulburn. So, I applied and about six months later, June 1975 I was promoted to Linesman Grade 2 on a wage of $6,693.00.

Sykes wasn't too happy about me doing that and one night after work we had a bit of a disagreement in the hallway in the Royal Mail Hotel in Jerilderie. We had a few words, and I don't know whether Sykes was going to hit my hat off my head or knock my head off that's when the words came to me of Jacky Rutter, a bloke I worked with in Wee Waa. Jack had told me if it looks like you're getting into a fight and you may get a flogging, at least get the first one in. That's exactly what I did and then we were pulled apart after Sykes got up from the floor. Next thing at work nearly straight away, Sykes was given a temporary position in the Narrandera Office in cable records. So now Pat Commins retired, the aerial fault man Denis Skates back home working in Urana, Sykes in Narrandera and there was only Jerry and I to look after three thousand square miles on aerial and cable faults from Widgewaa near Morundah, Bundure, Gala Vale, Mabins Well to Canargo Oaklands, Corree South, Logie Brae and nearly to Coleambally, Mairjimmy and much more.

One fault I had was a beauty, in those days the techs were to prove a fault out of the house. I was given a fault halfway to Finley on a dairy farm. I was testing cable at the break off from the road when I looked across the paddock towards the dairy, but the house was burnt to the ground. I went to house and through the rubble found what was left of the phone which was only the metal base and the bells. I gave them temporary service in the dairy and headed back to Jerilderie with the remains of the phone to front my German mate and as luck would have it, I caught him in the paper shop and a few local in there too.

With the phone behind my back, I entered the paper shop and asked the German if he proved the fault out at the dairy where I had just come from, and he said,

"Yes." I then said,

"Well I've just come back from there and the phone is stuffed so you haven't been there. So can you fix the phone?" He said

"Yes," and that's when I bought the phone from behind my back - what was left of it. I said I'd like to see him fix it. Then I said

"You haven't even been there. The house burnt down, you are lying bastard." I just loved beating that arrogant smart-arse.

The boss and me one sunny hot day went into the Royal Hotel Jerilderie, that at that time was more commonly known as the 'Swinging Tit' by locals and it was there the boss, even though we would like a beer, decided to stir up the barmaid. First, he asked was she on the dole, she said,

"No, why?" As she never wore a bra, the boss said,

"I can see you have no visible means of support." I told him to leave her alone. We got a beer then he asked her was it true she was suing the Jerilderie Council for building the footpath so close to her arse – she was a short girl.

It was in the Royal Hotel one day after work that a local named "H" Collier, a truck driver, came into the pub carrying a wheat bag with something alive in it. He put it down in the corner and we asked what was in the bag. He said kittens. I went over as a few blokes before me put my foot lightly on the bag and after a while one bloke did that and said,

"There's a snake in the bag." He opened it up by untying a bit of twine tied around the bag. I was sitting on a bar stool when the snake was tipped out on the bar room floor. It slid up to the bar under my stool along the bar and then out into the open. It was a bloody great carpet snake. That's when H said he was going to take it to the lady's lounge and a few ladies left the pub. Then that snake that had a lump in it about one foot from its head looks like it went backward to me but what happened the bulge in its gut moved forward and it unlocked its jaws and spewed out a half-digested water rat. I walked to the door and the smell was disgusting. I stepped outside, finished my beer on the footpath, sat the glass on the windowsill, noticed about six blokes being sick in the gutter and walked to the Royal Mail Hotel and never entered the Royal for a few weeks.

The snooker comps at the Royal Mail were always interesting, especially when we played blokes from out of town as we had a secret weapon to put the competition off their game in the name of Champ, a blue heeler dog. Champ loved to sleep or camp under the pool table, and he had some tricks up his sleeve. We trained Champ to jump up to the top of a door to retrieve an empty matchbox in his mouth. A couple of times, one of the locals would put an empty matchbox on the shoulder of a bloke as they were about to shoot, and Champ would jump up and latch onto the box. Champ would then go back under the pool table, which put them off a bit, as they never knew what Champ would do next or where he was exactly under that pool table. If I dropped a few paper notes Champ would always catch the twenty dollars. I couldn't trick him as he always caught what you dropped, but I found that when I dropped a cigarette paper, the way it floated and moved could beat old Champ.

The boss, me and the three blokes on the ditcher gang, Roy Bourke, Bunter Dowdle from Lochart and Jacky Stakedum from Urana went to the Royal Mail at lunchtime to see the World Champion, Mohammed Ali, fight. The fight would start at 1pm only have half hour to go at the most but the boss ordered us all back to work. Jack protested a bit and the boss said to him,

"How many kids you got?" and Jack said,

"Twelve." That's when the boss said,

"Back to work or I'll book you off, you need the money!"

That's when, after the gang had gone, I told the boss I was staying, and he left saying he would book me off. I stayed because he was always on the grog during working hours and it wasn't fair to treat us that way over half an hour, we would have worked later that day. I didn't go back to work that day at all and next day in front of the gang, the boss said I had to fill out a sick leave form and he sent the gang out to work. I sat down, pen in hand and wrote,

"Whilst watching world title fight in Royal Mail Hotel, I consumed a number of alcoholic beverages and considered myself not to be a fit officer to resume duties." The boss read it, tore it up, threw it in the bin and said,

"What are you doing, trying to get me the sack or something. Now get out and clear some faults."

Old boss was well liked, a rogue who like most returned blokes never spoke much of the war. He only told me that every year, he would go to Melbourne for the ANZAC March and would meet up with his gun crew. He used to be their Sargent in Milne Bay in New Guinea at the age of 19. I met his gun crew in Jerilderie once when they came to visit Jerry. There was a lawyer amongst them who said, and you could see, they all respected and loved their old Sarge. Jerry told me once that the Japs used to plant tins of fish under trees and they, his crew and others would put a hole in the tin and rebury it and it would poison the Japs when they ate it. He said he seen a fair few bodies and their stomachs would be really swollen up. It was only what Jerry had said about the war plus the words he said when we fixed the phone for those hippies that ever he spoke to me of the war.

Up at Mabins Well towards Coleambally, Jerry came with me to clear a fault. We proved it to be on the private part of the line, but we decided to fix it. We cleared a short circuit out of the two wires and bridged over a couple of dry joints on the way to the homestead. We arrived at the house to go in to test the line, then ring the technician to get a call back. A bloke opened the door to let us in to test the phone. He was a long-haired hippie type and he said he and his wife were looking after the place while the owners were overseas. I went to the phone which was on the wall at the start of a hallway, just around a corner from the kitchen, and heard the bloke's wife asked Jerry if we would like a coffee. As the phone was ringing out to the tech, I said I did. Then I spoke to the tech, asked him to ring back. Jerry called out from the table where they were all sitting,

"Steve, the lady said do you take milk?" Just as the phone rang, I looked around to say "Yes" and the lady was sitting at the table opposite Jerry with no top on at all. I answered the phone, and Pat Lafferty the tech was there. I whispered,

"What's going on?"

He said he had to go, and I was begging him don't hang up, "I can't go in there," but he hung up.

We had our coffee, and the bloke lights up a roll-your-own, a smoke he had rolled himself. He had a couple of drags on it and handed it to his wife, and vice versa. Jerry got out his pack of Viscount smokes and lit up while we had a bit of a yarn. As we were leaving, Jerry left them about 10 tailor-made smokes on the table. When we were off in the ute, Jerry said,

"Poor bastards, can't even afford smokes. That's the first time I've seen anything like that since New Guinea." The boss didn't realise those hippies were smoking dope! I wondered if it was breathing in that wacky baccy smoke that affected old Jerry and that made him so generous towards his fellow man.

One day old Bill from Cooree South rang and said his fridge was broke down, the glass was broke for the kerosene burner. The boss and me were going out to fix a fault at Gala Vale for a Mrs Bull who always said her name was pronounced Bule. Anyway, there were lots of old kero fridges used in that area for mailboxes. We searched each one 'til we found a glass for old Bills fridge. He was happy to see us arrive and specially to see his fridge working again.

Each year in Jerilderie, they would have the jackaroos and jillaroo's ball. This was always a wild weekend, always a few fights and a few injuries. I was having a couple of beers in the Royal Mail Hotel, and we were saying it's a bit quiet this year, when the local copper came in. He didn't mind getting into a tangle with those drunken jackaroos. Anyway, the Sergeant said to the publican Chick Cully,

"What sort of beer are you serving this year?" and Chick said same as usual. The Sarge said you'll have to start serving some of that fighting beer, I can't get a blue this year. There was a mob of those idiots drinking over at the Riverina Hotel when a jillaroo amongst them run into a bit of couple trouble and ended up in hospital. A group of the jackaroos and jillaroos were drinking on the balcony and when it was someone's turn to go downstairs for more drinks, they had a ute with a bale of wool on it and would jump down on that. This jillaroo hit the wool on the edge and then the road and luckily only broke her arm and not her stupid neck.

One day we had to ditch-in line at Gala Vale from a shed where this Italian family was moving to a mansion they had built over some time. The gang came over from Lochart and them plus Jerry and me were there to do the job which Jerry had said we would finish by 11am and be back in Jerilderie for lunch, so we only took a bit of morning tea to eat. The job was going to take a lot longer to do into the afternoon and Jacky from Urana was giving it to Jerry that we had no lunch. Jerry, true to form, the quick thinker he was, sorted that problem out. He got the paper bags and sandwich bags and a few scraps and spread them on the ground near our tucker boxes which were beside the truck. He waited his time till two of the Cockie's dogs were near the tucker boxes, screamed out for the dogs to get out of our lunch. The owners heard the commotion, and the dogs took off. The owners asked Jerry what was going on, then Jerry said,

"Those bloody dogs ate our lunch, that's what's going on." With that, the lady said she would make us all lunch and we enjoyed a beautiful salad for what their dogs did to our lunch. That one was Jerry at his best!

At work one day in the depot and the boss said he found a way to save some money – free board. I could be in it too, looking after a fibreglass boat building business in town. The bloke who owned the shed had put a bedroom, kitchen, shower, and toilet in the place and said we could stop there for nothing to keep an eye on the place, to deter dishonest people getting in at night. So, we took it on as night watchmen for the business. It was interesting seeing how the boats were made top and bottom and floated out of the moulds they were made in. The boss was a worry, always drinking and smoking, even in bed, which could be a danger I thought and found out one night I was right. I woke up half choking to the smell of smoke. Jerry was not in sight, and neither was his mattress. Next thing he staggered in. I said,

"Where's your bloody bed?" he explained that everything was alright. It had been on fire, so he got rid of it. I asked him where he threw it and he said he threw it over the fence. I asked which fence, and when he told me, I said,

"Great, you threw it in a petrol depot! Christ!" I got a hose going, got it back over the fence and said, "what a bloody great place to throw a burning mattress."

I was in the depot one day and Tom Dowdle came in and I heard, to me, the funniest thing. When Tom, who never swore, jammed his hand on the top of a jerry can under the lip below the back window in his ute, cutting his thumb badly, he shook and grabbed his hand and yelled,

"F it, I won't f'n swear as it won't do any f'n good anyway." Tommy was the Line Inspector, and you couldn't have found a nicer bloke, or a quieter spoken, non-swearing person; that's why I never forgot that happening.

If I saw an old bloke hobbling along in Jerilderie going to the shops, or doctors, or the pub, I would always give him a lift. This bloke's name was Lyle and he had badly injured feet. Before I started at Jerilderie, he was part of a gang south of Jerilderie on a road crossing, putting up aerial lines on a pole route under power lines. The job had been poorly estimated, and the power lines were too close. The phone lines had come in contact with the power lines, Lyle copping it, with the power leaving his body through the soles of his feet. Poor bugger.

At one stage, Jerry had borrowed five dollars off an onion farmer named Doug Drew. He had dodged Doug for a few weeks and one day in the Royal Mail Doug caught up with him. Instead of asking for his five dollars straight up, he was telling Jerry how that long-haired bastard he had given work to, had up and gone one night, plus half his tools in the shed. As I've said, Jerry was a quick thinker and like a flash, Jerry says,

"Did he give you that five bucks I owed you?" Doug replied,

"No" and Jerry says,

"I had a feeling I shouldn't have trusted that shifty looking bastard." How bloody quick Jerry was debt cleared.

I don't know where I got the idea from, but Ray Sykes was sent back to Jerilderie for a couple of weeks to work with me, cut some cables over and clear faults. Sykes and I were told by Jerry to go up to Mabins Well. Out in the ute ready to go, I said to Sykes,

"Let's make the boss think we are blueing again," so I stopped the ute outside Jerry's office and staged an argument between us, then drove off to Mabins Well. Me and Sykes proved the fault in the cable, across a paddock towards the homestead, caused by some bloke drilling small holes in the ground taking soil samples for the CSIRO. As Ray was repairing the cable, I was looking in the back of the ute and noticed a pencil and it hit me to stir the old boss Jerry even more. I yelled out to Sykes and said,

"How would you like to give me a black eye?" He said,

"Love to." I got my pocketknife out and shaved the graphite out of the pencil till I had a little fine powder and before we left to return to Jerilderie, I put my make-up on, a real shiner black eye and covered it with my sunglasses. Sykes was to tell Jerry I came at him, and he had to drop me. Back in Jerilderie, I told the boss the PMG could shove the job where the sun doesn't shine, and I'll never work with Sykes again. I left the yard to go to the Royal Mail and when I arrived at the pub, I told all in there what I was up to. Next thing, Jerry wanders in, pulls up a stool and sits next to me while the boys in the pub listen to see what he would say. Jerry asked what was going on when I said,

"Sykes is a bloody mad man." Then I took my sunglasses off and said,

"Bugger it, I don't care who sees my eye." We all thought he had caught on, but everyone broke into laughter when after some time and a few beers Jerry said,

"Mate, do you know that eye's getting darker?" Was it the power of suggestion or the beer working? I had put it over the master, the Flim-Flam man, quick when he was in trouble. He might have learnt that in the jungles in New Guinea.

On a fair few Fridays, Jerry would have a few beers and get a half dozen stubbies. He'd say they were his friends to talk to on the way home on the back road to Corowa, on the Murray River. He took the back road to try and dodge the cops while he was drinking. On the Monday, old mate was back to work, and he told me about his trip home and of his encounter with the highway patrol officer. Jerry said he was cruising along on that dirt road in his '63 EJ Holden Premier, when he sighted a bit of dust coming towards him and in that dust was a white Valiant Charger and of course our man in blue at the wheel. He watched in the rear-view mirror and a fair way back the Charger was turning around. He had to think quick and said he knew the cop would know he was drinking, especially if he smelt his breath, so he pulled over off the road in the gutter, flew out of his car, opened the boot, grabbed a shifting spanner, and crawled under the car tinkering with the exhaust. The cop gets out and asked if he was right? Jerry said,

"It's the muffler loose, it happened before, and I've nearly fixed it. I'll be right officer, thanks for your concern." Cop says,

"That's alright I've got to go. We're looking for a young bloke who we have to catch up with." Jerry said the cop could tell he was an old bloke and left him to fix the car. Who else would think to do that?

I used to act Line Foreman when the boss was off on leave and one day old mate Bill at Corree South rang. He sounded bad to me and asked if I was going out that way. Of course, I said yes, and he said he thought he should be in hospital. I raced out to Bill, who was on his bed in his shack. I got him up and he told me to find a tin that was hidden well near his wood heap and give it to him. I got him in the ute and headed back to town. He couldn't even get out to open the gates. We got to Jerilderie and to the Indian doctor in the Main Street. I left Bill in the ute and ran to tell the Doctor's secretary. The Doctor came out, checked him, and said to get him to hospital straight away. We took a quick detour to a shop and bought a couple of pairs of PJs, and shaving gear, then off to hospital. Bill was worried about his tin, so a nurse I knew there, Janette Malloy whose family came from the Harden area, booked Bill in, and locked the tin in the hospital safe. A few weeks later, I met Janette and she told me old Bill was dead and that she was going to Campsie to work. Turns out old Bill's tin had held about three thousand dollars.

One day, as foreman, I was showing Jack Stakelum a job and noticed a drum net I had seen a few days earlier was still sitting in very little water in the drained irrigation channel.

I said to Jack that I'd get that drum net out, as I'd had another set before and caught good fish like red fin, yellow belly and the sweetest of freshwater catfish out of it. We walked up to it, and I pulled it out, but Jack shouted to leave it, as there was a dead water rat in the bottom. No wonder no one had got it before us. I should have known better after the snake spat out a decaying water rat in the Royal Hotel when Jack said leave it, it stank. I said I can't smell anything and carried on loading the drum into the back of the ute. When I threw the drum into the back, the water rat broke apart. Pretty soon we both started heaving from the smell, so we jumped in the ute and started driving. I told Jack he would have to throw it out amongst a stand of small trees, and I would come back and get it when the rat had decayed. Jack flatly refused, telling me to do it myself seeing as I put the thing in there. I couldn't do it, so I thought like a true foreman. I asked Jack if drum nets were illegal, which he confirmed bloody oath they were. So, I said to Jack that if he didn't lift the drum out into that scrub, I would drive into Jerilderie down the main drag, park in front of the police station and tell Sarge that drum net belonged to Jack. With that, Jack tied a handkerchief over his face, looking like an outlaw from a western movie and got rid of the drum net. I did feel sorry for making Jack do that job, but about a month later, I went back, fetched the drum net, and caught heaps of fish.

At one stage, I had a good red fin fish in the fridge at the line depot, which I intended to cook up. A stores truck driver named Gill Botton, from Narrandera, was camping in the depot for the night. Jerry gave that fish to Gill, who cooked it that night for his tea. Next day, I was looking for my fish and Jerry said that Gill must of ate it. I mentioned it to someone in Narrandera, word got around back to Gill, he rings me up, blows the hell out of me as everyone in the area was now calling him Ricky Redfin and he said Jerry was drunk and gave it to him.

One Christmas time, there was a gang from Griffith working in Jerilderie. Dicky Hairs, Billy Fuller and one more bloke from Deniliquin. Pidgeon Perrin, the boss, had a bit of a run in with these boys at the Line Depot Christmas party. The next day, the boys from Griffith were heading home for two weeks leave. Jerry decided he would get them back for the trouble at the party. They'd left their truck behind, so Jerry got all the prawn heads and scraps, put them into wrapped up newspaper under the seat of the truck and left it locked-up that way for the very hot two-week Christmas break. Jerry was on leave when the boys came back. It was a bloody good thing he wasn't there; they'd have killed him.

I was acting line foreman when Gill aka 'Ricky Redfin' came to Jerilderie with stores from Narrandera for Berrigan, Deniliquin, and Barham. He camped in the depot for the night and what happened next was the biggest insult to my cooking I could ever have. Gill and I had a few beers at the Royal Mail, during which time I had a whole chicken boiling away at the line depot. We returned to the depot, had more beer, I added the veggies to the soup and a couple of packets of dried chicken soup and noodles, and had a few more beers. We had a tank loaf of fresh bread, sliced it up and enjoyed one of my best chicken soups ever, and even Gilley said it was the best. I left the soup to cool in the boiler, planning on removing the fat from the top the next day and freezing into containers. It was that good though, I planned on first heating some up for breakfast with a couple of bits of toast. I arrived at the line yard early, parked my Holden ute out front and was walking through the front gates, already imagining that tasty soup. Gill was on the move already and drove the international semi up to me, stopping to tell me that he was off and so was my soup. I said,

"What's wrong with it?"

He said, "It had all this muck on the top of it, so I threw it out." I couldn't believe it and thought he was having me on. He couldn't be that bloody stupid. Surely, he knew it was only the fat had set. Gill left, I go into the amenities room; sure enough, the boiler is empty and all washed-up. I looked for the containers thinking he must have put the soup in them, but no, nothing even in the fridge. My best soup was gone.

Just before the Lochart gang arrived, I was looking round the yard for signs of my soup, finding it on the dry ground near the pole racks. I was leaning there against the railway track (the poles would lie on about chest height) my head in my hands looking down at the moist circle on dry ground, bits of carrots, peas, potato, and chicken. I hadn't realised the gang standing near me looking at what I was looking at, the remains of my soup, when Roy Bourke the Party Leader put his arm around me and said,

"Boss, I think you're not too well, you go home boss. We'll cover for you." So that's the story of the Jerilderie soup. I don't believe you could receive a worse insult about one's cooking abilities ever!

Jerry had befriended a cocky who grew pumpkins along the river and had got us permission to put our drum net on his property. We would check it regularly, getting the fish out of the net and resetting it, always tying the nets to the root of a tree on the river's edge, underwater. One day after getting the fish out of the net and resetting it, we drove away from the river and Jerry said to head around to the left of a big open shed full of pumpkins.

"Smell those pumpkins mate, they're going off – pull up next to them as they're going off really quick," he says. I stopped the ute and Jerry flew out, throwing heaps of pumpkins into the back of the ute. It was then I knew what he meant about those pumpkins going off, and quick!!

We left there and headed back into town, driving down the main drag of Jerilderie, when we both sighted Frank Draper, a big boss from Narrandera, accompanied by Lionel Chapman, an engineer, and an old friend of mine. They were parked near to the old Telegraph office off the main street. Jerry told me to keep driving and pretend like we hadn't seen them. Telling Jerry, they were waving to us, so I'd have to stop, I purposefully parked right next to them, just to stir Jerry. Jerry flew out of the car and before anyone knew what he was up to, he had grabbed Frank's car keys and filled the boot half full of hot pumpkins. They were both stolen and that hot from the temperature they were all-but cooked, with the unsuspecting bosses now accomplices to the Great Pumpkin Heist of Jerilderie.

The boss and me had to clear a fault one day for a Mr Tom Cully, up towards Coleambally, north of Jerilderie, on his property named 'Wonga.' Tom was a nice old bloke who I believe had received an OBE for his work with sheep breeding. We chased the fault to a point where we proved it onto the open aerial pole route private line. Tom had spoken to us on the line, and it was noisy and hard to hear because it was earthing out, but Tom assured us they had checked every part of the line to the homestead and could find nothing wrong and desperately needed it fixed. We followed that line through paddocks of the highest Riverina Bluebell I have ever seen. I sat on the ladder on top of the ute, while Jerry drove, looking for faults on the line, as well as fences in the cursed Paterson's Curse. At one gate I had to open, I was about 30 metres from the largest big red kangaroo I've ever seen. He stood up tall and was belting his chest. We got through the gate, shut it and I felt better when back on the ladder on top of the ute, as that big bugger worried me a bit. Then after some time, there was the homestead and out the front was Tom and one of his sons. Tom asked how we went, and I said we had found nothing. That's when I noticed two phone wires heading away from the homestead and said to Tom what are they for? Tom said don't worry about them, they don't work, they go up to the new house. Tom's son got me aside and said that his dad had built the new house for his Mum years earlier, but his Mum had died before they could move in, and Tom wouldn't ever move into that house. While they were talking, I went to the earth lightning protector block on the homestead veranda and the new house line was connected to the line, so I went up to the new house in the ute and one wire was against a tree which Tom had planted there in the house yard and the limb had grown around the wire. I cleared the limb away from the wire, went back to the homestead and asked Tom to ring someone up. He came back and said that's the best that phone had sounded for years. Then Tom invited us in, and we celebrated with two German steins of beer each. I noticed Tom's son went out and put a carton of long neck beer on the seat in my ute.

We left to head back to Jerilderie with that box of beer on the seat next to Jerry. As I was driving out a different way, rather than through the paddocks going in, I got caught going too quick over a little rise and then in front of us two white gates and big white strainer posts. The quickest way I knew how to stop was swing the wheel and drag the handbrake on. The back of the Ute spun round, and the bumper got a little white paint on it, no damage. Why this was so memorable for me was really our lives were at stake, but all old Jerry did was a brave and admirable act. He didn't fear for his own safety, he threw his body over that box of beer and wrapped his arms around it so that if we hit the posts and the gates the beer would suffer from no injuries. He was always thinking quick. So those dirt roads and the two German Stein's of beer nearly brought us undone.

Every second Monday, Jerry and I had to do an aerial route inspection on the J route from Widgewaa to Canargo, to find any broken wires, flying insulators, broken spindles, or birds' nests in the transposition plates. The bird nests caused faults, plus if they were magpies, they'd give it to you by swooping you. Crows' nests were different, they never swooped me. I used to call this run the bottle run as while I was looking for problems in the pole route, Jerry would look for bottles. I would have to stop while my old mate was picking up the bottles. At the end of the day on that run, when we got on the last, long, flat stretch of road on a very hot summer's day, I would see the white, moving mirage of the Carnago Pub, shimmering at the end of the straight. We would always go into that pub for a beer. First thing you would notice was all the shearing shed scenes in painting around the walls and the second thing was Neville the barman, studying the horse form guide, sipping on a glass of beer. We would wait till Neville had finished his beer when he'd say,

"You blokes right?" and then we would get a beer. Old Neville wasn't too quick at serving, his race guide seemed more important than customers.

Back in Jerilderie, the boss would get me to drive to the Golden Fleece service station on the Narrandera end of town to cash those bottles in, then to Birchit's store, where he always bought a chicken, soup mix pack, three packets of Chinese chicken soup, a loaf of bread and margarine.

I always took time to go to Boorowa to visit my grandparents and stay the weekend with them. When I would get home, first thing I would go to the RSL club for a beer and would shout a few beers for my old uncle Jack and pay for a couple more for him when I left town. One time, I left Jerilderie to go to Boorowa to visit old Jack, he was crook and was in hospital. I had left Jerilderie during a big grasshopper plague, with the little feed that was about being taken by the hoppers. The land was like a desert, farmers driving round paddocks picking up dead sheep. The grasshoppers were all around Boorowa too and when I saw Jack in hospital, he asked were the hoppers bad at Jerilderie. When I said yes, he pointed to an old bloke in bed in the men's ward and said the reason he's in hospital is for his own protection as the hoppers were eating everything green and that's his last name. Jack then asked did I know the Greenethorpe railway station is now called the Thorp station, that they even ate the green off that.

I was very sad on one return to Boorowa for my old Pop Howe's funeral. He was only 69 years old, and I am sure he died partly from his treatment by the Japs for three years as a POW on the Burma railway, after being captured in Singapore in the 2/19th eight division. He suffered with malaria, starvation, anaemia, tsetse flies and tropical ulcers. Colonel Anderson VC read the valedictory at the graveside. With sadness and pride in my Pop, I sat down and wrote a poem for him. I also sat in Pop's chair much later and from my memory of it, jotted down a poem he once wrote. What I couldn't remember, I made up from the story his poem had put in my mind.

Pops 1975
I was out in the outback
From home a long way
When I received the sad news
That Pop passed away.

Yes, it all seemed to me
God must have needed this man
Who had fought for our country?
For which he'd made a stand.

And I still remember now
As he was lain to his rest
God had given him a job
And Pop had done his best.

I remember the kind words
That were spoken that day
How Pop was a good man
Yes, that's what they did say.

I felt sadness and pride
As he was lain to his rest
While the bugler played to his honour
As for his country he'd met the test.

And now many months later
I am placing flowers on his grave
Now I see and I understand
How much of himself he gave.

I found myself just looking
Out over this country he loved
At a land that he would die for
With unquestionable love.

Yes, there I was standing
Proudly up on that hilltop
And right there was a man
And he was my Pop.

<u>Mad Man in Bigga</u>

In a peaceful little country town
In the hills that's known as Bigga
Where excitement's hardly ever known
And that's not hard to figure.

The locals they're easy going folk
Have lived there all their lives
Had never yet been threatened
By rifles or by knives.

Into this town some linesman came
Up in the hills to bring the phone
Then after work spend time in the pub
To drink and laugh and talk of home.

He yelled and screamed at locals
To his words they all adhered
And to show the weapon was the goods
He shaved off half his beard.

The locals called out for his boss
To the rescue came Neville, Claude, and Mick
They calmed him down and took his knife
Then to his bed they got him mighty quick.

Next day he to the pub the mad man came
Yet again his mood they could not stifle
He threatened all with a bloody death
Then went looking for his rifle.

Now he has gone where madmen go
To the people of Bigga please beware
He's made out an application
To the Minister of the air.

He applied for his own F1/11
He's mad, the crazy chap
He says he will be flying over Bigga
To blow it right off the bloody map.

Pop Howe recited this poem to me once and a year after he died in 1975, I sat in his chair and wrote it out and the parts I couldn't not remember I had to make up. Pop wrote a poem for me when I was a little kid when out the back of his house in a thick fog that come up from the river behind the house, he told it to me there and I've never forgotten it. A kind of up-market more classical type of poem, and this is it:

Have you ever seen Steve?
Make water
He piddles for a mile and a quarter
He makes such a lovely stream
You can't see the backyard for steam!

✧

Chapter 13

Jerilderie Part 1b

I n those days to fix a fault, you would go across a line with a portable phone called a buttinski to ring the exchange for a line test and the tech would credit back the call to the subscriber. When doing a fault one day in Jerilderie, I put the phone clips across the line, and they shorted a couple of times. The lady on the phone, who was talking to her boyfriend, said,

"We better be careful, the PMG listens across the lines in Jerilderie." I nearly threw the button on my phone and said,

"Bullshit, we do!"

I had a fault for the sin-shifter in Jerilderie, the Catholic Priest in the Presbytery house, that could have killed me. Instead of testing line on the cable run where I would be sitting on the ground, I tested line at the mainframe in the exchange. Thank Christ I never touched the earth when the needle on the metre was shaking like hell. The reason for this was the phone power was only 50 volts and direct current, what I was testing, was 240 volts alternating current 240 V A/C. I got the Electricity Board to turn the power off and retested the line, and the 240 volts A/C was gone. With the power off, we both went up into the ceiling with torches and found where a power cable crossed over on the phone cable, and both had bare wires where a rat or mouse had chewed them. With the power off, thank the Lord I survived that close call.

Whilst Jerry and I were still acting as uninvited nightwatchmen in the boat building business, protecting the owner's property (vigilantly sleeping in the shed to deter dishonest people from breaking-in and lifting stuff), a funny thing happened one night. I'd had a few beers with the boss before he went "home" to the boat shed and I went to the line depot to make a phone call and cook some tea. On my errand, I might have had more beer – possibly too much more. My boiled jacket potatoes were ready when I heard some bloke yelling out to me. When I went to the front gate to see what he wanted, he asked me if I would like to give up drinking? As I had drank a lot, I said of course I do. He said there's a couple of blokes with him and would I like to go for a drive to Mulwala on the Murray River. I had nothing else to do, so I said yes, went and grabbed a couple of the spuds I'd been cooking and put them in the pocket of my bluey jacket.

Next thing, I am walking into this hall in Mulwala, and it hits me, people saying their first name and telling everyone all the stupid and bad things they've done while on the grog. Yes, you guessed it, those buggers from Jerilderie had taken me to an AA meeting. I was polite and listened to their stories, one said he drank away his farm, another drank away his home, one drank away his wife and one had lost his driver's licence, one had stopped eating altogether. Then they asked me to speak after the last speaker who was an Aboriginal and said she was there for her daughter, who was doing too much of that horizontal stuff under the bridge for grog. I said,

"My name is Steve, and it looks like I don't have a problem with drinking...because I've never lost my farm (I've never had one), I've never lost my home, (I've never had one), the same with a wife, as I've never married. I still have my driver's licence as I walk when I am pissed and well, I still eat." With that, I put my hand in my pocket and pulled out one spud and said, "as a matter of fact, I brought some of my dinner with me." After a little more talk, they started to take up collection. I opened my wallet and pulled out a twenty, but put it back into my wallet and said,

"Sorry I need that for beer this week." When those buggers who had kidnapped me let me out back at the shed, they asked if I'd like to go to another meeting and I said to them,

"No thanks fellas. The only way you will get me there again, will be to get me pissed first." I wandered into the shed, knocked something over, went to my bed and fell into it. Old Jerry woke up and said,

"Where the bloody hell have you been?" and I told him I'd been to an AA meeting in Mulwala, and he ought to go to one. Jerry said,

"Cut out the bullshit trying to put that crap over me."

Whilst repairing a fault on a phone line in Jerilderie, I was sitting down on the footpath at a pit in front of a low front fence. Next thing, bang on the fence. I fell backwards as I heard a snap of teeth, and this great Doberman Pincer nearly took my head off. A couple of locals told me that dog was trouble waiting to happen. A few days later that mongrel met his maker at the Golden Fleece service station on the left going into Jerilderie from Narrandera. I got out of my ute at the servo to see that mongrel dog ripping the service station owner's limbs to bits. The owner had gotten the dog off his little four-year-old daughter and the dog had then turned on him. There were a few of us pulled-up and luckily a couple of duck shooters were amongst us. One shooter got out his gun, walked up to the killer dog and put him down. The whole episode was bloody crazy, and I've never forgotten it.

Another person in Jerilderie I was lucky to meet while fixing his phone would be a story and a book in himself by the name of a Val Chappman. He showed me in his shed at his home (northside of the main drag, west of the swimming pool, towards the Billabong) some interesting stuff. One thing he had was a door, it seemed bigger than a normal-sized door, and had a little opening in it with bars in it. Val told me it was the door from the police station that Ned Kelly locked the cops behind in their own jail when they rode into Jerilderie after cutting the telegraph wires out of town before they robbed the bank of New South Wales in Jerilderie next to the Royal Mail Hotel.

Also, Val showed me an old car he was doing up called a Humberett and an old motorbike. Val had a couple of old aircraft; one was called a Rhine and another one could have been a Spitfire or maybe a Mustang. He showed me a photo of his double winger taken many years earlier, him with Smithy, and him parked under the wing of the Southern Cross. Val then showed me his pilot license and it said on it 'License to Operate a Flying Machine." That was his first license, and I would say Val would have been born in the 1890s. He told me that the Mustang plane couldn't be given full throttle on take-off as the power would roll the plane. I told him of the Mustang at Nowra that hit Dad's cousin during the Second World War, which nearly took Dad's cousin's head off. He had to have a steel plate put in his head. He survived but his horse was killed when hit by the prop. They took Val's license off him as he was supposedly too old to fly, but a few times his Rhine aircraft would fly over and the locals just would say, "There goes old Val."

One night in the Royal Mail, Jerry had a bit of a run in with Lance Biddle from Deniliquin and the next day, I thought that all had been forgiven. When we arrived at work the boss's ute was half full of tomatoes. Lance asked Jerry where he'd been so early to get them, Jerry said about 20 kilometres towards Finley on the left, there is painted on the gate the two triangles of the eighth division. He told Lance if he went in, just get what he wants and not to worry if the owners there, if he sees PMG on the ute, you're right. About half an hour passed and Lance was back, nearly as white as his ute. He told us he'd been threatened with a shot gun by the owner and ordered to never come back. Lance settled down and after he left the old boss said,

"Got him back from the blue last night." I asked Jerry what he meant, when he told me he had got in trouble getting his tomatoes out there and the owner had warned him that he would shoot the next bastard out there with PMG written on their vehicle. Old mate won again, but I must say basically he was a very honest man, that he'd just often find things before people lost them.

On another day when I arrived at work the boss's ute, a white Dodge Valiant that could really fly, you could say it was a good getaway vehicle, was full of tinned food. A truck had rolled on the hospital corner a block from the depot. Jerry was onto it like a crow onto roadkill. He had competition though, with two nuns filling up wheelbarrows with cans as fast as they could. Jerry pushed on 'helping to clean up the road' and did his best to do his civic duty to 'tidy up the town.'

We used to get a gang come to Jerilderie, which is when I first heard of them. Out in the flat hot dry country all around why they would be called the 'Ski' gang. I found out when introduced to them, that they were all immigrants, I think Polish, and their surnames all ended with 'ski.'

One Christmas I walked into the depot and there was a bit of a commotion going on in the amenities room – I didn't expect to see three turkeys. The boss had three wheat bags and said he got the turkeys the night before and they had been 'broken free.' He had a hole cut into the bottom corners of the bags and I helped him poke their heads out of the corner of each bag and tied the bottom so they couldn't get out again. As Jerry drove out the gates of the yard that day in his EJ Holden Premier, I can still see the three turkeys standing in the bags on the back seat looking out the back window heading home to Corowa to meet Jerry's family for Christmas.

I was given a school in North Strathfield in Sydney to do an 'Install school.' We had to learn about running cable in buildings and about terminating cable in homes and industrial buildings. One bloke in my class had an accident in the morning, he had sneezed, and both sets of dentures flew out of his mouth and smashed on the tile floors. We were in the cafeteria at the school for lunch when he said he didn't know what he could eat and so I suggested a nice piece of gummy shark. He wasn't impressed with my attempt at humour, and he said to me,

"I should belt your teeth that far down your neck, you will have to stick your toothbrush up your arse to clean them." There were two blokes in that class from the Rock out near Wagga and they were having a bit of fun with a bloke from Sydney. He seemed to think he knew everything, a real know-all. So, these two blokes told him they were working in a paddock near a river and they both saw a horse shagging a cow. The know-all slicker said he heard of that before and the two bush blokes said they had a camera with only one more picture to take, so they thought they would take a picture to prove it. The slicker said again,

"I believe you blokes, I've heard of it before." So, the bush blokes knew they had him and said,

"Yes, we climbed through a fence with that camera and don't forget we had only one picture left."

"Well," the slicker said again,

"Don't worry, I believe it. I've heard it happens." Then they said to the city slicker,

"Guess what happened when we were about to take the picture?"

Slicker said, "What?"

They said, "The shag flew away."

So, I passed that school and back to Jerilderie doing my normal job mainly clearing faults. The boss got me one day and said to clean my Holden ute out as the next day, I had to take it down to Villawood in Sydney and pick up a brand-new jointer's Ute. In one day, I drove it down to Villawood, went into the office, there was acres of vehicles there and they brought my new ute up to the office. I went out and said,

"Where's my vehicle?"

They said "That's it a flat nosed Ford with a 22-foot tray." I told them I was a cable jointer and they said that's the vehicle assigned to you. Who was I to argue and I drove it back to Boorowa that day and stopped the night. The boss's eyes nearly fell out when I drove into the depot at Jerilderie. He said what the bloody hell is that, so I just said that's my new ute. It was one of those stuff-ups that happen now and then, it was sorted out later – but I did enjoy my drive to Sydney and back.

I later happened to be telling a bloke from Balranald that story when he told me the story of Dick, alias Ali Barber from Balranald. His first time out of the area and first time to the city and having to take a truck to Villawood. He was nervous as hell and he said what if I can't find Villawood and they gave him the maps and the phone number for Villawood and said when you get to Sydney go into a phone box and ring them up, they'll send someone out to you. Ali did that, rang Villawood and they asked this bushy where he was, but he couldn't see any street names. The Villawood bullies said,

"How the bloody hell will we find you?"

Dick said, "Easy, I am in the phone box!"

Chapter 14

Back to Jerilderie after Barham Part 2

J erry organised a job at the Catholic school for the priest, alias sin shifter. It was ditching in some pipes for irrigation on the playgrounds. When Jerry told me about the job, I said, the grass should grow good, are they watering it with holy water. When we had finished doing all the trenches the Irish priest told us to go to the fridge on the presbytery's veranda and we would find some ham sandwiches. I didn't think priests would tell us lies, all we found in the fridge was beer. It must have been a small miracle; the ham sandwiches had somehow turned into beer. There was something like that in the Bible with wine. Word got round about that shonky job, so I started another story that Jerry sent me around to the Catholic Church as the old wooden cross was falling apart. I said Jerry had made a new cross out of cross arms and it didn't matter about the holes in them with the spindles went as it would only make the cross more holy.

I used to play in a pool comp, and in doubles my old mate Harold Winkler always did well. Wink was the father of my technician mate, but Wink was a good bloke. Sometimes I would pretend I hadn't seen a snooker, I should do when old Wink would shout out in his big German accent,

"No, no Shtephen, go for za Shnooker!" Wink was a big man like Sergeant Schultz in 'Hogan's Heroes,' and he would tell me of his life. He was a Commandant of a German U-boat during the second world war. When old Wink got enough jungle juice in him (Carlton Draught) he loved singing. He had a real baritone voice and two songs he loved to sing were 'Lilly Marlane' and 'Underneath the Arches.' He really could sing, and everyone loved old Wink and he could really play snooker and we could hold the table and play for a beer with Wink. It was cheap drinking. He told me once he and his crew boarded a ship in a harbour from their U-boat and confiscated heaps of bottles of wine and put back out to sea but were very upset to find they had only ended up with bottles of vinegar.

While playing pool one day after work, I heard a thud on the floor of the bar, and I just didn't take any notice and kept playing. Then one bloke says to me,

"Aren't you going to help old Jerry?" I got a shock when I saw him on the floor, not moving and a real khaki colour, not breathing. I just put him in the coma position bent his head back, next thing he was breathing and back at the bar drinking. I said thanks to the good Lord for that and especially for the fact I didn't have to give the old bugger mouth-to-mouth.

A stupid thing at the time, you only could get a beer in a pub on a Sunday if you were a Traveller. You had to drink drive!

Burnie Woodward from Berrigan who was a coaxial patrolman could be a bit nasty on the grog and on the day, Bob Menzies died, I ran into him in the pub and asked him if he had heard that Menzies had died. He just said in a loud voice,

"It's about time that bastard did something for the country." Burnie, at the old age of 50-odd, had some time off work with the mumps and as I had heard this could be painful when you're older, I asked Burnie how he was going. All he did was yell out he had just asked the doctor to ease the pain and leave the swelling.

Dad picked up a good caravan for me in Kiama and towed it up to Boorowa, where I picked it up and towed it back to Jerilderie. This meant I was on my own, away from the boat building shed, as the stink of the fibreglass was getting to me...and just in case old Jerry set the place on fire; I didn't want to go up in flames. I had an annexe and put cross arms down and built a floor out of cable drum boards. When we got those hot summers in Jerilderie at night, I would put the hose and sprinkler on the van and the annex. The idea was to cool it down like the canvas water bag. I even put the recall fault phone on in my caravan which was the first and probably only landline in that caravan park.

One day in early 1978, I went to the ANZ bank to get myself some drinking money. There was a young woman on the relief staff behind the counter who caught my eye and that afternoon we met up after work and went to spend my drinking money together in the Royal Mail, next door to the bank. Her name was Rachel[6] and she was from Grenfell, but her mother was born in Boorowa. Rachel said she worked all over the place with the bank and had a few interesting stories to tell.

Funny thing was, that bank was the one Ned Kelly had robbed back when it was the Bank of New South Wales, so it seemed that

[6]Name changed for privacy reasons

bank attracted robbers and thieves in general. Although I now had a girlfriend, while I was living in the caravan, old boss would ring me in the morning and ask what I would like for breakfast and when I'd get to the depot, my steak, and eggs or whatever would be cooked. I would sit down one end of the table eating breakfast and Jerry would be the other end of the table drinking a Melbourne Bitter stubby. Single life was pretty good really.

One day, not far from the depot in Mahonga Street, I was jointing some new cable when a house I was working in front of I notice the fence around it was about 10 feet high and I said to someone,

"Why is the fence so high?" and they said the owner built that and he did it after his little boy had got out on the road and was killed by a car. I decided right then if I ever had kids, I would build a fence in the yard so kids couldn't get out. As the old saying goes, it's a bit late to shut the gate after the horse has bolted.

I used to make a joke about the linesman in Griffith that you could always pick their trucks out easy because they had no ladders on them. This was because of all the drugs up there. If they needed to get up a pole, they just lit up a bit of that wacky baccy and they could just float up the poles. When McKay disappeared in Griffith, I along with all of Jerilderie was interviewed by detectives many times as someone had tried to get McKay down to Jerilderie to meet near the line depot. Just after McKay disappeared, I drove up to Griffith one weekend and it was creepy. No one would talk to me and there were coppers and detectives all over. No one trusted anyone. The only people who spoke to me were die-hard Salvation Army volunteers after donations!

One afternoon in front of the Royal Mail Hotel Jerilderie, I spotted an old bloke who I had seen before while at the training school in Goulburn. He looked like he was still wearing the same old dirty white shirt and carrying his swag and his musical instrument wrapped up in the swag. We had a yarn and he asked if I thought he could make some money playing in the pubs. I said yes and said I'd go with him to each pub and introduce him, tell the locals a bit about him. So that's what we did, I thought I acted like his manager and everywhere we went everyone tossed us some money for that nice old bugger who just tramped the track between Sydney and Melbourne playing his music. His musical instrument was what looked like a plain old, everyday wood saw and he used a bow on it. He would sit and jam the handle between his knees and stroke it with the bow like a violin, putting pressure on the end of the saw to get different bends on it and wobbling it a bit to get a vibrato sound. He was bloody good and when everyone was so taken in with what he could do, he said,

"Now I'll play a Soprano woman singing opera." I swear anyone outside those pubs who had no idea what was going on would swear there was a woman singing opera in the pub. The old bugger did very well and made a good lot of money, which he really deserved. Once again, I could only feel privileged to have met him and heard his music.

Another bloke I worked with in Jerilderie doing a couple of jobs, was Leon Curriarkin from Deniliquin. He came from Poland and had been with other Poles when they came as immigrants and were put in gangs building bridges until he got a job on the PMG. The story was Leon had run into a mob of Japanese in Deniliquin and found out they would like to get some European carp fish, and if Leon could get them some, they would give him a TV. Leon had been in Australia long enough to be a real Aussie and had already mastered the art of bullshit. The fact that those bloody European carp fish were everywhere didn't matter. Leon told the Japanese they were bloody scarce and not too many people knew where to catch them, but if they threw in a TV for his son as well, he could get all they wanted. Leon got the Japanese the carp they wanted and told them how hard a job it was to get them, and Leon got the two TVs plus his honorary membership to being a good Australian bull-shit artist. Leon told me in his accent one day about putting new carpet in his house and how his wife had invited all her lady friends round so she could show it off. Leon got home he said, and all those old ducks had left their shoes outside but when he went in, they had some music on and would go jumping up and down doing some Polish dancing and wearing out Leon's carpet.

Leon says to me in his accent,

"Leon is not stupid. I went out in the backyard and found a heap of bindis and cat heads." What Leon did was go back in the house and when no one was looking he flicked a few cat heads around and he said to me, "That stopped them jumping up and down wearing Leon's new carpet out."

One day at work, I got a call from the Jerilderie Council that they would be digging near the coaxial cable. I was the only bloke there and I rang the Coax patrolman, who was out at Hay and told him they are ready to dig and bloody eager to start. Poor Lance got into a panic and said to go and tell them they can't start until he got there. I shouldn't have done what I did, but I had a bit of Coax cable in the yard, so I went to the council boys. I knew where the cable was and located it, so they wouldn't hit it. By the time Lance got there a big hole was dug and either side of the hole was a bit of bashed up coax cable sticking out which I had stuck there from the depot. The council blokes could have won a Logie for the act they put on, so bloody devastated for what they had done. Poor Lance jumped in the hole bloody upset when I jumped in the hole and just pulled the two bits of cable out of the hole walls and told him it was all bullshit. I wouldn't have blamed Lance if he had belted me with the back of a shovel, poor bugger.

The following pages are about the 100 years celebration in Jerilderie, commemorating Ned Kelly and his gang robbing the bank. It was a good couple of weeks and people in businesses in the town dressed in period clothing. The Bushwhacker's Band was there and a couple of my mates when they had told a woman there the band was called the 'Bushwacker's Band and the Far Canals' got a good laugh when they asked her the band's name and she would yell it out, oblivious to what she was saying at the top of her lungs.

I went home one weekend and up to Grenfell to see my girl-friend and told old Jerry the boss. When I was in a paper shop, I just happened to see a box of confetti and it hit me. I might be able to put one over the old master, so I bought the confetti. Driving my ute back to Jerilderie I figured out a plan to put one over the boss with a little innocent fun. My plan was to park my ute as usual at the little gate in the back of the yard, where Jerry had to walk past to go to the Post Office. I sprinkled quite a bit of the confetti on the floor in my ute, a little on the seat and a tiny bit on the ground near the driver's side door – just enough to get old mate's attention. I was in the amenities room in the depot observing Jerry walking about the yard. I felt like game hunter waiting for some critter to walk into a trap. Then it happened. Old mate near ute, caught! He was looking at the ground and then in my ute, a look of surprise on his face, then he went through the gate to go to the Post Office. When Jerry returned, he said nothing about the confetti. I grabbed some faults and headed bush for the day. After work, I met up with Jerry in the Royal Mail. A few beers in, he asked what I got up to on the weekend. To build up the ruse, I told him I didn't want to talk about it and even managed to look a bit glum. This went on all week until the Thursday night, when after a fair few beers with Jerry, I 'let slip' that I had got married and it was a bit of a forced issue. I kept on just enough to let the master of trickery believe me then I stopped and said nothing more. Jerry said it was alright,

"None of his business, anyway." He didn't bring it up again and on Friday went home for the weekend to Corowa, on the Murray River. On Monday, the 'Master of Scam' came back from Corowa while I was cooking my breakfast in the depot. He walked in and handed me a card from himself and his wife, Jean...for my marriage. He then goes out to bring me in a stroller for a wedding present. That afternoon in the pub, I told Jerry he shouldn't have brought the lovely stroller as I had just put it over him. He took it well and said not to worry about the stroller –he had only picked the stroller up from the tip at Corowa on Sunday. I told him he was a tight old bastard, but I had got him!

I had done a fault on a Mr Sid Fishers phone and when he, his wife and daughter were down at Jerilderie, I had drinks and a meal in the Royal Hotel a couple of times. They were nice people. Later I found out Sid was a bit of a yachtsman, often in the Sydney to Hobart race. At some stage I think he may have had a boat with a concrete hull, and he may have been a doctor, but I am not sure.

Something I was warned about in Jerilderie was to watch out for the 'cattle dog' from Narrandera – though he bit me just once.

This cattle dog was very smart; he drove a small truck from the stores in Narrandera. Even after I was warned about his bite, he still bit me. I was in the Royal Mail Hotel when Kevin Hoy, alias Cattle Dog, approached me. I was asked for forty lazy dollars. When I opened my wallet and held out in front of cattle dog to show him and say I only had a twenty, the dog swooped on that twenty like a seagull on a chip and said, "That'll do," and took off with all I had. I told old Jerry and he said I was warned, and they don't call him cattle dog for nothing cause every time you turn around, that dog will bite you. He was also known as GMH, as he always asked people, "How's ya Holden?"

Another story about money and the cost of things in the seventies was a discussion I was having with an old bloke in Jerilderie. The way he explained to me how much prices had risen and what you got for your money. He told me how when you got 2/- two shillings worth of mixed lollies once, you got a big bag full but now he said he asked a girl in a shop for twenty cents worth of mixed lollies and all she did was sit two lollies on the counter and said, "Mix the bastards yourself!"

Whilst working in Jerilderie on occasions I would have to go to a little place called Oaklands to clear cable faults at a sort of ammunitions dump. I would have to show identification to get into that facility and to get out again. I would repair faults in cable which connected posts around the area that guards used a key for at each point to let a monitor always know where the guards might be. There were mounds above ground very big, above I think explosives and apparently large metal work lathes and artillery and other weaponry. I supposed this place was left over after the second world war as I believe there was an air force base and airstrip in Tocumwal not too far away.

In the Royal Hotel Jerilderie, some Saturdays I would team up in doubles on snooker with an old bloke named Charlie Reaper, and boy could he play. We sometimes held the table all day. Any blokes challenging us had to play for the table and for a beer each game. Old Charlie had a reputation for being able to play snooker but not such a good reputation for driving his FC Holden after a good day. A few times I heard the warning go out in the pub to move your cars if you were parked along the street which Charlie used to get home. Locals said Charlie had bumped the back of parked cars on his way home as he was technically blind from the Carlton Draught beer and would drive by braille and sound, not sight, as he felt and heard the parked cars as he bumped them. Yes, you couldn't forget old Charlie. He was in his eighties and not such a tall bloke who always wore his hat which was the type of those detective's wear like in Homicide on TV. Charlie always reminded me of a bloke back then called Clarence the Clocker.

Jerry would often get an invite for dinner on a Thursday night to Peter Starr's and his wife's house. Peter was the Postmaster. To do the right thing as an invited guest, old mate would take an empty flagon over to Birchit's store where you could fill it with a bulk wine. After a few beers after work, Jerry would go to the depot, have a shower, clean his shoes, have a few drinks of wine out of the flagon. I noticed a few times that the flagon wasn't full anymore, but old Jerry was getting there with it full. He would stop at the water tank and top up the flagon with tank water. He was an old dog and willing to have watered down wine. Reminds me of a song. If Jerry had done that to some people, he could end up seeing stars for real.

One day Jerry got word from one of his cockatoos in Narrandera that some bosses were coming down to interview him over a serious matter and Jerry didn't want to be questioned by them over whatever may be the need to see him, which seemed serious and urgent. He had to think quick and true to form, he come up with a plan. I called it a convenient heart attack. When the bosses arrived to interview old mate, they had to go to try and interview him in hospital in Jerilderie. This was made difficult for them as a heart monitor was on him and an oxygen bottle next to him. He didn't look or act in a good way for a fella who was to be interrogated as any extra stress may bring on another heart turn. Poor old mate wasn't too good so when they went to ask a few questions he pointed to his coat which was hanging on the back of a chair and with much difficulty said, "Need in pocket, need now." He was nearly breathless poor bloke not well. One boss reached in the coat pocket and pulled out old mate's rosary beads and Jerry gestured for them in an urgent way. The bosses gave up as they found it too hard to ask questions to a man that could only say his rosaries with very little breath in him - to all intents and purposes a good Catholic to the last!

After twelve months of dating, I suppose I had fallen for Rachel, and we decided to get engaged. We went to Wagga to buy an engagement ring, spending what seemed like hours going in and out of every jewellery store. When she had seen a ring she liked, even though she thought it was too much money, I bought it anyway, as she loved it. $1200 in 1978 was a lot of money, but I also couldn't come at any more shopping. It was worth it to me at the time – a Lady Diana-style sapphire surrounded by twelve diamonds and a happy fiancé. I thought I had found my true love.

I applied for a transfer to Orange as we were getting married and Rachel had gotten a transfer to Orange with the ANZ Bank. I was asked by Rachel and my mother-in-law to get confirmed, as they wanted a nuptial eucharist wedding, as per the Royals in the High Church of England. I agreed and had to do a bit of study and was confirmed by Bishop Leslie in Bathurst. He asked me what I would like to pray for in confirmation, I don't know why I said, "To the good Lord to give me plenty of patience," but that's what I got and though I didn't know it at the time, by God I was going to bloody need it.

I was given a send-off party from Jerilderie that old boss Jerry had organized - the old bugger. I couldn't believe it the number of locals and workmates who attended from Barham, Balranald, Hay, Griffith, Leeton, Narrandera, Lochart, Urana, Tocumwal, Deniliquin, Wagga, Berrigan. There even were some big bosses and my old boss, and mate, from Barham, Herb Klein. In my speech, I asked Herb if he remembered the day, I was early for work – he had placed his hand on my forehead and asked if I was okay – he thought I must be crook to be there on time. I then asked Herb if he remembered I was late every day for the next eighteen months, which he remembered well. I laughed and told him I only did that to save him getting an ulcer worrying about my health. Even the mayor of Jerilderie was there with a few nice words to say about me. I was certainly being made to feel guilty for leaving Jerilderie. I was given a mug with a ball and chain on it, with words to say, 'chained to the grog in Jerilderie,' as well as a service tray inscribed 'To Steve with Best Wishes from Jerilderie, 1979.'

I left Jerilderie to get married at Grenfell so I, transferring to Orange after. I felt a little sad leaving as I had always felt welcome and had met many great people there. It had all been a great experience in the Riverina, working over a large area and seeing a good part of our great country. Its people, its yarns, its characters, its land, and views. Living and working in the bush or the big smoke, I had found that Aussies are just Aussies – great people – just take them as you find them.

And so, it was I had to pack up my camp, take down my annex from my caravan, load up my ute, hook up my van and do one last lap of the main drag of Jerilderie. I received a few waves from locals and when I pulled up at the Golden Fleece servo on the way out, I noticed that for me, a telephone man, I had made a rough disconnection of my phone in the van. I had about 50 metres of black cable dragging behind the caravan. It had been my phone connection. I had run temporary cabling along the swimming pool fence for my fault recall phone. So, I wondered that some locals waving may have been trying to let me know about the cable dragging behind my caravan and my ute. Fuelled up, I left Jerilderie to head off to what life had next in store for me.

Chapter 15

Orange Part 1 – New Life Ahead, Married Life, Fatherhood in Orange

After being married in Grenfell 21-4-1979, I looked forward to married life. We lived in the caravan park in East Orange for a few weeks and then moved into a flat at Anson Street, one block from the Orange Base Hospital.

I settled in quite quickly to Orange and was pleased to be made one of the country fault men after working in small towns down in the Riverina. It meant I was working in the bush where I was at home; spending all day by myself never worried me. The big difference for me in Orange was that in Jerilderie most of the time doing faults it was just the old boss and me. In Orange, working out of the depot was one line Inspector and three-line foremen – one for fault clearances, another for new work pit/ cable installations, and the third for telephone installations/new services. It was a change for me going from those bush stations to Orange depot, which had all up 66 men working out of the yard.

One of my first jobs in Orange was a fault between Borenore and Boree station towards Cudal. I couldn't find an exchange and rang the depot for directions and got onto 'Hamburger Jack.' He was making a bit of a fool out of me, saying that the line came out of an old farmhouse, which was a manual exchange. I got stuck into Jack and told him I wasn't impressed as I was just trying to get a bit of local knowledge from him. He was a bush fault man and a smart arse. I told him if I was still in the Riverina, I would run rings around the bastard and after that he was always willing to help me instead of trying to put me down. Another bloke in Orange depot was known as The Doc, his name was Barry Nonemacker and he helped me out a bit. He christened himself The Doc as he fixed faulty phone lines in the city. He said he had a doctorate in telephony, so that's what he was. I learnt a saying from the locals in Orange, that 'Old Man Canobolas has his overcoat on' when the clouds gathered around the top of the mountain, meaning it was going to be a cold, cold day.

Pretty soon, my wife and me found out that a little person was coming to join us in the journey of life. Straight away I started to worry and wonder what sort of father I would be.

I had taken to the bush faults well, put with Jim Cunningham (alias Tricky Pig) as he had the local bush knowledge. Every morning, I would pick up our faults for the day; could be Euchareena, Mullion Creek, Lewis Ponds for instance, and Jim would say to me in the office before we left,

"Where are we going today, Mike?" and I would tell him where we were going, and I would call him Mal. This always got a laugh, and so Jim and I were known as the Leyland brothers. Jim and

I were one day doing a bush fault towards Ophir in some paddock, chasing a fault in the cable. It was freezing, a heavy frost still settled on the shade side as we topped a hill. I looked down the steep slope, dotted with boulders and rocks, and said to Jim as I put my foot on the breaks that we were not going down there. Looking at his face, I realised we were doing it, so I yelled "Hang on" as we dropped off the side. We made it to the bottom, no damage, and more luck than good management.

Another day, Jim and I had to drive to the top of Canobolas and the main track through Nashdale was blocked with snow, so I decided to go up the back way, which was a dirt track. This attempt to gain access to the top of Mount Canobolas was doomed and after a few kilometres up we found this out. We were making good progress and the track looked good, especially as I did not and could not see the black ice. I don't know how I backed down off that steep slope and bendy road off Canobolas and didn't leave the track, a lesson learned about black ice.

Terry Rayner came out in the hills on a fault one day, riding shotgun for me. He had a way of describing the hills and the boulders and the rocks on them. He would say have a good look at this country, they had plenty of rocks left over when they built these hills didn't, they? Terry would say 'there's nothing on these hills but rocks and sheep, and the sheep would be worth a fortune as they must have diamond-tipped teeth with only rocks to eat.' If we were stuck in a mob of sheep, to get them moving out of our way, Terry would yell out two words, 'Mint Sauce.'

An old bloke came out of his house to talk to me in Orange while I was jointing some cable and he went to a lot of trouble to tell me he had been a paratrooper during the war and had dropped from planes about 20 times. When I said,

"So you have jumped out of a perfectly good aeroplane 20 times," he said to me,

"That's incorrect, I was bloody pushed, I am not that stupid!!"

I went up to the top of Mount Canobolas and the place had about a foot or more of snow lying about, and it was freezing. I got my testing equipment out of my van and went through the snow and opened the pillar testing point. While sitting on my jointers stool testing not far from one tower, I heard a sliding sound and then a 'splat' into the snow not far from me. I was sitting as the sun was hitting the tower up high and big shards of ice were melting a bit and sliding down the tower and hit the deck not far from me. If they hit you, I'd say you would get a bit of a headache and you would stay hit.

I was given a Hi Ace van at Orange to work out of and that was no good for me as most of my work was on hilly country and those vehicles had a habit of rolling over and a few had, also they were not much good in the mud and got bogged easily. I had mostly driven Holden or Ford Utes, but I always had to drive a van and so everyone would know if I got bogged as over the radio everyone would hear my call for help for the only four-wheel drive in the yard. I would call, "Orange 15 to Hamburger Jack" always this was Jack's reply, "Where are you Steve and how bad is it?"

One day I was doing a fault for a bloke out at Kerr's Creek north of Orange and that turned into an unusual chain of events. When I had the bloke's phone working and went to his house, he asked me if I could get a bloke's phone connected from the other side of the valley, and said if I could, he would give me half a sheep. The bloke without a phone had been told there was months to wait because of the condition of the aerial cable on a long pole route into the valley. I rang E. J. Jones, my boss, and he said he would let me try to get a cable pair or line through but that I would have to climb most poles to push a line through the clapped-out cable. Then I told the cocky whose phone I had fixed that the boss said I could come back and give it a go. The cocky said, if I succeeded, he would give me a whole killer[7], as it was costing him a fortune getting the bloke across to his phone when people rang to get him. The neighbour was some kind of businessmen from the big smoke! I said,

"Is he costing you a bit using your phone?" The cocky replied,

"No, that's not the problem. He gets lots of calls and it's costing me a fortune letting him know to come across, firing off shotgun cartridges!"

It took a bit of work to punch the cable pair of wires through for the new service, but I got it to the house and then the boss sent the ditcher crew out with me, and we dug a trench from pole to house. The city slicker was leaving to go to Sydney, showed me where he wanted the phone and said when you have finished there's some beer in the fridge in the shed. When we finished, we went to the fridge which was next to a post in the shed with the most vicious wild Alsatian dog tied to the post and the mongrel would not let anyone of us near that fridge. What a city slicking bastard, so no beer for us! Mongrel.

Next time I was out that way, I picked up my sheep and I was told this story about when the poles were put in for that aerial cable. The cocky told me the gang doing the work stopped out there and he let them camp in an empty house on his property and they smashed a heap of windows while they were there, the PMG paid for the repairs. What happened was because of the

---

[7]Sheep for slaughter, for the meat

rocky ground, the gang had a powder monkey with them and now and then he would blow a hole out. He told me that gang had been giving it to the powder monkey, so he decided to get the lot of them one night while they were sitting in the house playing cards. The powder monkey got a bit of broomstick the same length as a stick of jelly, wrapped it in that greasy paper part of a real stick, put a wick on it. Lit the wick, got the card players attention at the window when he yelled out, "Got you bastards" and then threw the stick in the middle of the room and that's how the windows got broke as they jumped right through them to escape the pending explosion.

One morning we had a meeting in the depot and the Line Inspector, now called the Senior Lines Officer, Bruce Cassey, was giving us a talk. He wasn't too impressed with some blokes walking out under his office window for lunch at a quarter to twelve. The very next day I needed to pick-up my car after a service at K-Mart, so asked 'Bot Fly' Lance Copping for a lift. A bit worried about the boss's chat the day before, I said to Bot

"What about leaving early for lunch – it's only a quarter to twelve?" Bot immediately said not to worry, we would come back at a quarter past one to make-up for it.

Things were good at work and the Leader of the Opposition, my wife, wanted to move to Young, as she wasn't married to Telecom, she informed me, even if I was.

On a Saturday in late October 1979, a colleague, Dave Brown, and I, went out on a call installing new telephone services. It was 10.30am, but our whole day was about to change. I was driving, heading east up a street in East Orange, just before a T-intersection. If you turned right at that T-section, you would head up to McMertices, where they made headstones for cemeteries. Just before the intersection, out of nowhere I felt a pain in my chest like nothing I had ever felt before, letting out a blood-curdling scream and grabbing at my chest. Dave yelled back, asking what was wrong with me.

"I'm having a F'n heart attack, that's what's wrong with me," I screamed. I tried to veer the car off the road and saw an old bloke falling backwards. He was on a slope of the footpath, flat on his back with his mower rolling towards him. I stopped the car, flew out, pushed the mower away so fast I didn't even remember looking for other cars. Down on my knees beside the stricken man, I took in sightless eyes facing the bright sun, pupils large as they could be. Feeling for a pulse in the carotid artery I couldn't find one and started heart compressions. Dave couldn't do the breathing, so we swapped, me giving breaths while Dave took over compressions. A taxi driver stopped and called through to his base to get an ambulance. It felt like it took a long while to come, and just as the ambulance pulled-up, the old guy took a breath.

The next-door neighbour to the man, an elderly lady, took me into her house and gave me a clean towel and soap in her bathroom, telling me to wash up. I felt sick. When I walked into her kitchen, she said I'd done a good job and that her neighbour was a decent man – his wife had left him, and he had raised his son and daughter himself. After he was home from hospital, near Xmas, I visited him and met his two kids and grandkids. Dave and I were asked to come back for Xmas dinner, and when we said we couldn't, they told me there would be two places set at their table regardless. They were Polish people and I still wonder is that a Polish custom for someone who had been kind to them.

Well, the next amazing thing in my life arrived on the 20 of December 1979 and what a day that was to be. My son Matthew was arriving, and he took his time. His mother was in labour for a long time and was in a room with another woman, who was also having a lot of pain. She was an Italian lady and I thought if my baby could hear her, he'd certainly know how to bloody swear. That woman would make a wharfie blush. After waiting for most of the night in that Orange Base Hospital, a nurse said I should go and have a sleep. I grudgingly said I would...but I would be in the car in front of the hospital. The nurse came out to the car and found me a mess, blood all over my shirt from a nosebleed in my sleep. She said they were performing a Caesarean on my wife as the baby had become stressed and was getting weak, but that I had to go home to freshen-up and come back. I wasn't gone long and was back at the hospital in no time. Before too long, the nurse came to tell me I had a son and took me to see him. I put on a white hospital gown, tied at the back, and was taken in to all the babies in the nursery. I sat on a stool in front of a humidity crib, looking at my boy for the first time. He was a little hairy on his shoulders and had bloody big feet, with little blue booties on. I thought straight off that he was going to have a good hold on the old Mother Earth with those feet. I spoke to him and when he heard me, he was rolling from one side to another. I thought he'll be right, he's not as weak as I was told.

I went and saw my wife and told her all about Matt, and that he was okay. She was sore from the caesarean but doing okay. Eventually, I drove to work, about 10am and let my boss, E.J. Jones know about my new son before going to our flat for break-fast and a shower. I went down the street to buy flowers for my wife and didn't know what to buy for my son – most people buy babies a teddy bear, but for whatever reason, I bought Matthew a Bugs Bunny rabbit. I rang my parents to tell them, and my mother-in-law. I was very proud of my boy. Matthew and his mother were kept in hospital for two weeks. My first Xmas as a father, I did cook Xmas dinner, and my mother-in-law and two brothers-in-law came from Grenfell. I made a baked lunch with roast pork and dessert, and when the meal was ready, I went up to the hospital and picked up my wife to bring her home for Xmas lunch take her back that afternoon.

Well, back to work for me and a fault I had to repair was at Panuara, on a property where I met the owner, Mrs Sonia McMahon. It was a big, old home, made of sandstone, with a big brick shed that looked like it may have been built by convicts. When you looked at the house from its left and to the front of it, about 50 metres out there was a wooden post about 18 inches square, with an old bell on top. I had no idea what it was for, assuming it was maybe an assembly bell for the convicts and workers. There was a small cemetery not far from the area, an isolated place in the hilly country, south of Orange, near Four Mile Creek, Cadia and full of history.

I had applied for a transfer to Grenfell, to please my wife in her desire to move to Young, nearer her family. Barry Morris, now one of the big bosses in Bathurst, granted my transfer application, offering me the line foreman job in Grenfell. Unfortunately, my wife then decided she didn't want her mother living on her doorstep, so I had to knock it back. Made me look like a dick head! This was just one of many times my wife would ask for one thing, then change her mind in almost completely the opposite direction, making it hard for me to please her.

Another job I did out in the bush at Lewis Ponds, I must tell as I found it funny. I went out with a gang putting in some cable which I would joint in and cut over. Peter Campbell was the Party Leader and each day we took it in turn to light a fire under a plough disc, which was our barbie[8]. This day, Pete said to this young kid, Shane Phefly, about 18-years-old, that it was his turn to cook. I thought to myself that this was likely Shane's first time away from his mother in Albury. He bumbled around a bit but couldn't get the fire going. I felt sorry for him, so gave him a hand. Big Pete Campbell saw all this and was surprised when Shane asked him how do you cook the snags and chops? Pete couldn't believe it and asked if the kid had never been camping in the bloody bush? Shane replied that of course he had, Pete saying back,

"Where, in the Main Street of Albury?" and Shane said,

"No, way out in the back blocks." Pete asked,

"What the bloody hell did you do for food way out there?" We all busted ourselves laughing when Shane said they would just go over to the shop over the road. You probably had to be there!

Back in the depot there was a clerk named Vic Monaghan, and the boys were always setting him up leaving messages to set him up. One such message was left on his desk:

Mr. Line was enquiring about another extension to go into the den. Phone number 0678688213. When Vic rang, he said he wanted to speak to Mr. Line about a phone in the den. The bloke who answered said do you know who you have called, Vic said yes, Mr Line. Then the bloke told Vic he was a smart arse as that number he rang was the Dubbo Zoo and he hung up on

---

[8]Short for barbeque, to cook food over

him. Another thing the boys would do to Vic was to disconnect the earpiece in his phone, so that when he answered he couldn't hear anyone and would go off his head a bit. They would leave old Vic alone for a month or so and then they would disconnect the speaker in his phone so when he answered people couldn't hear him. Poor Vic.

I had worked with Ken Williams a bit, he was the Coaxial patrolman when his driver was on leave and somehow, I was given a Coaxial Cable school at Greta up near Maitland. Greta school was what was left of the Greta army camp. The day I left to go up there for six weeks, only coming home on weekends, I was sorry to go, as Matt was about 10 months old, and I didn't really want to leave. There was another bloke from Orange, Dave Cleal who originally came from Gilgandra, doing a school at Greta at the same time as me, so we shared cars each week. Interestingly, I believe Dave's cousin, Crusher Cleal, played for Manly. First day in that school, we were all in the class waiting for the instructor to enter when a bloke I had done an install with on a phone school at North Strathfield in Sydney walked in. His name was George Portous, and he was mad as a cut snake and well known for his antics. Instructors dreaded having him in their classes, as he was real stirrer! George moved a bloke off the front desk and sat right in front of the instructor's desk. He had his bib and brace overalls on backwards and ahead of his time wearing his cap on backwards. He was carrying on something weird and the instructor walked in, saw George said, "No way" and walked out. After a while another instructor came in and George said,

"I stooged your mate he thinks I am here for a school, I am just passing through on holidays." George left and we got our instructor back, all he said was,

"That George is a real bastard."

Back in Orange working again, it was decided by the Board of Control that we would stay in Orange. Knowing we would be staying put, I went looking for a house and found a bargain. I hassled over it for a while and had about half the amount needed in my savings already. I got it for $28,000 fully furnished in West Orange. We moved in and one of the first things I did was fence off the backyard so Matthew couldn't get out on the road and put a slide lock up high on the screen door. I had never been able to forget about the little boy in Jerilderie, killed out the front of his house when he was hit by a car – his dad built the fence too late for his little mate. I enjoyed living in that house doing it up, painting it through, and having my first go at wallpapering. I had no idea how I would go about it, so my first attempt was in the toilet room – I figured if I was no good at it, what better place to do than a shithouse.

I loved that home and taking 18-month-old Matt with me in my Ute, in his cold weather gear and beanie to get firewood in the bush, even in snowfalls. When Matt was very young, he would watch cartoons a lot. One was the road runner where lots of things got blown up. One night, I was bathing Matt when he stood up in the bath and looked like he was going to touch the electric switch on the zip heater over the bath. I yelled out don't touch that it will blow up. Matt took that literally, like he'd seen on the cartoons, and took for cover with a backflip into the bath full of water, drenching me with a big splash. Little things you remember!

Jim Cunningham and I went out to Bloomfield, it was called a mental home and we were to clear a fault on a phone service there. For me, I found what happened next very amusing, but Jim wasn't of the same opinion. It was a Wednesday, the day for the patients to go to the pictures. Jim and I were working outside the picture theatre. The patients all crowded around when Jim climbed up the pole. I was what was called the 'ground sparrow,'where Jim would ask me to throw tools and equipment up that he required, and I would throw them in such a way as that they stalled in front of him, within his reach. Jim asked for a pocketknife to strip back on the cable, and I threw it up, stalled in front of him and he missed it, allowing it to fall to the ground. There was a mad scramble among the patients to pick up the knife and throw it up to Jimmy. He'd miss it as the game kept going, those buggers laughing and Jim dodging the knife. I finally got the knife back as the inmates were ushered into the theatre. I'll never forget a whiteofaced Jim climbing down the ladder. He was shaking and said,

"Don't ever let them get hold of a knife."

I replied, laughing "I am really happy you never got hit, Jim, but that was one of the funniest things I have ever seen."

I had a few early night job recalls to Bloomfield, and I started to think it was a place where you should have a second man with you. One night, I got a callout and was looking for an office in one of the wards when a big, strong fellow grabbed me by my arm and asked who I was looking for. When I told him, he virtually dragged me up to the office. I was trying to get out of his grip as he was nearly breaking my arm, but decided it was better not to resist. A wardsman then stayed with me until my work was done and escorted me out into the dark. I felt relieved when I was in my van and off out of that place. The 'help' from the well-intentioned patient was somewhat terrifying. There was another patient who would always make a beeline for me to ask me to marry her. I asked a wardsman why she did that and he said she thought that if she got married, they would let her out of Bloomfield.

At a send-off party one night, a fault came in on Mount Canobolas for the police radio, and Martin Corby and I went up to fix it. It was one of the wildest nights, heavy rain, thunder, and crazy lightning. Marty was happy as he'd had a fair few drinks, and as I opened up an elevated cable joint near the top of the mountain, he held an umbrella over us, informing me that if the lightning hit the cable, it could give me a flash in the eyes from the joint and it would blind me. He was laughing his head off. He was as happy as a mouse in a bag full of wheat. I had never seen a bloke so happy to be working in torrential rain, thunder, and lightning. We had fixed the police radio line and next thing I found that bloody Martin was holding an umbrella over his head, wearing a yellow raincoat in the pouring rain, lightning flashes and him dancing and singing that song, 'Singing in the Rain.' It was the best impersonation I've ever seen of Gene Kelly and the most memorable.

I will always remember that it seemed like every day when I got home from work my little mate - from nappies, crawling, to a little man standing at the front screen door looking and waiting for me - just made my day. That is worth more than all the money in the world. You just can't buy that sort of thing. It's priceless. My wife was pregnant again, and all was going well. It looked like my little mate would have a brother or sister, but about four months in the baby was lost. Why, I don't know. Sad.

And so, it was time to apply for another transfer to Young. I tried to do this by applying for a promotion to Line Supervisor Grade One, which I had seen in the Commonwealth Gazette. I flew to Sydney from Springhill, a little south of Orange, on a

Fokker Friendship aircraft. I was driven to George Street from the airport in a Commonwealth car. An old bloke I spoke to in Sydney said he came from Grafton and was called Truckie. I flew back that afternoon and went to see my dad in the pub. I was sitting at the bar watching the news, talking to Dad and his mates about what I'd been up to that day and on comes Truckie on the tele, being asked a question in the street in Sydney.

"I was down in Sydney talking to that bloke," I said. I couldn't believe it – two or three million people in Sydney and there was Truckie. Small world.

I did not get the promotion, but in a few months, I was given a transfer to Young. Matthew was about 14 months old. My dad was working away, and mum had gone with him, so we lived in their house in Boorowa, and I travelled to work in Young each day. The house in Orange was on the market and hadn't sold in about two months. My wife decided she wanted to move back to Orange and take our son with her, whether I went or not. What could I do? She had wanted to leave Orange, then once we did, she wanted to go back. Stuffed if I knew what she wanted. So now I had to talk to Barry Morris, the big boss in Bathurst. He was on leave when I had left Orange. I had got the move to Young by writing a letter to the New South Wales Manager of Telecom, Mr Cullen, who had previously given me a letter thanking me for giving Telecom the credit for my CPR Training when used to save the Polish man, Kazimierz Zarnota.

So, to get back to Orange in my work and to keep my family together, I did something I didn't think I should. I rang Barry Morris at Bathurst on a Friday, told him my situation, and virtually begged him for a move back to Orange. To my great surprise he asked me to put something in writing to him through the Senior Lines Officer in Young, and fax it to him, and to report for duty at

Orange on Monday. All of which I did. I couldn't believe the way I got the move to Young and now the move back to Orange as none of this was standard practice. The only thing I could think of I must have been liked and the bosses knew I was going through a hard time, and they had some compassion towards me. Through all this changing of minds, I was under a bit of stress and had to call on the patience I had asked for when I was confirmed. Why I'd asked for patience at the time, I did not know, but by Christ I was starting to find out why.

During all of this, I lost my dear old Pa Oxley. I saw my grandmother after his funeral in Sydney, back at Haberfield where they had been living for some years with Pa's sister. Once again, I tried to write a poem to make her feel better. Nan kept that poem 'til she died. I always tried to write, even though I didn't read much.

For Grandmother – 1980

Our dear loving Gran with head hanging down
In your heart a sadness you cannot describe
You lift up your face we all see a frown
In your eyes those tears you cannot hide.

We are all so sad to lose our dear old Pa
From us he has been taken away
Although he still lives in our hearts
Such love the years will never sway.

I see you Gran you don't feel right
Like us, you miss Pa's jokes and laughter
I know your sadness is worse at night
Now Pa is in his life hereafter.

So, Gran be happy with and enjoy your life
Lift up your head, show us your might
And thank the Lord you were Pa's loving wife
As you'll meet in heaven when you reunite.

So back to Orange and our home, and back to work. Working on bush faults, I used that time to think, especially when I was alone, and it was like therapy for me. I met all different people and found some real characters. I loved doing the bush faults and there was always the chance of running into a snake, of which I have many stories.

I was on my own in a little bush exchange halfway between Molong and Orange. From the front door to the back wall of the exchange would only be four metres at most. I was testing a phone line when the hair stood up on the back of my neck, spotting a five- or six-foot brown snake on the concrete step at the door, head up to come in with me. As I was alone, I thought what do I do? I saw a tin waste bin on the floor, and threw it past the snake, landing on the concrete path behind it, causing a loud bang and the vibration of it scared the snake off. It turned and slid down the gap of the concrete step and the exchange floor. Now I had another kind of dilemma as I could no longer see the snake to know where he was. I took off from the back door with three of the fastest steps in a run I could do, jumped over the step, and landed on the concrete path. I kept going for about ten more metres to the front gate before stopping to look back. The snake was nowhere in sight, and I wondered at the length of my jump from a standing start. I could have entered the Olympic Games in Moscow if I had a Joe Blake[9] to urge me on.

---

[9]Rhyming slang for 'snake'

Another brown snake story happened at Springside, towards Springhill to the south of Orange. This time more of a scare by not seeing a snake after I jumped over a gate in a paddock. As I left the gate and was coming down for a landing, I hit the ground about four feet from a brown snake. The snake didn't move, so God knows why, but I decided it must be dead, picked up my gear and walked away. What scared me, was that when I came back to the gate later, the 'dead' snake wasn't there anymore.

Cadia Mines was not a big deal, as at that stage there weren't any mines started. I had to get a telephone line to a temporary demountable office. One day in the park in the centre of Orange, I saw Bob Hawke on the hustings. I spoke to him and got a photo of him. I recall him saying that 'If I get to be PM one of the first things, I will do is get rid of world parity oil pricing.' Never happened!

I added another back lounge room and a veranda to our little house. The house was great, although for my wife it was never classy enough. I put a vegetable garden out the back and grew plenty of tomatoes, which would always ripen before my neighbours'. I would go to the bedding stores and get plastic off them from mattresses they sold and put it over the frame I built from cross arms off poles like a hothouse.

At work, I somehow used to act in the position of Foreman of Works, supervising fault clearances and the clerks for both works and faults. I also did the other clerk's job, completing work reports for 66 men and acting as the Coaxial Patrolman. One morning, I overheard the Line Inspector at the noticeboard in the depot, talking about me putting my name down for overtime as a fault man for the Saturday, commenting negatively about me being paid as acting Line Foreman, but still putting myself down for overtime. I fronted him, stating how many others were doing the same thing, then angry, asking where exactly it said, 'List names for overtime, *excluding Steve Oxley.*' With that, the Line Inspector pulled me into the office once all the gangs had their work for the day and had left the depot. He told me he could make or break me, and I had better figure out which one I wanted. So, I did, straight away. I told him never to ask me to act in higher duties again, so from that day on, even though I knew how to get the best work out of the blokes, I was never asked to act as foreman again.

I guess I don't like being threatened or told to toe the line, so I was back out again to do fault clearances for my old boss, E. J. Jones. It was great working for Johnny, we really got on great. He let me out in the bush, and he had a bit of a sense of humour like my own. It wasn't too long after all the above crap that John sends me out on a fault at the Orange sewage works. There was a pole route going in there and a drop wire strung along on the poles. It had been hit by lightning, and I had to replace it. One span went over the big round holding tanks with things turning around and stirring up all you-know-what from Orange. The sewage works bloke approached me, driving an old Fergie tractor, and towing a box trailer with a shovel in it. He started talking to me and said to look at the contents of the holding tanks, which always put him in mind of Telecom – if you look closely, he said, I will notice all the big turds floating to the top. I went back to the depot and shared the story with Johnny, laughing and asking him

"Do you think I should tell Bruce, the Line Inspector?" John advised me very seriously not to do that.

Wasn't too long after that the Line Inspector asked me to see him in his office again. I thought *what the hell have I done now,* when he says he had received a letter about me from a member of the public. He said to take a seat while he read me the letter, which would be going on my file. I wondered what the hell this was about but thought it couldn't be anything good. Well, it was from a recently widowed lady, who wrote that she had observed me taking my hat off and holding it to my chest as the funeral procession for her husband passed me in the street. She wrote that she didn't want my mark of respect to go unnoticed, as she was deeply appreciative and found my gesture very touching. After this letter, my relationship with the Line Inspector changed considerably, to the point where from that day, we got along quite well, and I would even consider him a friend. In life, it is far better to get along with all people where you can, much less stress,

Out at Euchareena, I was fixing a fault which took my mind all the way back to Jerilderie. The aerial line on the open wire part of a private line, or PPE line owned by the subscriber, was very hard to hear because of all the dry joints, or un-soldered joins, in the GI wires. This service operated on a magneto or manual exchange. The customer, named Hubbard, was barely audible when I called them from the exchange to let them know I would be working on the line. I found the dry joints and bridged them over with copper wire, soldering the joints in span between poles by standing on the ladder on top of my truck. No one had ever done this for them before or explained what was wrong with their service. When I arrived at the homestead out in the hills, I was greeted by Mrs Hubbard and went into the house, asking her to ring the exchange and see how Neville found the line. I was about 10 or 12 metres from Mrs Hubbard when she rang the handle on that old phone and when Nev answered 'Euchareena' loud as he had to so they could hear him, I heard him and it nearly deafened poor Mrs Hubbard. She made a cup of tea and scones for me and for her husband, who was driving back to the house. She asked how I knew to fix the line like that. I was telling her it was because of all the private lines out at Jerilderie I had worked on. When Mr Hubbard walked in, she asked him to ring the exchange, so he got a good surprise. He grinned and said great job. Mrs Hubbard said I learnt how to fix those lines in Jerilderie and Mr Hubbard said he had met me before, when he was managing a property years ago between Jerilderie and Conargo. He had gone on to do some university courses and then after his father retired from the farm at Euchareena, he returned to take over the property. Bloody small world – I had worked on phones on the place he was managing at the time.

We had some fun with the two-way radios catching people out. One day, I heard E. J. Jones calling Bot Fly and asking where he was. He was supposed to be down at Four Mile Creek. Bot answered that he was at Four Mile Creek, then EJ he said that's funny I am parked right behind you, and I am in Summer Street Orange. Just how some people get caught out. The boss didn't know this, but through the day someone would always call a boss up and ask them where they were so we could all hear and keep tabs on where they were. I used to like writing stories about things that happened at work and putting them on the notice board, and I wrote about Graham Cullen alias 'sparrow' as his nickname. Sparrow run into a bit of trouble while installing a new telephone service for a lady. I wrote a story of Sparrow taking his nickname too seriously as when he was up in the lady's roof like sparrows often do, he took being a sparrow one step too far, fell through the ceiling and flew through the lounge room and was lucky he didn't break a wing when he hit the back of a lounge chair. He was not to be awarded a DFC (Distinguished Flying Cross) for his efforts, if anything, he should have been grounded.

I put another on the board for Sparrow after hearing another story of him. I wrote that he was having trouble in his mind trying to figure out whether he wanted to work for Telecom doing phone work, or for New South Wales railway. On the railway crossing, on the tracks on or off Piesley Street in Orange, Sparrow had run up the back of a car in his works van. So, I asked did he want to be a cable jointer with Telecom, or a shunter on the railway, as I thought he might be a bit confused.

When I had acted as foreman over the new work, there was a Party Leader they called *Pint Man*, and I was to find out why. When they finished a job, the gang would draw up a plan of all their work and put down all the measurements. The difference with Terry, the Pint Man, was I would have to convert all his measurements into metric, as Pint man was still in imperial measurements and refused to convert to metric. He got his nickname from the drinkers in the devil house, or pub where he used to down a few amber liquids, as they kept his glass there and it was all he'd ever drink out of. It was a real pint glass. The Pint man rode a Honda motorbike and got a 'miles per hour' speedo sent to him from Japan.

After installing a phone extension in a house in Orange for a Minister of Religion, I wrote another 'story' on the board. I had an interest in government and politics, and knew they had ministers for everything, and I had found the 'Minister for wet and dirty nappies' in that house. I was stapling cable along a skirting board, pushing aside stinking nappies lying all along the walls. I could not believe the homeowner was a religious minister and wondered whether the stinking nappies were talisman to ward off evil spirits, they smelled that bad. It certainly got rid of me; I couldn't wait to get out of there.

Out on bush faults as I was mostly, I was paired up with Brent Pilgrim. He had done his schools and been put with me, and we worked well together. I was training him on fault location and clearance. Brent enjoyed the meals I cooked in the bush on the shovel and learnt how to survive in the bush. I had a bit of a reputation for the tucker I would take out with me or for the food I would find. My old mate at Jerilderie had taught me well. I would get to know where to find mushrooms, especially in unploughed paddocks. I also knew where potatoes or spuds were grown, what fruit was out and where to find it on Canobolas, and anywhere else for that matter. Brent caught on quickly, noticing my ability to find food anywhere, and said to me that it was a mighty coincidence that our boss E.J. Jones (Johnny) would call us on the two-way about an hour before lunch to see exactly where we were in the bush, and would turn up for lunch. Brent started calling me 'Wishbone', as the cargo barrier of the Hi-Ace we drove always rattled with frypans and saucepans hanging off the barrier. They would swing and bash like mad while driving through the rough paddocks, so he decided to name the van. Brent got to work one day and very skilfully, using black insulation tape, put the words 'Chuckwagon' on the sliding door and the back door of the van.

Brent (or Bert as he was known) had a sleeping problem, and if we were sailing along on a bitumen road, he'd go out to it. He reckoned it was because he was a diabetic and that caused the sleeping attacks. I would be a bit of a bugger if Bert was off with the fairies, and I knew there was a good dip up the road, I wouldn't disturb him. I would slowly pick up pace and just before the dip I would yell out,

"For Christ's sake hang on." Bert would be waking just as the dip was hit and it would scare the hell out of him. He got used to it after a while and one day on the straight past Hazelton airport at Cudal heading towards Orange, I scared him again, but not with a dip. It was getting towards the end of a long drought, which hadn't broken yet. Just like Jerilderie in dust storms, you had to give way to livestock crossing the road. This day, Bert was out to it when I saw the biggest 'willi willi' I'd ever seen coming across the road. Before it hit us, I yelled out and Bert woke up in time to see us hit the little twister[10] Poor bugger, he never knew what would happen next.

There was a bushfire up on Canobolas, and some essential radio lines were down over a weekend. E.J. Jones rang me and up Mount Canobolas we went, finding a couple of elevated joints burnt out. We dug down around the joints, exposing the cable and repairing the faults. We drove to the top of the mountain to test the lines and get clearance from the technician in the exchange down in Orange. I was buggered and had seen enough of fires for the day, but old E.J. hadn't. He climbed halfway up the big tower to get a better view of the fires. He was a tough bugger, John. There was nothing of him and he would have been in his early 50s, then, and bloody fit.

One day I was working on my own down at Four Mile Creek and I went to lift a big steel lid off a manhole near the exchange and did my back in big time. I got myself back into Orange where EJ Jones got me to a doctor, and I couldn't work for three weeks. I lost about a stone in weight and got put on 'Indocin' tablets which gave me bleeding ulcers. After going back to work, I saw

---

[10] A small whirlwind of strong winds

a chiropractor every week for about 12 months. One day I'd had enough and was told about a doctor named Bleakly. He x-rayed me and told me, while showing the tiniest gap between his finger and thumb, that my legs were that close to being ornamental. After three visits, Dr Bleakly had me as good as I would ever be. He had toured with the Russian Ballet, apparently, and I was lucky enough to run into him. Bloody miracle worker in my book.

We had been through a long drought and my little mate, Matthew, had a yellow raincoat and boots, and hadn't got to try them out. It was almost 1982, when he was two years old, that he finally got to try them. I'll never forget seeing that kid dancing in the rain out the back of the house. Funny how things like that stand out in your memories.

I would never forget the driver I had one day doing the coax patrol job. We called him Captain, his name was Frank Kidd, and so was Captain Kidd. Captain, by coincidence, had worked with Dad years before in about 1960 in a big PMG camp at Wallgrove near Sydney in what they called Primary Works. Captain would tell me stories of the old PMG days camping out, and I told him stories my father and my grandfather, Fred Howe, had told me.

Dad once told me about the gang camping out in the hills from Boorowa, towards Darby's Falls, for weeks. Some people who owned a property near where they were working let the gang stop in the shearer's quarters, and as the owners would be away for six weeks, they said that if they fed the chooks and dogs, they could have the eggs. One bloke in that gang came from Goulburn or somewhere, and he was hogging all the eggs for himself and rubbing a thing called egg keep or keep egg on them, so they kept better. One night when he was not about, the boys got a kerosene can filled with water, lit a fire, and hard boiled all the eggs before carefully placing them back where the bastard had them stashed, because they knew he was going to make a big man of himself taking them to give them to his relatives back home. 'Top Stir.'

Another story I told Captain was one my grandfather told me, about all stopping in shearers quarters in the bush once on a property. Dad had told me this yarn too. There was a big bloke with the gang about six feet four tall. Dad said his name was Dick and for some reason he never felt the cold in his feet and would sit on the tray of the truck, legs hanging over in -5 degrees, big frost, and his feet bare. Sitting beside him, his boots, and socks. Then anyway, the whole gang camped in the shearer's hut except Dick. He camped in his bed on the veranda and one frosty morning, my grandfather observed that even though it was freezing both feet were hanging out the end of the bed when Pop went to wake him. Later that day, the lady who owned the place caught my grandfather and one of the gang was with him at the time and asked had they all settled in well. After they were alone this bloke said to Pop,

"Do you realise what you said to that woman?" He then told Pop it didn't sound too good when he said,

"They are all well inside the hut, but you couldn't believe the bloke sleeping on the veranda, as he had seen him on the coldest morning and there he was, not feeling the cold and two feet of Dick hanging out the end of his bed."

Anyway, my driver told me a story one day and after all my writing and stories that go on, he didn't mind telling a yarn either and this was the biggest yarn ever and it all started like this. "I will tell you a story Steve, and so as not to make it too long, I won't start from the very start, it would take too long!" Well, the Captain started his story as we got out of Orange. We got through Mullion Creek, Kerr's Creek, Euchareena, Lewis Ponds, Kings Plains, Springside, Spring Hill, Blayney Neville, Mandurama, Carcoar, and that story he cut short so it wouldn't take too long, finished in Cowra.

One of our conditions of work was if you had been working in a confined space or cramped position for some time during the day, you got an early knock off at 4pm instead of 4.30pm. A couple of the boys would save cobwebs from under houses in an empty matchbox and if you needed an early knock off, even if you hadn't earned it, they would hang the cobwebs in their hair for evidence to prove they had been under a house.

I had a fault on a lady's phone where the drop wire from the pole went to the eaves of the house, down behind the down pipe, in under the house, and up through the floor. The line was pulled out twice and the lady lost service before being harassed by her ex-boyfriend. She was sure it was her ex was pulling the phone wires apart. So, what I said I could do for her was I would take the line from the eaves of the house where it came from the pole on the footpath, take them from the block or terminal point, through the ceiling and into the house, so he couldn't get at them. The poor lady said he will know the wires are moved and pull something else apart up the pole. I explained to her he won't because I will also repair the wires he's been breaking and give her some joiners so he can keep breaking a dummy bit of wire which isn't working anyway, and she could keep doing a patch up on the dead wires – that way she would always have a phone and could stooge the ex. I never heard from her again.

As time went on, my wife and I were to be having another baby and I just hoped and prayed that this one would not be lost like the last pregnancy. When the last baby was lost, I was told by the Minister who had performed our marriage that I had to look at that loss as nature doing the right thing and that didn't really make me feel that much better. This time, all went well, and Danielle, our daughter, arrived about a month early. Boy was I so glad to see her. My wife was having a lot of trouble and it was decided by the doctor to do another Caesarean birth. A little baby girl came into my world. The nurse brought the baby to me, and she was screaming, and the nurse asked me to hold her, and I said no, she is too little I might break her. The nurse then handed the screaming baby to me and when she was in my arms the first words, I said to her was, "I don't think there is any need for that" and straight away she stopped crying and settled down. Then the nurse took her from me and said she had to wash her to get some fluids off her skin after birth. I waited and the nurse brought her back and put her in the humidity crib and she started screaming again and I said to the nurse, "Give the kid a drink," which she did. She got a bottle with about an inch and a half of milk in it, fed her in the humidity crib and the brat drank that and went to sleep. It had been a big day for the little one. I then went to see her mother and told her the baby girl was good and she had black hair and dark eyes like this French lady on TV at the time, whose name was Danielle, so we called her Danielle DeVere very French sounding name. The DeVere was a family name from Mum's side which hadn't been used for 100 years in the family.

I rang Mum to tell her and Dad they had another granddaughter. For the first time in my life, while nursing the baby I could see a baby looked like someone. Dead tired and after a couple of beers, instead of saying I could see Mum in her, I said something like she's a bit of an ugly mess and looks like you. Luckily, Mum took it well and could see the funny side. Thankfully.

Chapter 16

Orange Part 2 - After Danielle's birth

Six weeks after Danielle was born, I had an accident while trying to put her on the back seat of the car which was a two-door Toyota Celica. I somehow lost my grip on one of the handles on the carry basket and although I tried to keep the basket close to the ground, little Danielle rolled out onto the lawn. Because it was so difficult with the two-door car, I decided that it was time to buy a four-door car to make it easier to put a baby in a carry basket on the back seat as it had always been difficult with Matthew as well, but I hadn't dropped him.

I went over to Parkes and saw a car salesman at the 'World of Wheels' car yard. His name was Greg Corcoran, and I knew him as he came from my hometown, and about two weeks later he rang me happy with himself as he had found a car for me and was bringing it over to Orange for me to look at it. I just couldn't tell him I had bought a Commodore from Cameron's Motors in Orange, so I put the car in the shed, pulled down the roller door and then made a mistake of telling my 3 · year old son not to mention the new car in the shed to Greg when he turned up with the car, he had for me to look at. Greg parked in the drive-way, Matthew ran out to see him and straight away said, "Come and have a look at Dad's new car in the shed." I learnt two lessons that day – one, I should have been upfront with Greg about the car and two, don't ask a three-year-old to keep a secret.

"Acting Line Inspectors Prayer" – Lord's Prayer

Dear Lord, please forgive me
And let me get some sleep
For you sure cannot blame me
For floods and swollen creeks.

Dear Lord, please forgive me
For the faults in the main drag
I didn't know the buggers
Had cable joints in plastic bags.

Dear Lord, please forgive me
For the faults we have now got
Please you cannot blame me
For all this bloody rot.

Dear Lord, please forgive me
For cables all washed out
For that you cannot blame me
It was you who broke the drought.

Dear Lord, please forgive me
For the shit that's hit the fan.
I need staff and some fine weather
And I am doing all I bloody can.

I wrote and put this poem on the notice board for E.J. Jones, as he was copping it while acting as head honcho of the Orange Line Depot. The big boss from Bathurst seemed to be blaming John for all the phones not working, caused by the heavy rain. The big bosses name was David Lord. Hence for E.J. Jones, I wrote the 'Lord's Prayer.'

Danielle developed a breathing problem as a baby and would simply just stop breathing. I found that if I just took a real loud deep breath so she could hear it, she would automatically take a breath. I always wondered was this a cause of cot death, so even when Danielle was later put in her own room, for quite some time I would check on her a big number of times through the night. Danielle would have a couple of operations while we were in Orange, but these didn't fix the problem.

One cold and windy winter's day, I had to visit the dentist after work to have root canal therapy and a new cap on a tooth and I found it very painful and told the dentist if he was to drill any deeper in that bottom tooth, he'd probably strike oil. I wasn't having the best of days and when I was driving home, I heard the bloke on 2GZ radio Orange, saying that for people in Forest Reefs and Spring Hill area that Telecom was working to restore the phones and they might have them fixed by Christmas. That would have been me, as I would have been working on that in the freezing blizzard conditions if it hadn't been for seeing the dentist. I knew that the Orange Council had ripped up the trunk cables with a backhoe along the railway line, so when I got home, the news was on the radio, so I rang that smart arse up and gave him a serve and suggested to him that he was probably some mongrel out of university bagging out blokes doing a tough job in tough conditions and that he probably had never done one day of hard work in his life. I then rang my Line Inspector Bruce Casey who was now a friend of mine and told him what the clown on 2GZ radio had said, and what I said to him when I rang the station. Bruce thanked me for letting him know and said to keep listening to the radio for an apology and sure enough about 10 minutes later there was a big apology came across the wireless. Bruce must have really got up that bastard and good on him.

I never got used to people running us down on Telecom and that went right back to that smart-arse cow cocky Bill Street in Koondrook when I worked at Barham. One day I was chasing a fault up on Mount Canobolas on what appeared to be a cut cable, as there was many phones off the air. I'd been testing at a few points and had one lead of my meter put to ground and the other to the cable, which was showing me a fault but the needle on the meter was still. Next thing I hear an engine start up a couple of hills away over the mountain, and while it was running the meter needle was jumping around, seeming to be in tune with the engine. I packed up my gear and went to find that engine noise – I found Watermen Drillers, a mob who drill for water, sinking bores. When I got out of my truck, I approached the three workmen and told them I was looking for a cut cable and pointed out the cable markers on the fences either side of where they were drilling and said they lined up and said I think you might have hit the phone cable. One of those blokes was a bit of a character and asked me how deep the Telecom cable had to be any way. I told him about three feet and asked him how deep they had gone down with the drill, and he said about 60 metres. I just said I think you might have got it.

Whilst working on a fault in Orange late one of those freezing Orange days, I had been getting some testing done with a technician in the exchange and I was swinging up a pole in a cold wind. I had my phone across a line for about half an hour, my hands felt numb from the cold, and I was waiting for the technician to ring me with his results of tests when I looked down from the pole to the footpath below, and there was the technician riding home on his pushbike. When I called out and said,

"Where the bloody hell are you going," he looked up and said,

"Christ, I forgot you." I said I wasn't too impressed and if my hands weren't so numb, I'd throw my pliers at him. Just another story, all would be well.

In 1983, I was sent to North Strathfield to a fault school to learn what I was doing for the past 10+ years. I found it much fun and I could have taught the instructors a thing or two, which I did without making a smart arse of myself. For the last week of the school, I took my family with me, and we stopped with my grandmother at Haberfield and after school would spend time outside with the kids watching all the planes flying in and out of Mascot Aerodrome. I somehow passed that fault school, so back to Orange doing what I loved, fault clearance. I got a fault one day in town along the railway track, in a fuel storage area. This fault ended up putting the fear of God in me. The line was a drop-wire feed, which is one cable with two conductors (or wires) for the phone, and a bearer wire to attach to the poles. This line had been run-in using one of the high steel petrol tanks like a pole. I climbed up a steel ladder on the fuel tank and at the top, I saw at a breather point the two-wire joined with no cover, or plastic sleeve, over the bare conductors, only about 15 ml apart. If a spark was nearby it could arc, and I just imagined that happening at the point of petrol fumes from the breather pipe. Half of Orange would hear and see me go up in an explosion and flames. I carefully climbed back down and when back where my ladder was, I disconnected the line and called E.J. Jones. He came straight away with a couple of linesmen and had all those wires taken down. They should never have been run there and John said they were lucky never to have been hit by lightning or shorted out.

I was out chasing a fault between Orange and Molong on the lead trunk cable that fed that little bush exchange where I had the encounter with the brown snake, and the whole cable had faults on it. I could not get a reading on a distance to the fault and the only way to do it was to open the cable to see if I was past the fault or not. I had a young bloke with me who could teach me something about lightning strikes. He was Martin Corby, the bloke who was with me the night in those lightning storms on the Mountain, the one who had done the Gene Kelly impersonation. Martin's theory was that lightning preferred to strike white box trees, so we drove the route and picked a spot to test where white box trees were close to the cable run buried in a paddock. We opened the cable either side of those white box trees and hit the jackpot. The cable was blown there, and we ran cable across the ground, temporary jointed it in, and all worked. Whether that was a fluke or not, or Martin's theory was true, I don't know!

One night I decided to take my wife out to see a show at the Orange Civic Centre and we went with Jim Cunningham (alias Tricky Pig) and his wife to see the Four Kinsman perform. Through the performance I happened to say to Jim that the acoustics in the place were good and my wife looked at me. I asked her if she knew what acoustics was, and she got a bit indignant and said, "Of course I do, that's those sticks they belt the balls around on a pool table with." I didn't laugh – risk assessment.

There was another bloke I worked with, his name was Peter Fowler and we called him Chook. He was a bit of a stirrer to everyone, and one day Chook met his match. I was having a couple of beers with a few of my workmates in the Commercial Hotel in Orange when the Chook decided to give a bit of a stir to the new and very young barmaid, who he thought he could have a bit of fun with and put it over her or put her down a bit. That young girl wasn't to be fooled with and she sat the Chook on his arse when she asked him what the material was around his head that went across his forehead. The Chook looked at her like she was stupid and told her it was a sweatband, with that the young lady said,

"Sorry, I thought it was a bandage to cover up your circumcision scar." The boys and me had never laughed so much to see an innocent young lady shut the Chook up, he certainly had nothing to crow about after that encounter.

Whilst working in Cargo, a little town between Orange and Canowindra, Jim Cunningham and I were jointing some new cables up when speeding cars were throwing little stones up at us from the road, inside the town speed limit. I said to Jim I'd slow the bastards down. When he asked what I was doing, I got about five feet of black cable from my truck, it was about 25 mls thick, got some black butyl rubber (used to seal up phone joints) and shaped a snake's head and stuck it on one end of the cable and even fashioned snake fangs out of small wires from within the cables. Jim watched me and said,

"How's that going to slow the bastards down?" I said, just watch. I walked about 30 metres towards the traffic where there was some loose blue metal and set the snake up on the road and went back to where we were working and just waited. Cars would come flying in, lock-up their brakes on that poor 'snake', and by the time they got to us were nearly stopped. 'Top Stir.'

Well, it came around again, and I was informed by my wife that I had to start trying to get a move closer to Grenfell, like to Harden or Young. This time I had done more work on the home at 84 Cecil Road, Orange, and put it on the market.

Another lot of bushfires happened on the Mountain and down to Four Mile Creek. This was not good, and they were supposedly lit by some nutcase deliberately lighting cigarettes and throwing them out of a car. Col McMillan was a foreman at the time, and he came from the big smoke. He rang me to go up Canobolas to fix some lines, including Police and Ambulance radio. Col said he would go with me, and when we got halfway up the mountain, it was the real big smoke, I thought he could have felt a little home-sick! I was just sick of the smoke. There were trees burning and the cable run was along through trees, in from the edge of the road. It was a boiling hot day and the heat from the burning trees just added to it, the smoke thick and swirling in the wind. We found an aboveground jointing post that was blackened from the flames and when I opened it, all the insulation on the wires were a melted mess, and it turned out to be the one we had to repair to get the radio lines working again. As we dug out the cable from the ground, we got enough cable to do a short temporary joint nearly underground to restore service. I saw something I would never forget. About 30 metres away, down the slope in burning scrub and trees where the fire hadn't long passed through,

I noticed a dead kangaroo. That kangaroo was sitting up dead, down on his haunches, with his hands, or should I say paws, held tight over his face and eyes to protect them. I even thought to myself, poor bastard mightn't have wanted to see what was happening to him when he gave up trying to get away and he was only about 50 metres off the track. That picture is always in my mind, and the first thought I had of that roo might sound weird, but I thought of Christmas, I thought he looked like a big roast turkey. While I jointed the cable now and then you would hear a tree explode or fall and Col said if I hear a tree coming down, we should run, I just looked around at trees near us and said,

"See that tree, it's the only one that can hit us and while it stands, I am going nowhere." Another job done!

Another job I was on was on the top of Mount Panorama, Bathurst where I was jointing up some phone cables. My old boss, E.J. Jones, came up to see how I was going, and he said he'd take me into Bathurst for lunch. Mount Panorama at times through the year is used as a racetrack and the boss and I were driving down the mountain in his Datsun 180B station wagon, down through the dipper around corners on the wrong side of the road. I asked John does he watch the races on TV and when he said yes, I told him its two-way traffic now and someone could be coming up the other way and we could have a head on collision. I guess the moment had got to him. I told EJ that as I was a Holden man, I've watched the car races for many years on Mount Panorama Bathurst, and loved V8s, cars with guts; it would be a bastard of a way to have to die on this famous racetrack in a lowly four-cylinder Datsun 180B station wagon.

Time was moving on, and my kids were growing up fast and had learnt how to behave. They had good manners and were polite, good kids. One day I was taking them and their mother for a little drive out of Orange towards Molong, when I drove past the highway patrol on the other side of the road stopping cars to breath test the drivers. It was then I realised I had left my driver's licence at home, so I asked my wife to drive back in case the police pulled us up. We were stopped and the officer grunted and virtually ordered my wife to blow into the bag then snatched it back, bloody rude! My daughter Danielle was about four years old, sitting in the back behind her mother and must have observed that rude behaviour of the policeman and called out to him, he should say please and thank you! I couldn't help but burst into laughter. So, the cop then went right over the car to try and defect it for something but found nothing and had to let us go. Years later, both Matthew, my son, and Danielle both acquired their driver's licences in that same car and used to drive it.

I was out doing a job in the bush near Mullion Creek, north of Orange one day, and I happened to be working alone. There had been terrible news on my radio about two little kids being kidnapped from Orange. They were brother and sister, and there was a big search going on around where I was working. The little boy had been found near there in a haystack, left for dead after being hit in the head with a hammer by the low life friend of the family who took him. His sister was believed to still be with that mongrel bastard. Whilst I was off the track a bit testing the phone lines, sitting on the ground in a fair bit of dense scrub, I heard some dried twigs and sticks crack, which alarmed me, and for a split second I thought it might have been that son of a bitch. Instead, I was looking at five or six mountain men in jeans, long sleeve shirts and Akubra hats, mounted on their beautiful horses. They had a good deal of ammo on them, a couple had belts across their chests and looked like 303 shells, and all had rifles in rifle scabbards on their saddles. I said to them they had spooked me, they asked if I knew about the kidnapping and the little boy, I said yes. I asked what they were up to, and they said they were looking for the girl in case she had been dumped in the bush. I asked what they would you do if they caught up with that mongrel, they just said, it would be hard not to kill the low bastard. The little boy survived and was partly paralysed down one side and the police caught that mongrel in a town nearby and got the little girl back. I believe that bastard had some record in Queensland for some other offence of interfering with children. Something very noticeable for a few months after that terrible incident as I was always out in the bush, you never saw kids waiting on the side of the road, waiting for the school bus, or getting off the bus alone. Their mums were always there like bantam hens, very protective of their young.

When my son Matthew and my daughter, Danielle were little they had a couple of pets and where they got the names from for them, I don't know. One was a budgie bird named Timber and a cat named Kettle. The cat was different, as cats, I thought, didn't like water, but on a hot day if the sprinkler was on next-door's lawn, you would see that cat under the sprinkler. That cat was a beauty and one day down the track, it may have even saved my kid's lives, as a snake had killed that cat in my wood heap behind the shed. Sad as it was, better the cat than either of my beautiful kids.

On some Sunday mornings, Matt and I would walk a couple of blocks to the shop to buy the newspaper. It was on one of those days, Matthew was four or five, I gave him 20 cents on our way to the shop. I found out that day he would watch his money, because when I asked him in the shop if he would like some lollies. Matthew said yes and when I said he'd have to pay for them, he said he didn't want them, he'd rather keep his money, so I left it at that. He kept the 20 cents and no lollies.

Once again, I was up on Mount Canobolas, and when I went to the customer's home, I noticed on the veranda a few wooden legs. When I met the owner, I said I had noticed the wooden legs. He told me when he was a kid, he and his cousin from the city had decided to get the tractor going and were slashing over some fire breaks. They were kilometres from the main house when he stepped over the drive shaft from the rear of the tractor where the slasher was being driven round. There was no cover over the universal joint and his overalls got caught in the joint. He yelled for his cousin to stop the tractor, but the boy panicked and took off for the house. Left to his own devices, the then boy had to look after himself, with his leg ripped off below the knee, so he took off his belt, tightened it up on his leg to stem the bleeding until help came. It was then I really put my foot down with my mother-in-law that my kids were not allowed on tractors on her farm at Grenfell or on her boyfriend's place at Forbes, especially when I found out from the kids they had been on a tractor while haymaking was being done at Forbes.

I was called in on a Saturday, a recall to repair a cable fault in Orange beside the base hospital. It was a lousy day, and a good storm was brewing. The ambulance station was off the air next to the hospital, and it would be because of an old lead cable being wet from previous rain. By the end of that day, I was reminded of a story told me by an instructor in the school in Goulburn in 1972, about how we should know when we are across lines, people might hear us, so we should always be conscious of that possibility. He told me of a linesman working on the Sydney-Melbourne trunk route, the aerial pole route which I had helped dismantle. The linesman was listening to the ABC radio news across the wires with his bag set, portable phone and somehow let off a few swear words which came over the news.

Anyway, I had found the lead cable joint in a pit by just putting my hand around each joint in each pit along the footpath to find the joint that just felt a little warmer than the rest. I did that as if moisture in there or a little damp with the power through the lines would warm a bit like say an electric jug. I used a hack knife to open the lead joint, no heat, as that forces the moisture in the joint up into the cable. I had put a tent and guards over the joint as it was raining, got some tin and hung it under the fanned-out joint that had the paper insulation damp, used my hot flame to heat up tin to dry out the cable joint to restore service. When I went to my truck to get something, the wind blew my tent open, and rain came in on the cable I had nearly dried out. You could imagine this made me a little upset and when I went across a line to ring the technician in the exchange, I let out a stream of bad language, next thing the technician is sticking his head in my tent to tell me he got a call about bad language coming over the ambulance radio. Somehow, because of the damp cable, the radio line had picked me up, or I may have been induced across the radio line. Anyway, that was a good lesson for me, and I never heard of it again, but it did remind me of my previous story of the linesman on the trunk line aerial route and his transmission on the ABC radio.

Another fault on Mount Canobolas was a mystery for me for a while as well. I had been testing the line and was in some paddocks on the north-western slopes of the mountain. The last place I had tested the cable, the fault was onward, but I could not find any sign of the cable. Not only could I not find more cable, but I couldn't find a house, or even a shed. I rang a contact number in Sydney, owners of the land, and told them the problem. They said to look down the hill from my position and there would be a 44-gallon drum, the phone lines were in that. Sure enough, I went to the drum, found a phone blown-up by lightning. I left a new phone. It wasn't the pub with no beer, it was the phone with no house.

It was about the time of a bit of new technology coming in that I was on a strange fault at the same property in Borenore, west of Orange, for the third time. The previous times, the phone line from the exchange kicked 22 degrees to a clean open circuit and no one home, so I would leave a card to say call us to gain entry to your home to fix the problem. This time would be different. While I was at the house, the lady who owned the place drove up in an old Holden Ute with a couple of dogs in the back. She was about 90 in the water bag, I mean old. When I asked her about her trouble with the phone, she said she has no problem with the phone. She said she had been out in the paddocks with the dogs, checking the sheep all morning, but had no calls. That's when I saw her old push button phone on the seat of the ute. It turned out she had seen some shows on television made in America with phones in the cars and thought she would take the phone with her when out in the paddocks in case someone wanted to ring her.

Trouble with mice plagues is it made me so I would rather see a snake than a mouse. When you had to open a pit in the ground in the bush, you would have hundreds of mice run out and over your boots. For that reason, I would put rubber bands around the bottom of my trouser legs to stop the dirty little rodents going up my trouser legs. It sounds weird, but I would have to open the elevated jointing posts and huntsmen type spiders would fall to the ground and sort of stand on their back legs with fangs and front legs up high and charge you, that and snakes never made me feel as bad as mice or rats. It may be some type of phobia for me. Something I noticed about snakes and mice was that the snakes would get into the pits in the ground and eat the mice and frogs, but during that mouse plague I found that the mice were getting back at the snakes in the pits when the snakes were out to it for the cold weather. I found a few brown snakes in pits that were very dead, killed by mice. What it looked like was when a heap of mice came across a sleeping snake, they would attack it in a group with their sharp little teeth and the first thing they did was chew the snake's head right off. In that plague I had heard of babies in cots being chewed on their ears by mice. Parents would put the legs of the babies' cots in saucepans or buckets of water to stop the stinking mice getting at their babies.

What I really loved and enjoyed in the home in Orange, especially in the wintertime, was coming home from work, getting wood into the fire, lying on the lounge and Matthew and Danielle cuddling up to me and reading their books. I always thought there was nothing in the world worth more than that. Danielle was still having trouble with her breathing while asleep and had an operation in Dudley Hospital in Orange. After that operation, I went to pay the doctor's bill in Orange and said to the secretary I was there to pay for Danielle's Oxley's operation. The secretary asked me which Danielle Oxley? I couldn't believe it a Danielle Oxley from Bathurst operated on in the same week by the same doctor for the same problem, and both the same age, how unreal.

I got in touch with the Oxley's in Bathurst and found they were descended from the brother of my great grandfather, John Oxley.

One day whilst working in Orange city, I had some builders doing a bit of an extension on the back of the house and for some reason I drove past my house. The side gates were open, and I spotted my boy on the front lawn screaming. I hit the skids, flew to him, threw him on the ground under a tap turned it on and held his eyes open and washed his eyes out. My little mate had found an open bag of lime that the builders had left out and somehow got a heap of it in his eyes.

The home was sold, and we moved to a unit just around the corner for a short time and then I was worried my wife would want to move before I could get another transfer. Then another minor miracle happened, I received a transfer to Harden about 20 miles from Boorowa. I was given another send off from Orange in a joint send off in the Commercial Hotel with Peter Devlin, who came from Goulburn and who had got a move back home to Goulburn. So, I was to start work at Harden on the 22/05/1985. We rented a unit in Franklin Road, Orange after the house was sold until the transfer to Harden came through.

Chapter 17

Move Boorowa 1985 - Part 1

T he time came to leave Orange again, and so the move to Boorowa took place. Somehow, we found a farmhouse just out of town to rent. The place was called Eastwood. I was back to work in the Harden/Boorowa area. There was an old depot in Boorowa that we worked out of for a few years, even though it was closed years before.

After selling our house in Orange, I was left with about $38,000 in the bank. My wife had agreed that we stay in Boorowa, so I had been looking for a block of land to build a new home on. We were offered a half-acre block in a new subdivision called 'Boorowa Heights', up on a hill, but I had found another piece of land on the edge of town that I thought would be great for the kids and into the future. I had no desire to live too close to neighbours and wanted room for the kids to run around. The half-acre block was $20,000 and the three acres I wanted instead (covered in this-tles and a few big old trees) consisted of six, half-acre blocks for $12,000. Admittedly, I had some work to do, and when I bought it some local said I was ripped off. I love being ripped off like that. I bought six 1/2-acre blocks for the princely sum of $12,000. I now live in a house on one half acre and one-half acre is left to sell at this time, so worth a bloody lot more than I paid for the lot.

I found out about a company named Paal Frame which made steel frame kit homes you build yourself, just a bloody big Meccano set you have as a kid. I got good pictures and plans and a few good talks to the company and they advised me they would help me all through the process of building. So, with a stick on the dirt out the back of our rental home "Eastwood", I scratched out a plan of the house I said I would build, and the kids picked out their rooms. I gave the floor plans of the house to Michael Cassidy, a builder in town, to put the foundations and the floor down, and I would take over building from there. I paid cash for the kit home, and I still had money in the ANZ Bank, but I wanted to keep that there and instead borrow some money for a concrete tank, fencing material and a shed. I had been with the ANZ Bank for years and they knocked me back because I didn't have a credit history. I said, doesn't that tell you something, I pay my way so you can shove your bank and I went and joined another bank up the street, bloody banker wankers!

So, I was working full-time and working on the land around the house, fencing and cleaning up the Scotch thistles and Paterson's Curse, and the kids were always helping. The first fence I put up; I got my boy Matthew to sight up the fence for me. He did a good job. I sat two Quick Eze tablets on the top of the strainer post and he sighted over them over 100 metres while I put some posts in, good job he was only six years old. My father set up a little trailer/ caravan type thing, and we filled it up with all the tools and gear, ladders and power leads I would need to build the house. Also, the plans of the house and all the instructions to build on a table in the van, which we parked under a tree on the block near the building site. I used to get some smart-arse remarks from locals while they were fuelling up their cars in the service station next door. One local yelled out to me,

"You wouldn't know how to build a house. What do you think you're doing?" I yelled back,

"At least I am having a go and I'll find out. You wouldn't even know what's past the 60 kph speed limits either side of this town, you know nothing, you've seen nothing, been nowhere and done nothing, piss off!" I had enough of the odd know-all know-nothing experts.

The whole time I was building the house, a friend, the local doctor, would call in and see how I was going and give me some advice and tell me I should slow down a bit and watch my health. I remember once while building, I ended up with painful haemorrhoids on the weekend, a good time to get them on a weekend! Get it. Anyway, I knew the doc that weekend was having a big party for his father in law's 80th birthday so I wouldn't go and annoy him, even though I was in severe pain. I finally went to see the doc on the Monday and when he checked me out said I had acute haemorrhoids and I asked him,

"What's cute about the bastards?"

Anyway, enough of that but I owe Doc Kenneally for what he did for my daughter Danielle, who was still having a breathing problem that after two operations hadn't been fixed. The doc knew people and made an appointment with a surgeon friend of his to see Danielle and said he believed in him, and he also believed he could fix the problem. Thanks to the doc, Danielle was finally able to breathe properly while she slept. Danielle was at the house and only about three years old, and I was screwing up the lining in the ceiling with an electric drill on the front veranda. I would never forget. I heard an aluminium stepladder being dragged along the concrete floor and when I looked, I saw my daughter climb the ladder with Philips screwdriver in hand and put the screwdriver in the screws I had put in and turn the screwdriver. When I asked her what she was doing she said,

"I am the checker." So, I thought I had a quality control on the site. I hoped she didn't find anything wrong with the place.

Back at Eastwood one night I had run a bath for my son Matthew, and that night he told me he would love to learn to play the piano. The kids would mess about with the piano by dragging a piece of paper with a piece of wool, start stop, fast, slow along the keys and get the cat chasing it and playing the piano. That cat was great for the kids and Danielle would put that cat in the tray on the back of her dinky and take it for rides. We got Matthew taught to play the piano, he was so proud of his piano playing and would ask me to hold his music book over his face so he couldn't see the keys and would still play, and well. He told me that some boys thought he was a sissy playing the piano. He was seven years old and could play football, so I told him to say to the bullies that there wasn't a lot of boys who could play football that could also play the piano. Matthew did get to play at an Eisteddfod at Cowra, he was bloody good at piano.

One Saturday, I was working on the house when the doc came to see how I was going and said he was going out to Binalong, a little town not far away, to an antique sale. He asked me to go with him and when I said I should keep working on the house, he said a break would do me good. I gave in and away we went, and the doc brought an old wind-up gramophone and I found him three cardboard boxes of cylinders of music at $10 a box. We headed back to his place and got that old machine working and doc explained to me with that big funnel speaker how the saying 'Put a sock in it' came about. There was no volume control and the way to lower the volume was to put a sock in the funnel, thus, to shut someone up you told them to put a sock in it. Anyway, we had a few beers and tried to sing a few songs with that machine, and I said to the doc I better get a lift back to my motor bike at the house and get home or else I would be in for it with my wife. Doc dropped me back and when I got out of his car and was getting ready to get on my bike to go and face the music, this time at home, he handed me a bit of paper and said give that to your wife when you get home, which I did. She was not impressed. It was a doctor's certificate and he had given me the afternoon off on stress and sick leave.

I kept working full-time on Telecom fixing faults on phone lines and all my other time I spent working on the house looking forward to the time it would be done! Once again, we were expecting another baby, but after about four months of pregnancy, my wife was put into hospital by the doc and I won't go too much into it, but I had to get her to Young Hospital when she came home in a hurry. When I got her back home from the hospital it really hit me hard, we had lost another baby. That night on the side of the road outside Eastwood where we were renting, I went and sat in the dark with my back up against a wooden guidepost. I just sat there bawling my head off. Why another baby? Why didn't they make it, why? Then I said to myself, you just must think about and care for the kids that you have and think of what a priest had said to me when we lost the first baby. He had told me that it was probably nature working right as there may have been something wrong with them. I don't know why but after the first baby was lost, I found out that I could if needed, baptise a baby before it died if it wasn't going to make it. So, I had to get past that, get back to work, and back to building our home.

I had never stopped to think before how much timber in metres was required to fit out a new house with skirting boards and architraves and how much work it is to cut every join with a tenon saw and mitre box and then fit it all to the walls and windows. I went to Canberra and took kitchen measurements and had a kitchen made and delivered in flatpack form, and built it as well as bathrooms, showers, and laundry. Painted the house, got floor coverings, carpets, and fitted all internal doors. It was when I had to install the fireplace and the chimney, I was talking to one of my workmates and said I had to figure out where or how I line the chimney position in the ceiling in the lounge room with where it should protrude through the roof, he thought he would be a help and gave me the following bullshit advice.

"All you do mate is get your spirit level, then get your old Lithgow.22 rifle and attach the spirit level to the barrel of the rifle, put the end of the barrel of the rifle on the centre mark of chimney on ceiling, make sure by spirit level and rifle pointing straight up and all you have to do is pull the trigger, done!" After not listening to that advice, I went ahead and put in the wood fire, including the chimney, without the use of the rifle.

Meanwhile at the rental home on the farm I was having trouble with a couple of possums. One had got under the tin in a flat roof and on the ceiling. I got my dad to come and give me a hand to catch the possum. Dad came up with the idea to put the possum in a plastic garbage bin once I caught it by the tail with my snake catcher. I just made a metre long pike with a loop of rope out the end which I put over the tail of the intruding possum, pull it tight and he was caught, hang it over roof into garbage and dad tied the lid down so it didn't get out. Now for the funny side of this story. I put the garbage containing the possum in the boot of the car, put my four-year-old daughter in the back seat of the car and took the possum miles away in the bush to release it near a big tree. When I took the lid off the bin the possum didn't come out and I thought it must be dead. I had a little concern for his teeth and his claws, and next thing he flew out of the bin. I went flat out one way and the possum the other up the tree. My daughter was watching and was having one of the best laughs I've heard in my life. I even felt like doing it all over again. Anyway, those possums were still giving me trouble and one got me in the outside dunny one night. I was sitting on the throne minding my own business and for my first time I heard the scary creepy sound a trapped or scared possum could make, he was on the wall and above the door and it did scare me a bit, especially as I wasn't expecting it, although it was a blessing that I was sitting on the throne at the time.

All the while I was working and building, there's a story I must write about - my dear son Matthew, who was about seven years old when I picked him up off a bus in Harden from a visit to my mother-in-law's farm at Grenfell. I was working with Jonny Fisher, and we were cutting over some cable in town and when we were having lunch Fish asked Matt what he was going to do when he grew up? My little mate said he was going to play football! Then Fish asked what for and Matt answered,

"Money." Then Fish asked,

"What about after football?"

Matt then said this, "When I am too old to play football and too old to work, I am going to get a job with Telecom." All I could say was what a good boy he was, and he gave Fish and me a good laugh that day.

I was working with Fish another day and he told me I was a bit of a ratbag when I gave a carload of Japanese some directions to Young and Cowra. I thought as they couldn't speak much English, I would give them directions in Australian as it's a more descriptive language. I said,

"Head off that way on the frog and toad and go up the jack and jill, turn right at the marble forest, watch out for the fowls and the geese and head towards wombat." The only thing they kept saying was,

"Are-so, are-so, wombat, wombat" and took off. Fish just said to me,

"You're a dead set mongrel," and I said,

"You too! They just called me an arsehole! And a wombat! the Pricks! Twice." Anyway, they must have calmed down a bit and understood after figuring out what I had told them, took off along the road, went up the hill, turned right at the cemetery going steady so the police didn't book them and headed towards Wombat. I was just trying to help some strangers in our country and do my civic duty. They probably got back to Japan and told all their friends how helpful the Australian people are.

We finally moved into the house and settled in there.

My father had a 17 · hand high retired trotting horse named Boofa, and we put him in the paddock next to my house on two acres. He was a big, quiet horse and the kids could get up on him, but it was a long way to the ground if you came off, as my boy Matt found out sadly one day. Something spooked old Boof and he stepped quickly to the side and little mate met the ground and snapped the bones in one wrist. I raced him to the hospital and all they did was give him a couple of pain killers and put an ice pack on while we waited for the only person in town who could perform an x-ray to do it. She was in church, and we had to wait for them to come out. It seemed that God was more important than my little mate. The doc arrived as the x-rays were developed and said to me to take him straight to Canberra Hospital and when you get there, there will be four people waiting for you. True to his word, there they all were. More x-rays, setting the broken bones and said if not right we will have to knock Matt out and set again, keeping him overnight. That's when Matt brought a tear to my eyes when he told them

"Do what you have to do and don't knock me out, cause I'm going home with Dad," tough little bugger. Anyway, it was all okay first go so we came home.

Poor Danielle not long after moving into the house had to go and get a birthmark off her jaw before she got much older so the scar would be hard to see on her jaw line as she aged. Matt and I picked her and her mother up off the train at Yass and I thought Danielle would break her stitches when I squatted down when she saw me and ran to me and crashed into me with arms around me for a cuddle. That night Danielle woke me from my sleep, she was sick and maybe it was to do with the anaesthetic she had for her operation. I could never forget that when I walked into her room, her rag doll was covered in sick and Danielle said,

"Dad, I've spewed all over Wendy."

It was about this time that Danielle was about four and did what I think was two ballet concerts, her first and her last. I did my best to video her but the tears pouring from my eyes I found it hard to keep the camera in focus from laughing. In her tutu and dancing gear she wouldn't watch the other little girls and when they stopped would crash into them, and when each little kid took their final bow at the end of the concert she raced out, stopped, slipped, and fell over. She was sent back to bow again and... same thing. It was the best ballet concert I've ever seen, and as with my daughter, for me it was two ballet concerts in one hit, my first and my last.

One day whilst working, I saw what looked like a big shed that had had been pulled down and stacked in a paddock. I went and found the owner and asked him if he is selling it and he said no. So, I offered him $800 for it and left him my phone number. A week later he rang me one night and said I could buy it, so I got a big four-wheel trailer off my father and got it onto my land and paid for it as quick as I could. It was a 48 foot long and 20 foot wide with an 18-foot-wide tilt door all, with no plans for the building of it. I got the ground levelled and had to figure out how to square it up. I did that probably the way the ancients found. To do a 90-degree bend was by three numbers (three, four and five). If you make a triangle when the sides are a length of three, four or five metres, you will have your right angle. If your measurements from opposite corners are equal both ways, you have a perfect square or oblong, simple eh! It took me six weeks to build that shed completely by myself and it was square and straight, and the hardest part of the job was fitting the 18-foot tilt door, but I managed it with the door across a big trailer and a series of ropes. It all fitted so the house and shed were done on our three-acre block.

I was offered some work down at Cooma, Berridale, Dalgety, Jindabyne, and the Alpine Way, and up on Blue Cow in the high country, jointing in some new phone cables. I didn't really want to go but my wife wanted me to as the dollars for working away were very good money. The dollar signs were showing in her eyes like a cash register, and as it was only for six weeks and I would come home each weekend, I took it on. The cable jointing was good, and I enjoyed seeing that part of New South Wales, I had not seen before. The work going up to Blue Cow, a new snow resort, was a bit hard because we had to drag heavy telephone cable up steep slopes and attach it to high telephone poles. We had to work in snow and before we finished that job, I got myself bad sunburn off the sun's reflection from the snow. When I came home at the end of that six weeks, I was looking forward to being home, but my wife thought I should keep working away to make more money. All I just wanted was to be home with my family.

I will now write very little of what next happened in the life of my children and myself as it is all written in the big suitcase I have from years of fighting in the Family Law Court for my children, and it was a very painful time. After finally returning from working in the snow country, I was told by my wife there was a place for me to rent on the other side of town. I took my kids on holiday and was picked up for kidnapping my own kids. My wife had taken out interim custody orders and I was allowed no defence. I just kept working, stayed in the family home, fought for my kids until I finally had them back. Even then I did not get custody in that biased family law bloody court. Now, I will try not to mention the court again other than this, after three days in court and after not having custody of my kids for 12 months because of the interim custody order, I was not granted custody of my kids and that was on my 35th birthday.

I could never forget that day and when I arrived back home, I went to the pub and a man whom I now consider to be a friend, Ray Pocock, the Church of England Minister, walked into the pub to see me. We had a few beers and he said he was so sorry for me and the kids, and I said this fight has only just begun. Ray said to me then something I would never forget,

"Steve don't drink too much beer mate. It does not drown your sorrows mate it only irrigates them."

My daughter Danielle made me laugh one access visit. On a Sunday morning, before going to church, Danielle was pulling faces about going and I told her that when I was a kid, I was told if the wind changes your face will stay that way. Armed with this newfound piece of information, just as we walked into the Church, Danielle spotted an old lady, raced up to her and told her if she passed wind, her face would stay that way.

With a bit of stress in my life, I started to smoke too much, smoking up to 80 a day. I knew I had to stop smoking, and my daughter did too. I would often come home from work and sit a roll of insulation tape on the fridge and the girl would use the whole roll of tape around and around the packet of smokes to try and stop me getting at them, "Thoughtful kid eh!" I found a way I could give up smoking when a lady I knew told me that every time I go to light a smoke that meant I loved my mother-in-law, it worked, I gave up cold turkey. I used to say that what was black and gold and would look great on some mothers-in-law would be a Rottweiler. One bloke I ran into said his mother-in-law told him she would dance on his grave, and he told her that made him so happy because he knew she couldn't swim, and he always wanted to be buried at sea.

While working in Young one day, ditching in a bit of cable along a footpath, there was a little tiny dog in the front yard of a house on a chain yapping and barking its head off, going round and round in circles. I told the little mutt to shut up and Ray, the bloke I was working with, warned me to be careful of that dog because he was a watchdog. When I said he's no watchdog just yapping and running and circles when Ray said he is just look at him he's winding himself up!

One Thursday night, I rang my kids as I was allowed to once a week, and my daughter was so sad that the dog she had over there had been skittled on the road by a car. As she was very sad about Shep, and I was getting the kids the next weekend, I thought I would try and put a few words together in a bit of a poem and to hopefully make her feel a bit better.

Poem of Shep for Danielle – November 1988

Danielle my daughter dear
Now, I know you've lost old Shep
It was so sad for me to hear
From you old Shep had left.

So Darling, please don't you be sad
Though I know your dog has gone
Short time, but happiness with you he had
So don't be so forlorn.

Just like old Shep in song we sing
From heavens he'd been sent
To you from God happiness he'd bring
Now back to God he went.

So Darling, please old Shep's okay
He's up there guarding gates
But in your heart, he'll always stay
So be happy knowing he is safe.

It's hard for you to understand
For you're not even seven
But Shep is giving God a hand
Because he now lives in heaven.

Time for a laugh. I just thought of that old paratrooper I mentioned earlier in Orange. He also told me of a story he said his uncle told him. His uncle was flying Sopwith double wingers in the RAF in the First World War, and he told him about the Baron Von Richtofen from the Red Baron fame. It seemed that the Red Baron painted his plane red so if he got shot, the blood wouldn't be visible on his plane, so people wouldn't know he'd been hit. His uncle had been told there was a big chance he would one day come up against the Baron in a dog fight, so he requested his plane be painted brown!

On another day at work, I was working with me old mate Ray in Harden. When we were having smoko, he asked me a weird question and at that time I saw the boss driving up towards us. I said to Ray,

"You ask the boss that question, I double dog dare you." The boss drives up, gets out of his ute and straight away Ray says,

"Boss can you get the sack for thinking on the job?" The boss said of course not, Ray said,

"Are you sure?"

Boss said "Yes," then Ray said,

"That's good because I think you are a dickhead and you've no idea about anything and you're a pain in the arse." Lucky for Ray, the boss had a good sense of humour.

I met a lady who needed some work done on her house on a small property out of town. She was doing it tough on her own with three kids, and I felt like helping her and her kids out a bit.

I had the kids home on access and thought I'd take the kids out to her place on weekend. Before we went out, I told the kids a bit of a story about them. I said the lady had 20 kids and told my kids not to comment on the buckets through the house on the floors as they were poor and couldn't afford to fix the roof which leaked badly in the rain. On the way out I saw an old house, not too far off the road with one wall out and no windows and stopped there in the driveway and said to the kids it looked like there was no one home. Then I drove to the real place. I also told my kids before taking them out to the goat farm to meet the lady and her kids that the lady was a big tough woman who sits in the lounge room on the farm knitting wire netting with a pair of crowbars, and she was covered in tattoos. Poor kids didn't know what to expect, but we had a good laugh over it. The kids met the lady and her three kids and were wondering where all her other kids were 'til we introduced them to a heap of baby goats, that was the rest of her kids. There was a time the lady who owned the goats was having a lot of trouble getting them shorn and they needed shearing badly. Now the goats, unlike sheep, get shorn twice a year. The shearer had failed to turn up several times and things were getting desperate. So, for this hobby farmer, I thought I would write her a poem about the problems she'd been having getting the goats shorn and so it follows, and I hope it describes the scene.

<u>Hobby Farmers Lament</u>
Shearing's on about bloody time
The shearer must have had a fit
I 'spose he can't find grog or wine
Or he's broke and cannot buy it.

The shearing is just two months late
Cause that shearer wouldn't come
At last, he's finally kept the date
To shear those goats and give them some.

Kids mustering and penning them
Then bring them to the shed
We hoped the shearer now could do some
Or she'll get another man instead.

The gear was warm and running hot
As the shearer puts them through
While we hope and pray to God
That he knows just what to do.

If he's a bloody shearer
Who only shears them rough
The time is getting nearer
When he's told enough is enough.

After a real big day's hard work
The shearers all but done
Sweating and thrown off his shirt
I am sure he ain't no gun.

Now I hope that it is never said
That hobby farming's always great
For shearing time, you sometimes dread
But this is part of what you must take.

And while the shearers working
As though shears they really go
That new buck he is there lurking
And he lets his feelings show.

He lines up for the shearer
His feelings he doesn't disguise
He wants to get much nearer
To get the hair cleared from his eyes.

For he's been having trouble
Just seeing all his harem
Missing them and seeing double
But cripes he sure does scare 'em.

As a kid I had remembered that story on an old 78 record dad used to play, it could have been called 'the poor old workingman' it was from England.

One day in 1988, I was jointing in some new cables between Boorowa and Cowra, near a property named Woolpack. It was a warm spring day, blue skies, and long grasses in the paddocks, magpies singing, and the laugh of the kookaburra. I felt a warm breeze which seemed to wrap itself around me, the country looked great, and the bush flowers were well and truly out. It seemed that all was well in the world. At that time, all was not well for me, or for my children. I won't go into that too much other than write that after some time, all that was sorted out and we all, that's my kids and me, were put back together. So, I had to see some good in the world. What I saw in that paddock, those hills, the warm breezes blowing across those tall grasses, was like the ocean going towards the beach. Something in my thoughts told me not to forget that day and to write it down, how good the country I love is. Sitting in my truck at lunchtime I tried to put it down on paper. Some of the poem also had pictures or memories of scenes from my life at Ophir, Jerilderie and places between Cowra and Orange and Gerringong and the high country.

Australia

Look at our country, we're Australians
At its trees and undulating hills
It's sweeping sometimes barren plains
Those of us who love it always will.

This land to us is just so good
This land to us a way of life
We must all love it the way we should
Though sometimes to us, it causes strife.

Sometimes our country makes us sad
With floods and wild bushfires
We've learnt to take good with bad
Though our love for country never tires.

Our country must mean to us all
The same as does our lives
It can be kind, it can be cruel
For Australia we should always strive.

For us sometimes it gets too hot
So sometimes we take a break
High up in forest mountain tops
Holidays on golden beaches, we will take.

We have good springs, we get long grass
Gentle breezes through grass and wild bush flowers
Makes it sway and move like ocean waves
We could dream and watch for hours.

We see great boulders sitting still
They protect our hills and sit in clover
They say that when they built those hills
There were stacks of rocks left over.

With peaceful parks, tranquil lakes
Tall trees reach to bright blue skies
Peaceful times on rivers we can take
And all receive our natural highs.

Along the beach around the rocks
Most wear thongs not riding boots
Aussies kick off shoes and socks
Sink feet in the sand like trees that take up roots.

One time I was bringing my kids home for an access weekend when we were pulled up at an accident on the Canberra side of Murrumbateman. I noticed some cars turning around and heading back towards Canberra, turning onto a dirt road called Dog Trap Road. There had been a lot of rain and then it was snowing, and my kids thought I was pretty good, just sneaking along in the mud driving past car after car that had slipped off the road and were bogged, I said typical Canberra drivers, as soon as it rains, they put their bloody foot down.

Back at work though, I had a reputation for driving fast and being able to take a Falcon panel van through muddy, boggy paddocks. I found on a slippery hill I could back that van up when you could not drive forward, so over the years I had learnt more than fixing phones. I drove hundreds of thousands of kilometres in the bush and off road, saying I was a rally driver sponsored by Telstra; they paid for my fuel and running costs, and if I was on a dirt road and no one about, it was not natural on a bend if you weren't slightly sideways.

I was chasing a fault on a phone line north of Boorowa, heading south, when I came over a hill on a dirt road. No one else was on the road, no dust, so I went a bit over the legal limit. Suddenly, on my right at the gateway into Sheridan Park, I saw the ditcher gang from Young, and the big boss waving me down to come back. I stopped a good way down the road, turned around and went back. The boss had gone out with the gang and wanted a lift back into town to get his ute, he didn't say much on the way. Later my mates that were with him at Sheridan Park said the boss was screaming when he waved me down and when my brake lights came on, he told them all to wait for the drag chute to come out.

It was a few kilometres north of Sheridan Park where I came down a hill towards a low-level crossing, near a property named Bonanza, that I nearly came to grief. It was a dirt road and before you got to the crossing there was a hump about 50 metres before the low-level crossing. There must have been a gully-raker there the night before, and I wasn't expecting about a metre of water over the road. My 'rally driving' came in handy. I braked, then handbraked, right lock to wash some speed off, hit the water sideways and it washed the rest of my speed off. That worked well, but although there was no damage, my speed would be washed off for a while. I was lucky to get 50 kilometres an hour out of the van until I got it to a Ford garage in Harden, where they found that when the catalytic converter on an unleaded fuel vehicle gets that hot, when I hit the water the baffle plates let go, creating back pressure. Hence no revs, so no speed. Another thing I had a good laugh about in the Young Line Department was me old mate Ray back at it stirring one of the blokes in the yard. Ray knew this bloke lived not far from the cemetery in Young and asked him if he had heard the story about the Young Council putting a ban on people who live within two kilometres of the cemetery being buried there. The bloke went off big time that the Council was a load of crap and after a couple of hours he figured out Ray was shit-stirrer. Go figure.

I have told people this following story and I hope I can write it, so you get the picture. We had been to Crookwell from Boorowa to do a job and were driving back to Boorowa and Reg Crocker was the pilot of the Land Cruiser troop carrier. Reg and I were both speed hogs, and for years had raced each other from Harden to Boorowa depot of an afternoon to knock off. We were flying along on that dirt road and the dust had been stirred up by a truck and a few cars. To make it worse we were driving into a setting sun. If you have been in such a situation, you would know my low flying pilot was flying blind. I don't scare too easy, but I couldn't see too much, and the road was lined by gum trees, and they don't give much when you hit them at a speed between 100 and 130. I just had to say something to Reg and as I couldn't see much, I asked him how he knew if we were still on the road. He just looked across at me and said,

"Can you hear us hitting any trees?"

I said, "No,"

Reg said, "Well, we must still be on the road!" As you can imagine those words put me at ease. They helped me so much, the fact he took his eyes off the road didn't even worry me because you couldn't bloody see it anyway.

I'll now go back to my home on the three acres where old Boof, the retired 17 · hand high ex-trotting horse was taking life easy and had slowed down in his retirement. I got home from work one day and a dirty great limb had fallen from a big pine tree which was about 40 metres high and was near old Boofs water trough. A quick check on old Boof and he was okay. He often stood under that tree. A few days later, I ran into my neighbour, who had a farm diagonally opposite my land on the edge of town. George Wales told me that he heard that limb crack and he saw it come down and he thought old Boof was going to cop it big time. Then George, in that great Aussie way of telling you a good descriptive story, put a picture in my mind I can't forget. He said,

"Stephen, as that limb came down, I saw Boof prove he could still really run. He raced up that hill at your place in that big of a hurry that he had his arsehole around his neck for a collar." Every time I thought of that I could see it in my mind. It's good how words can paint a picture, that was one horse in a hurry.

Now for another snake story. Working out in the bush most of the time you just can't avoid them. Working for Telstra you still now and then receive a bit of stick from the public inferring we were a bit slow and even bludgers, which we were not. I drove into a property between Boorowa and Murringo, and when I drove around a circular driveway and garden in front of the homestead and got out of the van, I was greeted by a woman on the front veranda screaming her bloody head off. A big brown snake had nearly got her in the garden, and she was screaming for me to kill it, so I grabbed my banjo from the van, and she pointed where it went and for that woman in some distress, I flushed it out of the garden. It took off down the driveway and I chased it and just as it seemed to turn back on me, I accidentally hit it in the head with my shovel and the poor thing was deceased. I walked back to the poor lady and asked where her video camera was and she said why and I told her if she had videoed what just happened, me chasing the snake, it could have been worth a quid really, a Telstra bloke moving fast. Unheard of!

On another job in the bush, I had to meet up with a couple of technicians in a little bush exchange. One was an Australian and the other was an Indian I think his name was something like Rami Swami. We were testing lines that had bad noise levels on them induced from power lines, and I would have to open the cable at certain points so the tech in the exchange could check the level. The Aussie tech told me to go with the Indian tech, and he beat me to the driver's seat of my Falcon panel van, so I jumped in the passenger's seat. That Indian got in the vehicle and started it, but to my surprise I quickly found out that was about his full knowledge of driving. As that vehicle was a manual and what we called three on the tree, I quickly found out more of Swami's knowledge of driving when he asked me in his Indian accent,

"And where would the first gear be?" I said pull that lever back towards you and down. He did that with a grating of gears because he didn't have the clutch fully down, but we got moving. Then Swami said,

"And where would the second gear be?" I told him up forward up, he did that with only a little trouble when he tried to get reverse first. Then Swami said, and where is the third gear, I said straight down, he did that well, we were on the open road doing about 125 kph, he could steer well and I even had calmed down a bit when he yells out,

"And I am knowing where the fourth gear is," and threw it into second with no revs and bloody near threw me through the windscreen. First place we stopped for testing, I made sure Rami wouldn't get a chance to drive again. When we got back to the little bush exchange R.A.X when it was just me and the Aussie technician, I told him about my adventures with Swami and all he said was,

"You didn't let that mad bastard drive did ya!" Later the Aussie technician told me that Swami had worn a clutch plate out in one day in the city by just keeping the revs up and controlling the speed with what pressure he had on the clutch. He also told me a linesman jointer up around Armidale had gone out in the bush with Rami to do a similar job as what I had been doing. The 'liney' left the Indian in a little bush exchange and said he would ring him when he got about 30 kilometres away for him to do his testing. The linesman rang the exchange, no answer and he rang and rang and rang. The liney started to worry about the Indian and drove back to the exchange. When he got there, all was okay, so he asked the Indian didn't he hear the phone ringing and Swami said,

"Yes, I have been hearing it ringing."

The liney said, "Why didn't you bloody answer it?"

The Indian just said in his lilting accent "But how am I knowing it is for me?" I can't vouch for those last stories, but I believe them after my experience with the Indian.

I was shopping one day, and as I had just acquired a new Falcon panel van for work, after about six months of driving a

Ford econovan. He had his name on him, as Con the fruiterer used to say. Anyway, the new Falcon had a cassette player in it. The thing is, I found a cassette of a storm, you could hear the rain hitting the tin roof and occasional thunder. My boss would often call up on the two-way to see how I was going with a job he had given me, and I would be miles away. If it looked stormy where I was, I would use the cassette. When he called on the two way I would put the cassette in that Falcon, turn it up loud and answer him, he'd say,

"How's the weather over there?"

I'd say "It's pissing down. I am sitting in the van; can you hear that?" It was a good stir; I don't know if I ever told him.

I had fun with that cassette player and my son Matt thought he would too. He was only a bit of a kid and he got hold of a tape and didn't tell me and he slipped it into the Falcon. The song on it was I think by John Williamson about nutting the family cat in a gumboot. The next day, I was jointing in some cable or chasing a fault in the monastery at Galong a little place not far from Boorowa. The place was crawling with nuns wandering about in the gardens when I had the van opened, when I dropped the cassette in and a couple of nuns walked past the van just when the song about nutting the family cat down a gumboot came on. I just walked over and got the cassette out, put the radio on and went back to my work, nothing said! But that was not the story I told my son when I got home. I told him all what happened, and Matt asked,

"What did the nuns say?" and I said,

"Nothing."

Matt said, "Oh well, if they said nothing then you should be all right." I then said I didn't think so, because I had heard from a plumber out there that for them it was a Day of Silence, and they would have heaps to say when they could. I'd probably cop it next day from work. I didn't leave it too long before I told my little mate he had nothing to worry about, that I had made up the last bit of the story.

Just a little story about me getting the new Falcon and getting rid of the Econovan. I had somehow had Falcon vans for years since I came back to the area from Orange, and linesman weren't to have them, when I ended up with the Econovan, or 'bread bus', as I used to call them. I whinged and complained to the Supervising Officer, and he must have got sick of me and said go and ask Martin Corby for a Falcon, thinking I'd never do that. Although Martin had become a big boss in Canberra and a big part of New South Wales, he was a bloke I had worked with an Orange, and you may remember the story of Martin and me on Canobolas in that big storm. I had been told to ring Marty, so I did, and two days later, the boss rang me at home early, told me to empty the Econovan out and go to Telstra House in Canberra and swap over to a Falcon panel van and wondered how I did it. I always say sometimes it's not what you know, it's who you know.

There is another snake story that's a bit different. It's about a snake I didn't see. I was sent out to do a job in the bush to install an extension of a phone into a lady's bedroom in a big old homestead. When I got to the place the lady of the house showed me where she wanted the point to go and where to get under the house at a trapdoor which was left open at the side of the house. It was late spring and as usual I had thoughts in my mind of snakes whilst I crawled under that house. When I was all finished, the lady asked me if I had seen the big brown snake? I said what big brown snake, and she said the one she had seen the day before going in the open trapdoor under the house. I said nothing but I thought a lot and I should have said something then.

Three months later I was chasing down a fault and was sitting at a joint with an echoplex testing machine, and the house where that lady was could be seen about two kilometres away. I was thinking fondly of that woman when a ute pulled up in a cloud of dust and a cocky came over and said G'day. I decided I would tell him the story and said this big ugly bitch had let me go under the house with a brown snake and it was in that house down there with those tall trees around. When I said what sort of a bitch would do that, he said that's my place, and took off. It was a good thing I held back on what sort of a bitch I thought his wife was eh!

Chapter 18

Boorowa Part Two

One more day I could not forget while working with my old mate Ray at Harden. We were working near the high school at Harden. I had met Ray there, and he brought the truck and ditcher over from Young and I had picked up a line for a new service to the front of the new home. I ditched a lead into the house when Ray discovered we had no 90-degree 20 ml PVC pipe bends. Ray filled a bit of pipe with sand and got the flamethrower going to heat the pipe and bend it and the sand would stop the pipe closing in on itself as it was bent. All that was a great idea until we had a little emergency. On the back of the truck was a lot of empty pillar tail boxes made of cardboard, and it was on the truck where Ray had bent the pipe. Ray was fitting the pipe to the house, and I was sitting on the footpath working on the cable joint when a young school kid tapped me on my shoulder and this is exactly what he said, "Excuse me mister, but is your truck supposed to be on fire?" The flame thrower hadn't been turned right off and had set all the cardboard boxes on fire. If that truck with fuel on board had gone up, it might have not only of been the truck that got fired on that day. My old mate

260

would sometimes have little problems or errors of judgement and I heard him one day order three new billies for the gang truck and when the boss said why three, he answered one to run over, one to lose and one to boil the tea for smoko.

I call this a true story, 'Tony and the Gazunder!' I had been on a fault in Murrumburrah, and it turned out that the fault was in the house, and no one was at home. I left a card for the subscriber to make an appointment for someone to gain entry to the house to fix the phone service. This was a time when I would often be working around the Goulburn area and it worked out that Tony Gorham got the job to clear the fault in that house, and he never forgave me for what was to happen when he was working, but I knew he could handle any problem. There was an old lady lived in that house alone, she was not to fit a woman and had to find ways to not go fumbling around the house at night. It turned out she was a very inventive old dear. Tony had to rewire some of the internal wiring in the old dear's bedroom and as he was stapling a new cable along the skirting boards towards the bed, he was moving things out of his way as he went and putting them back. When he got beside the bed, he discovered a long handle attached to a large saucepan sticking out from the bedcover, which was almost down to the floor. The handle was pointing up and out. He was on his knees and in a bit of a hurry, he dragged the saucepan out towards himself. When it stopped, it splashed up in old mate's face. It was a gazunder the bed. The handle may have been guide for its use in the dark. Tony never forgave me for getting him that job and was somewhat pissed off about the whole ordeal.

Now I will tell you one time my mate Johnny Fisher and I got bogged at Phil's Creek near Boorowa. It was not a wet or rainy time, and the last thing you would think of was getting bogged in a paddock, let alone on top of a hill, but we did! We were out to fix a fault into a property and when Fish drove his Nissan Urvan to the top of a hill on that property, it just sunk and was well and truly bogged. I walked a couple of kilometres down the hill towards the homestead and when I got there, I was greeted by a bloody angry cocky. He went off at me and said are you bogged on top of that hill, and when I said yes, he said what kind of idiot would drive there. I said we don't know your property, but you do, you don't usually get bogged on top of a hill. I just turned away and said don't worry about it and I hadn't even asked him for a tractor to pull us out. I started walking up the hill towards the bogged vehicle. As I was walking, I heard a tractor start up and the cocky pulled up beside me and yelled to jump in. It was a bench seat Chamberlain tractor, and I had a bit to do with that type in Wee Waa years ago on cotton farms. When we got close to the stricken van, he once again said what type of idiot would drive there, just as he let that out, I was about to say I wouldn't go any closer and you guessed it, down the tractor went, there in the spring on top of that hill. With a few expletives the cocky abandoned his tractor and headed home on foot back down the hill. We rang our boss and Reg Croker and he brought us out a turfer to winch the van out, which we did. When we fixed the phone line temporarily, we drove down to make sure it was working. The cocky was still cranky and suffering from high blood pressure and said, "I see you got out and now my tractors stuck up there". So, I did the right thing and thanked him for bogging his tractor there and told him it worked beautifully as there was no trees or anything up there to hook the turfer on to winch us out, so we hooked the turfer to his tractor. Before we left, I thought I'd better calm him down and told him we had to run some temporary cable on the ground and big Dick Knowles would be out next week to plough some new cable in with his bulldozer, and we would pull his tractor out then.

I have now got to write another story of being bogged on a property, but this is a story of a cocky with a good sense of humour. This happened while I was in a property about halfway between Harden and Jugiong, where I had driven in from Talinga Mines Road towards Garangula Exchange. That time, there had been lots of heavy rain and you could get bogged without too much effort – as was said you could bog a duck anywhere. It was on top of some high ground and the land cruiser I'd been given to take through that place went down big time. I'd have been better in a Falcon panel van, less weight. A gentleman cocky had been watching me and came up to me on his motorbike. First thing I said to him was that I felt bloody stupid getting bogged and asked him if he had a tractor to get me out. First thing he said was not to feel stupid and the next was that yes, he did have a tractor. He pointed down the hill and across a couple of paddocks. He then said to me

"Do you see those three tractors down there parked in a row?" When I said yes, he once again told me not to fill stupid getting bogged because those three tractors were his and there all bogged!

Now it's time to write a story about a mouse plague and I swear this story is true. I went over to Young depot from Boorowa one morning for a meeting, and it was a time when I thought there was that many meetings, we would sometimes have meetings about meetings. Anyway, during the meeting in the lunchroom, a mouse raced across the cupboards from the stove, over the sink and disappeared. Old mate Ray said to leave it to him, he would get some traps and get that mouse and any mates he might have. Next meeting, old mate shows me he caught a mouse and a steady flow of mice previously, and that's when I started calling him Trapper John. I couldn't believe it. Next meeting Trapper John was well and truly living up to his new name and showed me a trap with two more mice caught in one trap. When Trapper John wasn't about, the boys told me what they had done about putting those mice in early from their own places, so they had now trapped the Trapper. I didn't think it could get any better, but the boys stepped it up one notch and after another week the master mice catcher had caught three mice in the one trap, and the excitement of the hunt had really got him hooked. The next catch that Trapper did was amazing, I wasn't there for this one, but the boys told me all about it. One of the boys bred birds and he caught a rodent and stuck it next to a trap which had gone off, and Trapper John next time I saw him told me all about his latest catch. He told me that he had killed a bloody rat with a mouse trap. I told him that would be impossible, and he said oh no, he wasn't in the trap, he was next to it. He must have set it off and it hit him in the right spot, got him in the temple. So, there you go, true story no bullshit.

How about a dirty story! Okay, this is what happened one day when myself and a school kid working with me on work experience went to do a job at a piggery between Murringo and Young. We went from Boorowa to Young to pick up the truck and the ditcher, and back to the piggery to ditch a new line into the piggery. When we got there, we took the ditcher off the trailer as usual, and the next thing to do was make sure there were no services such as water, power, drainpipes, and such, so I asked the boss of the piggery. He was what I would call a hands-on boss. After being assured there was nothing in my way, I backed the ditcher up to the wall of the piggery, threw the digging chain into gear, gave it some depth, and started digging a trench away from the wall. Everything was going well when a bad smell wafted up from the trench and it was rotten. I stopped the chain and lifted out of the trench. In the trench cut in half was a white PVC pipe with a little dribble of a dirty fluid just leaking slowly. The boss fella from the piggery came over and inspected the damage and said he bloody forgot about that pipe and asked us to clear around it and leave it for him to repair it later. He told a bloke next to him to let everyone know not to turn the pump on at 3:30pm in the afternoon. When I asked what the pipe and pump was for, he said it was to pump all the pig waste and swill down to a big holding tank where they took methane gas from it. We had finished the job and were just dogging the ditcher down on the trailer when we saw the boss man in the bit of open trench with a hacksaw trimming the pipe for repair with a couple of slip sleeves and a bit of pipe. We were in the truck and the boss in the trench in his white overalls, and it was then it hit me he was a magician, one minute he was in white and next second he was in brown and black. Some dick head had turned the swill pump on, and that poor bastard was wearing it big time. We heard him screaming out and watched him chase the bloke down who had turned the pump on, he was going to kill him with the hacksaw he was holding up above his head. I started up the truck and said to the work experience school kid you heard of the shit hitting the fan? He said yes, and I said, this is one of those times and it's also time we got out of here!

Time for another snake story and this story I told to the boys about the low flying Reg Croker. On this day, poor Reg was not well and suffering badly from an overdose of an anaesthetic the night before. I was plumbing up a lead sleeve next to a fence in the bush and before I lit up the gas flame Sir Reginald Ansett, the speed hog low flyer, was flying low to the ground. In fact, he was lying flat out on it. Reg said to me he was that crook that he was laying out on the ground, and he didn't even care if a big brown snake slid up beside him, he wasn't moving. Next thing, as it's a bit hard to hear when your plumbing with the flame going, I heard someone screaming,

"Get the bloody shovel, get the bloody shovel!" When I looked around, Reg was perched up on the top barb squawking like a cockatoo. I just kept whipping up the joint and I just said to Reg,

"I thought you said you wouldn't even move." That sort of a thing you just couldn't plan for that big brown snake to turn up when he did and Reg had said earlier, he was giving up the evil drink so now it was a snake, which had driven him back on the drink to calm his nerves.

Anyway, I was doing a job in a pub in Boorowa, and two Aussie blokes were telling each other stories. One said,

"Have you ever tried to crank start a T Model Ford" and the other bloke told him that he cranked that hard it flew off into the bush. His mate asked, the handle flew off into the bush? No was the answer, it was the T Model. Being good Aussie bullshit artists, the other bloke had to spin a better yarn and he said that in the winter of 1930 he was trying to crank start a T Model Ford, it was -12 degrees. He cranked so hard and so fast and for so long it was boiling before he even got it started. And some people say Aussie's tell lies. It's not true that some would tell a lie when even the truth would do or couldn't lie straight in bed. It's true we are of convict stock, and we must live down our past of stealing stuff. It's like a mate of mine puts it, they weren't stealing stuff as they were basically honest, they would just find stuff before people lost it and that's not stealing.

I did research on my ancestor William Oxley, and all he did was highway robbery in Nottingham. He was given two choices, the colonies of New South Wales for the term of his natural life or he would be invited to a necktie party. If he took the latter, I suppose it was a way back then in 1827 to make sure he didn't reoffend. He amazed me that bloke. He was supposed to be illiterate, but I saw proof on his marriage certificate he wasn't completely illiterate cause where it said his mark there was an X so at least he always got the second letter right of our surname. He was sent out here on a little ship called the Albion for highway robbery – you remember the Oxley Highway? I don't know how he did it, but somehow, he must have sneaked it over to Australia with him. Enough bullshit, I just wanted to prove I am a real Aussie. Now a real 'true' story about drought in our country. The 10-year drought in Boorowa meant water was that scarce we could only have four lanes of the swimming pool open. During those cold winter mornings and early starts to drive down to Goulburn for work I would see the stalactites growing down towards the bonnet of my truck from the steel ladder rack over the bonnet. The radio aerial would get thicker with ice as I drove along the highway, and you could see frozen cobwebs on and off the trees beside the highway. If the ice slipped off the truck and you looked in the rear vision mirror you could see it break up and bits and pieces flying up from the road and the sun would hit it and the pieces would shine like diamonds sparkling in the sun for an instant.

I remember going through Gunning early one morning, and what I saw that freezing morning gave me a great appreciation for the people from that little town for their kindness for animals. You know, those fitness fanatics that walk early of a morning, I always thought they were sticky beaks just checking out whose car is where at what house and what clothes are on whose clothes lines. Well, not so in Gunning. The walkers were, on that cold morning, walking through the frost and fog carrying thermoses with warm water in them, freeing up the town dogs which were frozen to the trees, there you have it, another true story.

Now I've just mentioned a thermos I must write down this yarn and then get back to writing my book, my life story, probably the bit of Irish blood in me but if I don't get back into it, I might cark it before I am finished! Here is the yarn. A blonde sheila went to see the doctor and she noticed a thermos on the doctor's desk and asked the doctor what it was. He told her he brought it to work with his lunch in it and he explained that they kept hot things hot and cold things cold. Well, the blonde brought one to work and her workmate, another blonde, asked what it was for and was told

"I bring my lunch to work in it, it keeps hot things hot and cold things cold," and when she was asked what she brought today, she answered "a hot cup of soup and an ice cream!" Wonder if that yarn is politically correct these days.

Back to work with Telstra, I was getting my work through a computer, and the fellows that gave me my jobs knew I would go anywhere like Yass, Goulburn, Jerrawa, Gunning, Windelama, Moss Vale, Bowral, Crookwell, anywhere I didn't care, and I was enjoying being what I called a paid tourist. I said to the fellows from the work management centre I enjoyed always going where I'd never been, and I always like to see what's over the next hill. I also felt those blokes who didn't like being sent any distance from home probably couldn't let go of their mother's apron strings. It was months after I had said that, and I was logging onto my computer at home in Boorowa when I got the following job. It was to replace a pillar cover which had been left off in a street in Darwin and I could never forget what day it was, it was the first of April.

I knew the boys in the work management centre would be watching or wondering what I would do, so I selected the job. I figured I really would be going down Goulburn area, so I headed off and ignored my mobile phone as I knew it was the fellows who put in that job for Darwin. At about 9.30am I answered the phone and I said I was just through Molong heading towards Wellington. They said there was a job behind that Darwin job for Collector. Top stir. I had worried them a little. They were good blokes, and we all had a good sense of humour.

The story I had written earlier about whether you can get the sack for thinking, I found out while clearing a fault at Collector was partly true. I didn't get the sack, but I found out you can run into trouble for thinking on the job. I am sure I was getting my work from a work management centre in Newcastle at the time, not my mates in Canberra. I was trying to find a fault up that hill West of Collector, which was leading me onto the road towards Gunning, where an old bloke stopped and asked me if I was working on his line 'phone.' I told him no, but I would as that lead cable took a bit of time to open, test and close. That's where I did a stupid thing. I thought I rang cable records and got cable plans for the old bloke's phone. Then again, I thought and put a tone on his line, so I could fix his phone while fixing the original fault I was on. Now the work centre blokes were following the policy of not being able to think on the job, so they didn't think to ring me and tell me there was another fault in the cable I was working in. So, because I had allowed myself to think on the job, I'd cleared both faults and I thought that was good thinking. So, I hit complete on my computer on the job I was given and straight away the old bloke's fault was in my computer, so I thought again and hit select, on-site and complete. Next thing I thought again and this time I was thinking my mobile phone was ringing and I thought I should answer it as I thought it might be a call for me. I thought right that call was for me, and it was the work centre from Newcastle telling me I couldn't do what I had just done with the second fault because the computer couldn't handle it and they had decided to think, and they thought, as did the system, that I could not clear a fault in the time I did, it was unthinkable. I thought for a couple of minutes and told those blokes that from now on in the future if this is to happen again, especially if it was a hot day out in the bush, I would give it some serious thought to select the job I had used my brains to fix before it came on the computer, and I would find a shady tree, lie down under it and rest for two hours, and practice not thinking. It seemed to me that was what was expected of me. At least that was my way of thinking.

This was another story of thinking, but the story is of a customer or subscriber who used the power of thought when she reported her phone out to be sure it would be fixed quickly. It was a Friday, about 2.30pm, and I had just cleared a fault at Breadalbane. I got a call from the work management centre in Canberra, and they asked would I be able to do a fault at a place called Myrtleville, up near Oberon. The fault had been escalated to what they called 'Ministerial.' I asked if it was Alby and they said yes, Alby Schultz, local member. I said to send it to me, especially when I was told it was for an old lady who lived on her own out on a property and she was blind, poor old bugger. Off I went and when I proved the fault on the phone line, it was going down a dirt road off the bitumen road, so I headed down that track. As I was driving down the track, I slowed near a line of poplar trees where there was a couple of drovers with a mob of cattle in the long paddocks. As usual, I always ask locals for information and directions, so I stopped and went over to the drovers, told them who I was looking for. They told me where the place was, then said there was no one home as they had just been talking to the lady I was looking for, and that she was heading down to Goulburn. Okay, so she had someone taking her to Goulburn, to which they said no, she was by herself. I thought how good that is: I've heard of people driving blind drunk but never just plain blind. I went down to a T section, turned left and up to the old blue painted weatherboard home the drovers had directed me to. There I proved the fault on her phone was in the house, and had a look under the house, seeing the cables that run to a few points in the house. I crawled under the house, tested things, and left the faulty cable off, so at least that blind lady would have a phone when she got home from her drive in the country. While I was still under the house and I was lying on my back thinking the lady had come up with a good story to ensure her phone was fixed, something happened, and I thought if someone had been beside the house, they would think I was a bit suss. I rolled over and I was face to face with that lady's dog. I noticed it had a scar on its face and it had one eye knocked out. I just let out a laugh and shook my head and said that's close enough and maybe its owner was looking at her dog when she came up with her bullshit story to make sure her phone service was fixed quickly by saying she was blind alone in the bush.

When I was working with Telstra, I always believed in getting things done and I had no time for stupid games made up by modern engineers or what I called educated idiots figuring out ways to waste my time. Some engineer from North Sydney was paid to ring people up at random and she would ask a heap of questions like how long you should take to clear a town fault or country fault or some other time-wasting crap. She was probably working for those three Amigos we imported from America to just create havoc to help sell Telstra and make it a more slimmed down business with less staff through redundancy or people getting out to do other things with their lives other than being annoyed with bull dust! Anyway, we were given a sheet of paper to put on the sun visor in case that bird rang up to interrogate us. The paper we were given was a copy someone had made up of all the questions and answers that annoying woman would try and catch us with - bloody waste of time.

The day she rang me on my mobile phone was on a late spring, hot sunny day. I was chasing a fault in a paddock between Gunning and Belmont Forest, towards Gundaroo. I had just pulled up beside a few boulders, enjoying my day and my mobile phone started ringing. It was that woman who would hit me with all those questions about the daily running of Telstra. I should have said to her that if she had to ask me those questions, she shouldn't be employed by Telstra, because she should have known herself without asking everyone else. Anyway, I pulled my sun visor down in my truck and there for me to read was the questions and answers 1 to 25. The lovely lady had informed me that she would be asking me some questions and I imagined her to say "We have ways of getting out of you the information vitch ve vont to know" – like an SS guard. Anyway, I said let it rip and questions 1 to 5 I answered with flying colours, too easy. Then this lady threw a spanner in the works and asked a question out of sequence with my notes, I needed time to read it, I was caught. My old boss Jerry in Jerilderie must have taught me to think quick and I played the old OHS (Occupational Health & Safety) trick and said to the lady to excuse me for a sec that I had just seen a big brown snake slither round the boulders and I had to test the cable near the boulders when I was off the phone, so I wanted to see where he went. She said to check it while she waited on the phone. I grabbed my list of questions, got out of the truck, read until I found the answer she wanted, back to the mobile phone and told her the answer. Then she said what about the snake and I said not too sure where he is, she said I'd better let you go. I don't want to trouble you while you have that snake situation. So, I asked how I went with the test, and she said I've passed it very well. We said goodbye and I was very happy with myself for putting that one over!

All I ever wanted to do with my job was to get on with it, but with the government pushing for Telstra to be privatised and all the changes brought in, I have to say I was getting a bit disillusioned with what was a good and satisfying job. People were waiting months at times to get a phone connected for really no reason at all, and with new systems of getting phones on with pair gain[11] systems instead of just getting in and doing the work how it used to be done. This slack way of connecting new services or repairing services that were reported out became so slack that

---

[11] Digital Pair Gain System - a linesman's trick - useful if there were no free main pairs in the pillar - allowed two telephone services through one pair of lines, also helped internet to run better on long lines.

I would spend a fair amount of time my time doing PR work for Telstra and a slack case in point follows. This is a sad story of a phone service which had been left off for six bloody weeks at Belmont Forest area, south of Gunning. I received a job to install lightning protection on a service and while I was doing that work the bloke asked me a question. He asked when his old father's phone would be put back on the air as he was on the property over the road, and he was not well with cancer. His elderly wife was looking after him and a bush nurse was visiting them to attend to his needs. When I finished the installation, I rang the boys in Canberra at the work centre and told them and they said they would put a job in my computer first thing next morning. There had been a big lightning strike six weeks earlier and a kilometre of cable ploughed in with a bulldozer, then cut over to the new cable – 915 metres to be exact. I went to the old folk's house, put tone on the line at the point in the kitchen, and chased out the fault. I found it open circuit in a sealed up joint and that joint had been done six weeks prior. Those poor old buggers had reported their service about ten times, and how it didn't get in the system for repair, I don't know. I restored the phone service and when I went to the house to remove the tone I'd put on their line, I got the boys in Canberra to ring me back and thanked them for send-ing it to me as a fault. I would have expected the old folk to have some abuse for me or for Telstra, but instead I sat at the table to have a lovely lunch with them. Lovely country people.

This was another unusual job to get service restored at the hos-pital at Boorowa. I had heard fire sirens and thought it sounded like they went to the hospital. I was there when they had got the fire out and they could only save the emergency section of the hospital. All I could do while the brigade was still there, was crawl under the building and push the lead in cable back up through the floor for the technician to set up temporary phone services for the saved part of the hospital.

The days of being watched over everything you did have arrived, and even the gas detectors you used to detect gas were being interrogated at random by some prick with a computer to make sure they were being used. Most of my work was in the bush and some in towns and cities, you would use it near a fuel depot or station, but for me not in every bloody pit I might open, and that's what the powers that be wanted. I would turn the detector on as I travelled to Goulburn and that would be it, to satisfy the thing being interrogated, but then they found a way to tell when it was used what time, and for how long. Big brother was watching.

This story will, I hope, not make people wonder about me, but it really happened one morning, early on the dirt road between Gunning and Collector. I was about 10 kilometres from the bitumen road that led down to Collector when I saw a big black cat with a very long tail crossed the road up the road in front of me about 100 metres ahead. It well and truly got my attention, and I stopped when I watched it go under a netting fence and go about 80 metres down a slope and into some briar bushes. I got out of the truck, picked up some rocks and threw them in to those bushes to try and make it come out as I just wanted to see it again. After that incident I asked a few locals around Collector and Yarra if they had ever seen anything like that, and a lady on a property towards Yarra, from Collector, told me a story. She said that there was a paddock on the family farm, and it was well and truly full of trees, on a hill. Her father had seen a big black cat in there, and she said real big black cat that scared the hell out of him. He had never liked to go back near there again. So, who knows, but it stuck in my mind so much that to this day of writing at least 22 years after the event I could go back and find the very spot where I saw that bloody big black cat, make up your own mind!

One of my last jobs I did in Telstra was a job putting in an extension in an old double brick home at Boorowa. When I told the lady of the house, a quiet-spoken lady, that I didn't believe I would fit through the trapdoor to get under the house, she said that young Michael Cassidy had gone under the house alright and had been up to where I had to go. As I knew the bloke of which she spoke, I let myself into believing that I could also find enough room under that house. I dropped a bit of jumper wire through the floor and was ready to go under with a cable to tie onto, to draw up through the floor. As I was working alone and was still a bit worried about getting through that trapdoor and the house was so low, plus I knew those old houses often had the internal walls built by bricks that went all the way to the ground. I thought just in case I rang my son, who was home from university at the time to come over and stay till I got out. He and his mate Brendan came over. They were both big strong young fellows in case I needed help to get out. I went under and how the bloody hell I made it through the trapdoor I didn't know and then through three little holes through those brick walls to the ground into what seemed like little solitary jail cells. I got through and tied the cable I had dragged through with me and was freaking out, getting through the holes in the brick walls on my way back to the trapdoor all the time thinking of the time I was dug out after being caught under that house near Forty Baskets beach on the North Shore of Sydney in 1972. I made it to the trapdoor and my son Matthew and Brendan were waiting for me luckily, as I could not get out. At least I was where I could see light and the blue sky and not stuck in those tight spots in the walls under the house. The situation had me worried, and the boys got an arm each and couldn't pull me through the trapdoor. I then laid on my back and put both arms out and the lads tried to pull me through but to no avail once more. I threw my wallet out and took my belt off and this time the boys dragged me out and at last I was free, although I had a bit of bark knocked off my chest and especially my hips. Then the lady of the house appeared, and I said to her that I was buggered if I knew how bloody Michael Cassidy got under there. Michael Cassidy was about six foot four, tall and pretty broad shoulders. That's when Mrs J said in her soft, almost whispering voice,

"Oh, did I say young Michael Cassidy, I meant young Michael Keefe." I said thanks a lot but thought a lot more. Michael Keefe was a plumber in Boorowa and at the time was built like a bloody greyhound. I couldn't believe I had been fooled or fooled myself by the power of thought or suggestion.

Now I must write a story which started in 1983 to do with my work on Telstra and includes this day, the day of writing it down the 18th of October 2019. In 1983, I was repairing a phone service for a Mr David Ogilvy of Mullion Creek North of Orange towards Kerrs Creek, Euchareena and South of Stuart town. I found the following correspondence about that job yesterday.

I read the previous pages last night and I wondered, as Mr Ogilvy had written that great letter about my work on his property, 'Brittle Jacks.' If like me, he was still on the right side of the grass, and it hit me that it was 36 years ago. It also hit me that I had no recollection of thanking David for those kind words.

When I rang the land line phone David's wife answered. I told her my name and she put David on, and I said I had a belated thank you for his letter to Telstra. David remembered that occasion and as soon as mentioned the power, it hit me remembering the cable had come through the earth mat at the power pole. I asked David if you would like to see both the letters, if so, I had his mobile number and I would send them to him, which I did so after 36 years. David asked me to call in and see them next time I was in Orange, which I said I would. So, there's another story of part of my thirty year's work on the PMG, Telecom and Telstra.

One more truly memorable fault which Telstra sent me on was on a property named 'Springfield,' towards Braidwood, from Goulburn. That fault meant a lot to me, as I was being sent to a vast property, which I had never seen before. I had started chasing down my family tree in 1981 and I had found that my great, great, great grandfather had worked on that property way back as far as 1857, for the Faithfulls. Also, my great, great grandmother had worked there. Her maiden-name was Mary Silk, and she met my great, great, grandfather, who was also working there at Springfield. Great, great, grandmother started working there in 1863, and the owner of Springfield, a descendant of the Faithfulls, helped me to get my great, great grandmother's first payslips from 1863. She married my great, great grandfather, W Oxley. Mrs Maple Brown showed me through then and said for me to just look over that beautiful property, including outbuildings and the shearing shed, which had a big open fire in it. I fixed the phones in one of the many cottages, and before I left, Mrs Maple Brown gave me a lovely big book with many photos and the history of Springfield. When I asked her how much, she just said for you, Steve, nothing. So, I felt like I owed Telstra one for sending me there.

One more job in Collector I just must write. It was another one of those jobs where you wished you had a camera, so I will try and write a picture in your mind. I was given a job in the police station to install a new service for the policeman's wife, for a little business she was starting up. After I had the new phone line going into the station, I went behind the counter and was confronted by a bloody big Alsatian dog. I got the feeling he didn't like me when I walked between him and the lady, his owner. As was the policy, I asked that the dog be tied up, and the lady grabbed a bunch of keys and said come this way I'll show you where I want the phone to put. The dog followed us, she stopped, called the dog up, opened the cell door and locked the dog in jail behind bars. I felt bad with the look in that dog's eyes, poor bastard, and each time I had to walk past him in that cell he looked at me and I could imagine him just saying "You prick, it's your fault I am in here." Just as I was packed up and leaving, I saw the dog in the yard and thought he must have got out for good behaviour.

Chapter 19

End of My TELSTRA Career

I was really enjoying myself clearing faults all over the place, from my home at Boorowa out every day to all kinds of places: Manildra, Orange, Canowindra, Cowra, Grenfell, Murrumbateman, Bowning, Jerrawa, Yass, Rye Park, Dalton, Rugby, Frogmore, Bigga, Lagan, Crooked Corner, Jueena, Taralga, Marulan, Bungonia, Windellama, Lake Albert, Reid's Flat, Tarana Ville, Binda, Collector, Lake George, Wyangla Dam, Bowral, Moss Vale, Berrima, Harden, Galong, Binalong, Cootamundra, Gunning, Bannister. Barwang, Yarra, Crookwell, Goulburn, Belmost Forrest, Robertson, Kingsvale, Wombat, Burrinjuck, Grabingullen, Gundaroo, and there would be many more towns, places, and areas which I have missed oh, and Bundanoon, Robertson, and Burrawang. I would always go and enjoy a couple of beers each night and a couple of old mates whom I would drink with always asked where I had been on the day, and I would tell them, so they started calling me lucky, after Lucky Star and his song 'I've been everywhere.'

Since I had thrown my hat in the ring for redundancy, my time with Telstra was growing closer to the end. I must say I had enjoyed my 30 years and I don't knock the job, but I didn't go much on the way it was being run, government interference, imported rat bags from America. I was fixing a fault in Burrawang between Moss Vale and Robertson and was at the little exchange at the centre of that little town. That's when I received a phone call on my mobile and it was my boss from Crookwell whom I had known since 1972, Graham Stephenson. Stevo told me that I should get ready for redundancy because I would be finishing up in three months. I was happy with that and a little sad as well, but I knew I had to go as if I stayed much longer it would not be good for my blood pressure. I would have to stand by and watch the company bosses and the government take apart and take down a company which my grandfather, my dad and my brothers had worked for and helped build with a certain amount of love and pride in and for the job! I could see the writing was on the wall and not long before I finished up, Stevo told me that the head honcho, Barry Morris, had told him 'Steve Oxley was not to go.' Graham told him he has known Steve Oxley for thirty years, and he wasn't going to be the one telling me they have changed their mind about me going. Graham Stevo told Mr Morris he could tell me himself, and Mr Morris changed his mind, and I was let go!

And so it came to pass that after over 30 years, at the age of 48, I was back out in the big wide world. Really, I had done well if you remember back when I had started on the PMG on the dismantling job of the Sydney to Melbourne trunk aerial pole route. I had only been promised 12 months' work, so when I finished up, I told the mates at Telstra that I either just took my time, or I was a slow worker, because that 12 months' work took me 30 years to get it all done! At the time I was close to finishing up I was given a medal for my service and was happy it was a copper medal and not a lead one between the eyes. As there were a few redundancies at the time, jokes would be made of it that you weren't too popular. For example, for your send-off they didn't need a big venue, they would organise your send off in a phone box. I was doing a job at Boorowa, and somehow the local paper caught up with me to do a bit of a story, so I asked them to give me a bit of time to go home first. I found an old sleeveless jacket, put it on with the collar turned up to show the PMG for the picture they wanted, rang the reporter, and asked them to meet me in the public telephone for the interview and I could check it out for my send off.

Chapter 20

My Life and
My Kids to University,
Two Degrees Each

As mentioned earlier, the completion of building the new family home was also the finish of my marriage, as my wife had informed me, she was finished with me. She had been very kind in finding me a house to rent on the other side of town while I was away working.

Anyway, that's enough of that. After a bit of a hiccough in my kids' lives and a cost of $88,000 to me, after two years my son Matthew was back home with me and a further four years later my daughter Danielle was home with Matthew and me. I believe I drove about 192,000 kilometres either for access to my kids or allowing or providing them access to each other. So finally, I had my family back and together, and now it was time for the kids to show what they were made of and what they could and would accomplish in their own lives.

As I wrote this, I was watching the movie 'Mrs Doubtfire,' and it struck a chord with me. Watch it and see – the kids are the most important. When I first got Danielle home, she came home once sad because some kids teased her for having no mother at school, how bloody cruel some kids can be. There was no way in the world I wanted my kids to be like that. I had seen how kids could be cruel when I was a kid. How could a kid tease a kid with callipers on because of polio? I had seen just that. My kids did not have to suffer or see cruel stuff again, and I knew then and there that in the future neither would my grandchildren. If my kids were to have kids, I had hopefully taught them and shown them how life should be, so they will know how to love and protect their own children. Kids must know they are loved and valued as precious little people. To be encouraged to show their potential, not only for themselves, but also for what they may give to others, but especially what they can give to their spouses and their own children in later life. Kids should have faith in themselves and their ability, whatever that may be, and as I used to say to my kids, just be good and nice, as people like nice people. My kids were told that millionaires sometimes don't have what they need, and that's someone who loves them, a full belly, a warm house to live in and their health. I tried to show them that a sense of humour was also very important in life. You must know how to laugh and sometimes laugh at yourself; it doesn't hurt much.

In life today, a person may do another a favour or good deed, and then that person passes it on. That is exactly how it is raising kids. If you get it right, they pass it on to their kids. Sadly, that works to the detriment of kids who are brought up in unsafe, violent homes, teaching them violence to sort things out. Children taught to be selfish, greedy, or uncaring for others will grow up being that way too. I have always said there is not a bad kid born in the world, if they turn bad then they are made that way. I suppose I was in a way lucky to see the love between my kids, and Matthew really proved it to me when I found out after he had been home for a while, he asked his mother if she would let his sister come home to me and he would go back to his mother, which he didn't want to do but would do it for his sister. That was the sort of love you just can't buy.

Matt would not go near the piano again once he came home, so I paid a real guitar player to teach him, and I would mess around with the kids and have little concerts at home, and they would record them onto cassettes. With both kids back home, I was given the easiest thing I was ever to do in my life after the previous six years, and that was raising the two best kids in the whole world, or as Danielle used to say the whole, whole world Dad, as a little kid! Danielle was taught guitar at school and played in the school band and the music, and the love of music, was with us always. I believe my Mum helped with that. Both kids also had a love of reading and I believe my mother could have helped with that, as she loved reading and had many, many books. My kids could read with encouragement from their grandma.

I think as I am writing the story down that these modern times, we are in now in 2019, that the government or some interfering person would be saying I should have bought my kids up differently. Shock horror as latchkey kids I had shown them how to put wood in the fire when they got home because I worked full time and would be often late home. They even had to get a bit of wood in, feed the chooks, collect the eggs, bring drinking water in from the tank, feed the dog and let him off to run with them and tie him up. They had to find some food to have and then do any homework they had from school and even make their lunch to take to school, and then would spend time studying their school lessons. They were also encouraged to do well and learn how to work their way through life, working together as a family, but also to know money doesn't grow on trees. I would tell them the only way I know how to get what you want in life is to work for the bastard.

For some people today, I would be labelled as an abusive, being too tough on my kids, but they had already seen the tough side of life and they were enjoying life, were ready and willing to do their very best in life with their school, studies, exams, which showed in their results. They were two smart kids and the only advice I gave them about that was that people don't mind smart people, they just don't like smart arses.

One day Danielle got 98% in a maths exam and when I spoke to her teacher Mrs Gilbert, she asked what I said to Danielle when she told me. I said I was lying on the lounge and Danielle came from her room and showed me her mark. Then I told Mrs Gilbert, I said to Danielle,

"What are you doing out here, get back to your room and study." Mrs Gilbert got to know me and knew I wouldn't do that, and after a few years of her seeing Matthew and Danielle going so well she would embarrass me a bit over the town when shopping and ask in front of others if I would like to raise her children. Matthew was into football, rugby league, and I remember one game he got hit in the head, came off with a chipped tooth. He cried a bit about it, got himself back together and said,

"I am going back out to get him." The last year Matt played he got most of the points, and when I took him to presentation night, somehow, he never got a mention. He would play well and if he was caught with the ball, he would have three or four trying to tackle him and like Mick Cronin, he could always get a pass away. Anyway, I wasn't impressed with that presentation night and took Matt out of football, mainly because he was getting tall, and he was small around the neck, and I was worried he could get a broken neck. I was badgered for a good while by people wanting me to let him play again, but I had made up my mind and unlike some I had no desire to live my life through my kid's achievements.

As my kids and me had always played cricket together we decided that Matt would be a good cricketer, and he got right into that. He was tall and a good fast bowler, and not too bad with the bat. I held the record at backyard cricket of the longest hit and to this day don't know how far away from where I hit it that ball next hit the ground. I used to wait to see a truck going past our house, tell Matt when to bowl and I landed one in the back of a truck. Someone saw Matt bowling somewhere and somehow, he ended up with my uncle Keith Oxley going to Turramurra in Sydney for a week or two at the cricket academy in Sydney for his bowling.

Danielle was a good swimmer and was the best at backstroke but didn't really want to swim that much and that could have been because of her continuing ear problems and the grommets in her ears. Danielle told me one night after the school had a swimming carnival the following story about the teachers having a race in the pool. Danielle said it came over the speaker that lane one Mrs so-and-so, lane two Mr so-and-so, lane three Miss so-and-so on up to lane five and then over the speaker in lanes six, seven and eight Mrs so-and-so. I won't say names, but I think there may have been some inference there to someone's size or weight.

Danielle also loved to play netball and was good at that, and both kids were busy with their music, sports and school and study and were always kept busy. In the paddock next to the house, we sometimes had a few sheep in there, or a horse, and I had built a set of goalposts in there to kick the footy. As Matthew was getting into the cricket, he found a bit of wire netting and wired it across the goalposts and called that our wicketkeeper. The two kids and I would get in there on the two acres, and we would take it in turns batting and bowling. I made sure Matt wore the box, mouthguard and gloves, pads, and helmet with mouthguard but for some reason I couldn't wear any of that gear and I paid for it one day from Matt. My boy had started calling me a 'grown down' and not a 'grown up' as he had reached six foot and with his height and pace, he could really send one down. Matt sent one down and it came up like a bullet off that shiny dead yellow grass and got me fair in the forehead. I felt it and the noise I heard was like being in a tank and someone bashing it from the outside with a sledgehammer. I staggered about and with my cricket bat knocked my stubbie of beer over. When Danielle saw what had happened, she knew straight away her dad must be in trouble and yelled,

"Dad, are you alright, what can I do for you?" Luckily, I recovered quite quickly and asked her if she could nip into the house and get me another beer. So, then it was time for Matt to bat and he always loved to hit more boundaries than me so as he was getting close to my score, I told him I was appealing against the light. Matt said the light it's alright, and I said it might be the knock he put into my head, and we pulled up stumps.

One day I was watching Matt in the cricket grounds in Boorowa and as they played a lot of limited over cricket, he was down the order in the batting and often didn't get a bat, which he would regret. This day he got a bat, and they had a few wickets in hand and needed three runs and Matt said to me,

"I am getting the runs today," went out and put the ball over the Creek and close to the swimming pool grounds.

My kids had to grow up watching all the news on television, A Current Affair, 7.30 Report, even Parliament. Danielle used to win a lot of debating at school and represented the school in Boorowa, and away. Danielle told me once she learnt a bit of debating skills by watching and listening to Matt and me having a few battles over the politics of a night-time while watching the news.

Around Christmas time I could only afford a few days down at Gerringong each year and would always stop at Mick Cronin's motel. We would always buy fish and chips for lunch at Werri Beach, and set up at the headland at Gerringong, at the cemetery looking down on Boat Harbour, to have our lunch. It was great views of the ocean and of course it was peaceful there. A few times I told my kids that I would like to be buried there when I cark it.

At this time of writing, I found about five years back when I was about 62 years old, I was hit with a bad flu which was a surprise as I rarely ever get sick. My daughter rang to see how I was going and must have remembered what I had said all those years back at Gerringong when she was a kid. Danielle said,

"Dad, you don't sound very good, you sound terrible, do you still want to be buried at Gerringong?" I just loved that and believe it or not, I had a good laugh afterwards and I think it made me feel a bit better!

The kids and me would mess about writing poetry and Matt and I had a go at the following poem in 1990, just before Anzac Day.

<u>Where Anzac First Began 10/4/1990</u>

Those Turks were good, could surely fight
We were always under constant fire
For our position was so very tight
Machine guns, cannons, bullets never tire.

We knew for us this shouldn't be
From the start we were in a trap
Dropped here because they couldn't see
A deadly mistake made on a map.

We've got many dead and wounded
For eight months it has been hell
The wrong place that we were landed
Thou in loss we have fought well.

They must not know we're leaving
For in darkness, we must go
As we have done some screaming
And we have put on quite a show.

25,000 we would evacuate
Though thousands left there sleeping
In what hell' oh what a state
And loved ones all left weeping.

The Anzacs gone not left one
As Turks found out just how we left
We left some proud Aussie and Kiwi sons
Who paid the price with death?

Now our retreat it was amazing
For in our trenches, we were not
As we had left our guns a blazing
And not one of us got shot.

Before we left our trenches
We left those Turks a note
To read and ponder in wars trenches
And this is what we wrote.

To Turkish foe a fond au revoir
Please keep our trenches clean
For a while these trenches will be yours
By now you'll know just what we mean.

So, we hope that all Australians
Will never forget our deeds
For we fought for our Australia
And we never fought for greed.

All over Australia on our Anzac Day
Come together in your groups
Proudly hold your heads up high
And remember all our troops.

I asked my son to help me write this 10-4-1990. Matthew was 11 years old at the time and he read this out on Anzac Day at the service at the memorial in Boorowa. As always, I was very proud of my son for being who he was and who he is today.

Danielle sprained her ankle once and because I couldn't get her to school because I was working, she had about two town blocks to get to school on crutches. That was a good sign to me of her desire to go to school to learn, do well and to improve her lot in life. With both my kids there was rarely any sibling rivalry, and they both had a sense of humour. They both had study practices and would listen to music, even classical music, while they studied or did school assignments. One day, Matthew's music was a little too loud for Danielle, and he let me know that there was something wrong with the volume on his CD radio machine as it kept turning itself down. Danielle explained and showed me that as the kid's rooms were next to each other that she had discovered that the remote for her music machine also worked on Matt's as well, smart kid eh!

Both kids had learnt that if you want something in life you must work for it, you must give or be prepared to make a little effort to acquire what you seek. Danielle set up her own business, detailing cars at home and did well out of that after making up these flyers which she walked all over town delivering to people's mailboxes. Every presentation night at the school, we would go – my mother, the two kids and me, and the kids would always get awards and certificates, and more books, and sometimes sports awards. Both Matthew and Danielle had their study procedures, and when they got home from school would run a few kilometres, have something to eat, do their chores and then any homework, and study mostly with background music to suit their study time. Both kids found work at the little supermarket stacking shelves, working on checkout and Matt also on the unloading of trucks at the store. Matt did well with his cricket and got a few awards for the junior's cricket and from the senior's cricket at the same time as he played for both simultaneously. It was so easy bringing both my kids up, as they just naturally wanted to work, play sport, netball, basketball, cricket, and the music was also a part of their lives as was school and their home chores, so bloody easy!!

Matthew and I always had our own ideas on politics and policies and when it came time for work experience at school Matt put one over me big time. He asked me what I thought he might do for work experience. At the time I was watching Paul Keating telling some university student in Adelaide to go and get a real job on the news on TV. I said to Matt go and ask Pauly to take you on for work experience, he'll look after you and teach you a few things, he's a good bloke! I only said that for a stir as I knew Matt was leaning towards the Liberals at the time. Matthew was having none of that, and about a week later I was lying on the couch and Matt came up to me and dropped a letter on my chest with a Commonwealth letterhead on it, which I noticed straight away. Then I read it, saying he was getting a week's work experience with Alexander Downer in his office in Parliament House, Canberra, with Downer's Secretary, Mr Greg Hunt. Matt got me on that stir and good on him as he applied for that himself and got it, good one mate! Danielle and I took Matt over to Canberra on the Sunday, met Greg Hunt at his unit and he was looked after by Greg and stayed with him for a week and travelled in commonwealth cars to work experience at Parliament House. When Danielle and I went to pick Matt up on the Friday at Parliament House, Greg was still asking Matt a few things about computers, so he gave Danielle and I some identification cards to put on so we could wander about in the bowels of Parliament House.

I taught Matthew to drive the car and the motorbike, and he used the old postie bike to get himself to work and sports, and to visit his friends in town. I could always ask Matt to drop me at the club and pick me up when I had a couple of beers. Matthew finished year 12 and was Dux of the school. He'd just scraped in at top 10 percent of the State in English, maths, and economics with a TER of 87.95: he put in the work and got the results. Matt was helped get to uni by the Boorowa Education Foundation. He also got three-months work on the Boorowa Council, where one of his favourite jobs was on the garbage truck. He worked on the roads and cleaning up the cemetery and it was while working for the Boorowa Council he received his first diploma. This was after first year at university! He said to me they wanted blokes to go in on a Saturday to train as traffic controllers and I said to do it, so he got his certificate on the stop-go sign. Matt would say to me if I heard of any work he could do, he would do it. The day after the Council Christmas party, I woke him to go and do some grape trellis building, I think that was the day of Matt's first and only hangover. He went to work and put in a hard, long, full day and made me very proud not only for doing the job, but he refused any pay for it because he could have worked a lot better had he not been crook.

So back to Canberra University to get into economics and a law double degree. One day Matt was explaining to me that he knew about economics and how good the GST was that every-one had to pay. I had met up with Matt in Canberra and left the car parked at the Family Law Court, and we grabbed a taxi to the V8 racing cars. We got into the taxi, and we had a bit of gear on, so the taxi driver said as he reached to turn the meter on, 'I 'spose you blokes are going to the races' and when we said yes, he said, bugger it, I won't turn the meter on just give me five bucks, Costello is getting none of this. I could never have planned that, but it was another lesson for Matt in the GST and how it can work, or not work.

Meanwhile, Danielle was in year 10 at school when she did some work experience at an optometrist in Cowra and was able to stay with my Mum's sister and her husband and they looked after her. In year 10, Danielle told me that she thought year 10 would do for her and she would leave and get a job. I told her she was better off doing years 11 and 12, as they would be the best years of your life. I just said that but thought, who am I to say that as I had no certificates from school, and I wasn't much better than a kindergarten dropout. Anyway, Danielle made up her mind to stay at school and worked part-time as a checkout chick and gained her certificate in responsible handling of alcohol and took on waitressing for the cook at the Ex-Servicemen's Club. My daughter put everything into her work, school, and sports. She took up Rugby Union football and I am pretty sure the girls played a game one weekend up Bathurst way and made their debut the next, I was so proud.

Danielle went on one of those wilderness camps out in the bush down Canberra way and explained to me that a couple of girls there had missed out on their formals or the debuts that time, so the girls made them up using garbage bags and whatever they could find and gave them their ceremonies in the bush. I taught Danielle to drive and to get her licence, and as she was doing year 12, I would sometimes get her to drop me at the club and pick me up and bring me home. One Friday night Danielle dropped me at the club and returned home to study for year 12 and forgot to go all the way over town to pick me up. I decided I would walk home and not bother her and figured out on the walk home what I would say when I got home. When I walked into the house, Danielle was sitting at the table, books, and paper everywhere, she looked at me and probably thought I might have something to say. What I said was,

"You are a great caring daughter for putting your father on some kind of health or fitness test, I just love ya!"

One thing about teaching Danielle to drive was she always took in what she was told. I asked her one day if she was driving around a right-hand bend on a dirt road and the rear of the car was slipping or sliding to the left which way do you turn the wheel to correct the slide and then I told her that you correct to the left. Straightaway we went out on a dirt road and Danielle had to make a hard right turn on dirt, up a hill, hit the accelerator, the rear of the car went left, she corrected to the left and drove up the hill, it was good as I knew she listened to what she was told, well done.

Matt came home once from uni, and as usual at about three in the afternoon I would start thinking about what I would cook for tea or figure it out on the way home. This day, I was working north of Crookwell and driving home it hit me that I would do veggies and Danielle could have a steakette, which she liked, and Matt and me would have the two big T-bone steaks in the freezer. When I went to get the meat from the freezer, the two big steaks were nowhere to be found, so I asked Matt had he seen those steaks and what he had for lunch. He said he hadn't had steaks, but he had eaten a couple of bloody big chops. I just thought he'd come a long way since I got him home, as then he was hiding food under his bed, at least he could get a feed for himself, and had never planted chops or steak under his bed, thank God! The boy could eat, and I would always be amazed to sit at the breakfast table and see him devour 10 or 12 weetbix, two would do me. He was a growing lad.

Danielle dropped me at the club one Friday night after I had put the washing machine on. She was going out for something, and she had real high heel shoes on, and I said to her they were that high if she fell out of them, she would need a parachute. I also said they wouldn't be safe driving in them. Anyway, when I got home, I had a few more beers than I remembered I would have to put the washing out and it was dark. As I felt my way, I found I was pegging onto the line I was getting closer to the ground as the clothesline was on an unusual angle. You guessed it, the girl I had taught to drive had backed into the clothesline and had put it on a bit of a lean. My father rang me and when I said to him,

"That brats a silly bugger, she's put the clothesline on an angle," my Dad said, "She's been here, and she is not as silly as you think as she told me that she thought about backing into it from the other side to straighten it out but decided not to in case she made the situation worse." Dad and I just had a good laugh. Thanks for that my darling daughter.

When Matt and Danielle were young, I used to have a bit of fun with them and would sing that Billy Thorpe song the Aztecs sang "Some people I know think that I am crazy." It was good to see my kids had a sense of humour and they would say

"Yes Dad, but we know you are." Love it!

Sorry Danielle, but I just must write the story about your little problem while backing the car out the drive... when it went over the pipe in the gutter, and the back right wheel went down beside the pipe, and the car was stuck. I got my work truck, put the winch on the car and pulled it out. I explained to Danielle that I had a look under the car, and all looked okay, but to try the brakes a few times to make sure they were good still. I watched the brake lights come on a few times while standing on the roads edge and people driving past probably thought I was crazy as I was laughing my head off. I had looked up in the sky and nearly straight up above me was a big bright sun, which could only be the same sun my daughter claimed got into her eyes and she found it hard to see. Not a bad effort for an excuse on the spur of the moment – I was very proud of my little girl! I shouldn't have been telling some people down at Dad's place about Danielle's car problems. I got what I deserved from a daughter who knew how to shut her old man up. Danielle piped up to say that *she* had not jack-knifed the trailer into the side of the Commodore while reversing, and *she* had not backed my work vehicle into a tree in Harden. A nice and cheeky way of telling me to shut up.

Danielle worked hard at school, and when she had completed high school, she missed out on being Dux by only a couple of points. She did well and in her ancient history exam, she scraped through in the top 2% in the state in Year 12. So now it was time for her to go to Wollongong University to get a degree in psychology and economics. The day came when I loaded my father's Ford Maverick with all Danielle's things and took her down to the Gong to leave her at East Campus of the Wollongong University. When I got back home to Boorowa that night I went to the club, had a couple of beers, came home and was having a few more quiet beers as it sunk into my head that I was now an empty nester. The house now was as empty as I had known it some years earlier, and it was not really a good time for my ex-mother-in-law to ring, which she did. When I picked up the phone, she said I want to speak to Danielle, like an order, but I told her Danielle was not there, she was at Wollongong University. With that she said that'll cost you, two kids in Uni. That's when I said I could always count on her daughter to pay the maintenance over the years, and she said that's good. It took her a moment to notice I was being sarcastic. She said she didn't have to listen to that, and I said, F'd if I must either and hung up. That felt good!

When Matt finished school, he had just two days off work before going to university. Matt went over near Young picking cherries to earn some money, and after some time he was sent home because the weather was so hot the cherries were stewing on the trees. After that, Matt was picking peaches for a quid or dollars, I should say. When Matt finished the first year of uni, we got him on the Boorowa Council for three months during his break. Back at uni, Matt did security work for Harvey Norman, fencing, installation of air conditioners, graveyard shifts in service stations and even a bit of work with a shovel and crowbars. He would have a go at anything.

Danielle had to work to get through uni too, waitressing in a restaurant in Wollongong and as a checkout chick for Woolworths. I could never forget that she was having a lot of trouble trying to get work at Woolworths. Danielle rang me one day excited and pleased with herself, as she had finally got to meet a manager. She had hatched a plan and it had worked. In the Woolworth's store she put on a bit of a stir, raising her voice, and demanding to see the manager. She must have put on quite a stir, and she was ushered up to see the manager to quieten her down. Once she was in talking to the manager, he asked her what the trouble was, and what her complaint was about the store. Danielle said she had no complaint about the store, her problem was she'd applied at a few stores and was just asked to leave her application and her resume there – she was never allowed an interview or to meet a manager. That made a good impression, and she was given a job. It just goes to show if you are sure of yourself, have confidence and can show those qualities, you will get on in this world. I used to say Danielle was doing psychology to figure me out, but whatever, maybe it was to figure out managers from Woolworths. Either way it had paid off!

Anyway, Matthew and Danielle got through uni and when Matt got his economics degree, I took Mum over to Canberra with me to a dinner and presentation in the Great Hall, and when I asked Matt where we should meet him, he told me he would be easy to pick out as he would be wearing a funny hat, ratbag! Matt was admitted to the bar of the Supreme Court in Canberra after he got his law degree. This happened before he turned 25, a kid any parent would have great pride in. I went with Matt and the Barrister who stood up with him in court for a celebratory drink at the Ned Kelly Tavern. After I'd had three light beers, I said I'd better leave it at that as I needed to make it back to Boorowa later. The barrister said why not have another beer, and when I said no, I don't want to be done for DUI, the barrister laughed and said

"You'll be right. Matt will get you off." I just said bugger that, I've had enough! I put Matt's hat in the ring with the Lions Club in Boorowa for the Australian Day Awards, and he was presented with an award and named Young Achiever of the year!

Danielle received her degree in psychology at Wollongong Uni, and I went down to see her graduation. I was so proud of her. I remember Danielle telling me she didn't want anything written in the local paper and NOT to put her name in for any Australia Day awards in Boorowa. On reflection, I hope that wasn't because of me telling the kids that people don't mind smart people, they just don't like smart arses.

All I can say is my kids had both worked bloody hard to achieve what they did, as that kind of success doesn't just fall out of the sky. They had both learned to work hard and apply themselves to get to where they were – a huge credit to themselves. To this day, I praise them. I wonder if my Mum had said to them as she often said to me, 'Self-praise is no recommendation,' as they both say very little of their own achievements.

Now I will write about my working life after my redundancy from Telstra in 2001, at the age of 48.

Chapter 21

After my Kids,
plus Uni from 2001

W ork, Private Phone Work and Retirement Village Handyman Part One

Well, 2001 was a year of change. I had lost my job as the head of what was then called a 'dysfunctional family,' as well as becoming an empty nester. It felt like a bit of a demotion. Later in the year, I was given another tag after thirty years working for the old Postmaster General's Department, Telecom and finally Telstra. After thinking of making a career of it, I was now redundant, surplus to requirements. Telstra had decided to improve productivity by cutting down on staff. I believed, as did many that could work, it should have been the modern, brain-washed, brain-dead managers that were to go, because the idiots couldn't organise a piss up in a brewery! The bosses were singing to the government's song book, written to the tune of the government's desire to sell off all our country's assets, which seems to be all the bloody lot of them know how to do, local, State or Federal.

So now, I was given another tag of self-employed. I got myself an ABN from the government, brought an invoice book and did telephone install work for myself plus for local builders on most new homes and renovations. I couldn't get away from communication work, it must have been in my blood, and even that brought up a few stories for me to tell. I had a job for Margie M in Boorowa, where I had to crawl under the house to run a telephone extension. It was very late spring. Even though it was hot, I put a winter jacket on as I found it helped to stop me knocking so much bark off my arms. I was crawling on my belly and got stuck under a bearer holding the floor, and that was when I noticed the slide marks on the sand that was beside me. Luckily, I was on my belly and dug the sand out below me with the knowledge that I may not be alone under that house giving me much encouragement. Not a good idea to run into a snake under a house, as it's hard to stand up and run! When I had finished my work there for that day, I was carrying my half extension ladder out the front when one of Margie's kids screamed out that a big brown snake had come out from the front of the house. Margie screamed for me to hit the snake with the ladder. I kept an eye on the snake, put the ladder in the trailer, picked up a length of steel pipe, followed that snake and he turned on me on the road, and somehow it spooked me, and you wouldn't believe it, the pipe I was carrying drop hit the snake on its head and the poor protected species was immediately deceased. The fact that I had to return the next week to go under the house again had nothing to do with the actions I had taken. Before I left, I asked Margie if she thought when she saw the snake that in her mind it had been a serious situation, and she said,

"Yes," so then I asked her as it was a serious situation, why had she asked me to play silly games. She just looked at me and I said,

"Games like snakes and ladders," then we had a bit of a laugh about the whole thing!

I did another phone job for a Mrs Gay out in the country and when I had run the phone cables under the house, I was offered a cup of tea and cake. Mrs Gay was looking at her mail, having a bit of a laugh, and said her daughter was on her honeymoon in Fiji had said she was having a wonderful time and was not Gay anymore. Good one, I said with a laugh. On the way back to town, I was thinking about how word meanings have changed. I used to tell people I slept with a tranny at night, meaning that that listening to the wireless at night was the only way I could sleep. Years back, if you were gay, you were just happy. I'm just bloody confused by it all.

I was doing the phone work for a couple of years when I got a job as a handyman at the retirement village in Boorowa. It was permanent part-time, so suited me well doing two part-time jobs. After working at the village for a time, we had to do an OH&S course. The lady instructing us asked that we each say our name and describe what our employment entailed. As I listened to people's names and stories, my mind went back to that AA meeting in Mulwala, when I was working out at Jerilderie. When my turn came, I said my name and that I was employed as a handyman. When asked what I did, I said I was supposed to clean leaves out of the gutters but couldn't as I had a fear of heights; supposed to mow the lawns, but had bad ears, so couldn't stand the noise; should weed the gardens and dig them up, but my bad back didn't allow that; should be painting the buildings but couldn't as the fumes affect my lungs. I said to the instructor she must be wondering how I got the job of handyman at all, and she said yes, she was. Well, it's because I only live around the corner, so I'm always handy.

There was a bloke named Jack who used to do a bit of voluntary work at the old folk's home, and he had a real sense of humour. Jack and I got on well. Jack wasn't a young bloke and even when he found out he had leukemia, he would still have me laughing. Jack told me he had been diagnosed for some months, and his doctor in town had gone on leave. A young lady doctor was taking his place, so he had an appointment with her instead. Jack being the bloke he was she asked him what his doctor had told him, and he told her his doc told him not to buy any more shirts and to buy toilet paper one roll at a time, and she was shocked. Then he said he had to see her for an oil change. Apparently, he had to spend a day in hospital now and then and be bled, then get new blood in a transfusion. Jack said the doctor had several goes to get into the vein to take the blood and when she was putting the new blood in, she noticed Jack looking seriously at the arm she took the blood out of. When she asked Jack if he was all right because he looked concerned, Jack said he was, he was checking to make sure the new blood wasn't running out of all the holes she had put in his other arm.

I would always go into the village even on weekends if there was a problem, and one weekend I got a strange call. When I answered my phone, I was asked could I come in as Mrs Smith in room six had a leak in her toilet. I couldn't let this one go by, and I tried to explain that they shouldn't be calling me in for that after all that was only natural and they should think themselves lucky that she was using the toilet and not the floor, it all worked out in the end! I enjoyed working there and talking to the oldies, as I did my many jobs as a handyman. I particularly remember one situation on the veranda at the front entrance, when old Nancy spoke to me. It was a spring morning around 10am and she was sitting in the sun in an armchair when she said to me,

"Steve, I've nothing to do and now there's not much I can do, and I feel so sad." I went to her and told her that she should think of something nice from when she was a kid, down on a river where the water is crystal clear, flowing over some big smooth rocks and you can see the water droplets popping up off the rocks, sparkling like diamonds in the sun. Willow trees reaching down into the water, moving slowly and a soft, gentle breeze upon your face as you hear the birds singing to you from the trees. Noticing Nancy's eyes were closed, I softly said,

"I'd better go" and she didn't open her eyes, just quietly and slowly said,

"Thanks, Steve."

I went to a Christmas party at the pub for the village staff and told this story to a couple of the ladies. I said to them how quick time flies and it didn't seem 12 months since the last Christmas, then I said to them, it didn't seem that long that just after last Christmas that I was fixing a leaking tap for old Mrs Smith in room nine and how generous a lady she was as she caught me looking at a jar of peanuts and asked if I would like them. I said that was nice of her, but she should keep them, and she insisted I have them because she had no teeth and couldn't eat them, the girls said that was lovely of her. Then I said, that's not the whole story, I had to go and put a new light bulb in for her a couple of weeks later and she asked if I had enjoyed the peanuts she gave me,

I said yes, and she said that's good dear as I told you I couldn't eat them, but I did suck the chocolate off them.

One day at the retirement home I did my one and only piano recital for a few of the residents, as I had been joking around with them while doing a bit of painting and told them I had studied the piano for 20 years and had learnt that it had lots of black and white buttons on it. Then I felt bad and remembered when my son was learning piano years back that I, to encourage him, had taught myself by sound the first few lines of Amazing Grace and did that for them. They were impressed but I told them I had better get back to work.

I told one of the ladies working at the village that there was an old gentleman in the home who got a little unwell and had to go to hospital for a couple of weeks to recover. I said I'd been talking to the old bloke's son and asked how he was going. The son said he had asked his father if the staff were looking after him, and the old bloke told him how the nurses would put pillows up behind his back so he could sit up as it was better for his breathing. If the nurses saw him leaning over to the side, they would rush to straighten him up again. The son said,

"So they're really looking after you, then Dad?" His dad went off a bit and said,

"No they bloody aren't, they're bloody well annoying me! Every time I lean over to fart, they straighten me back up!"

Time for another snake story, you can't make this stuff up: One day, I was at home, and I got a call from the village people to come up as there was a problem with a brown snake in the bedroom of a resident in the retirement units. I grabbed my stick with a T piece of timber on the bottom and went into the unit, and the old dear in the unit said the snake was in her bedroom, she had locked it in and put a towel under the door, so it couldn't get out. When I opened the door lying on the carpet in front of a big window which went nearly to the floor, sun streaming in bathing in sunshine was a five-foot-long brown snake. As I approached the snake, which seemed to be asleep, a hand grabbed me from behind, then took my stick which I intended to pin the snake with and gestured for me to leave the room as the second bloke entered the room. These blokes were local fireman and the first one pinned the snake down and the second bloke sprayed the snake with the fire extinguisher with the black funnel on it with. That cold stuff from the fire extinguisher put that snake into what I saw as suspended animation or hibernation, straight to sleep. The snake was in a coil and carried out the front of the unit on the lawn and I went and got an empty wheat bag to put the snake in, when I was asked not to get a shovel. There was a person over the road filming us and the fiery explained that snakes were protected species and they would take it and release it into the natural environment. I jumped up into the fire truck and asked the men in the truck what they were going to do with the snake, and they all said we are going to take it out and release it into its natural environment. I said that snake would be lucky if it saw the sun go down.

Meanwhile my old mate Jack and I would talk about the news of the times, and one day, the subject of football came up. I said to Jack I wasn't impressed about that bloody Hopoate sticking his fingers up bloke's backsides in tackles. Jack as usual with his humour told me Hopoate wasn't the only bloke on the field doing the wrong thing, as some tight arse had stolen Hopoate's wedding ring during a game.

I often drove some of the old residents from the village to hospital and doctors' appointments in Canberra, or Wagga. One old mate I could never forget. I picked him up from a Canberra Hospital and he didn't have a great prognosis. On the way home he told me he just wanted to see his 93rd birthday on the right side of the grass. He'd been an old digger and fought for his country, and I asked him about his treatment. He said he'd decided he's not going to have any of that "radar" treatment. That old bloke had spent all his life on the land, and I noticed him on the way home really looking at all the paddocks and the sheep, and cattle, the creeks, hills and trees, skies, birds, and clouds, and really taking it all in. I was taking it all in too, and I was wondering if the old mate was thinking to himself that could be the last time he would be travelling through and looking over a country he loved. Old mate gave me a heavy piece of metal that he used to tie his pet cat up to when he was outside, a weight out of an old chaff cutter. He also sold me his table and chairs when he moved from his unit at the village to a higher care facility. I would see him sitting on the veranda in an armchair with his mates, feeding them a couple of magpies. As I write this, I have been sitting at my old mate's table, working away. Good on you, Claude.

As I am writing this, I wonder how the old people are coping in villages now. When I was working in the retirement home, the oldies would ask me about food supplies in the country and we would survive; they watched and listened to the news, then in drought times, and were worried. Once they worried about what their kids were seeing on television and now, they needed to be reassured themselves. I would tell them all would be well, that we could always get food from overseas these days. The television is and always was delivering bad news and it can get people down a bit. There is not enough content to help make old people laugh or smile these days. When I think of TV now, the Skyhook's song 'Horror Movie' comes to mind. So, the old folks need cheering up a bit more, and people should understand that they like to hear a good yarn and could tell us a few too, might even surprise with some of the yarns they told me over the years.

I did learn a bit about old age, and a few of the oldies were able to teach me a couple of things about being old! If you're smart, you can use your number of years you've been given on this planet to get out of trouble or doing something you don't want to do. You can always, when not wanting to do something, just say you're getting old, and your memory isn't what it used to be, and you just plain forgot.

That brings me to a day when all the old residents had put money toward buying a heap of flowers to go into a garden bed I had prepared in the courtyard of the village. I was in the garden on my knees, and I got the feeling there were people behind me. When I turned around, most of the residents were there with their walkers. They sat on them and asked me questions about the garden and the flowers to go in. That's when Dot, a lady of 80-odd years, asked me what the smell was, and added it was a putrid smell. When I told her it was a fertiliser called Dynamic Lifter, she exclaimed loudly that it smelt like shit! With that, I pretended to be shocked, and I said to Dot that I was embarrassed to hear such a nice lady speak with such vulgarity. She immediately came back at me with an apology by saying she was so sorry as she had never sworn like that before, it's just because I am old now and I don't always know what I am saying. Apology accepted you old bugger! All that sort of thing I put down as part of my apprenticeship of how to handle getting older!

Another day when I was at the village, old mate Jack and I were having smoko and I saw in the local paper Doctor Scott and a nurse were putting on a men's health night and free check-ups for the blokes. I asked Jack if he was going and he said he might, but it's a bit late for him, and he asked me if I was going. With a straight face, I said no, because it was going round town that Hopoate would be there to help the doc out, as he had lots of experience doing the digital examination, with plenty of field training. The main thing was that old Jack got a good laugh out of all that.

Another story at the retirement village was one I will never forget. Each year, I would prune back an ornamental grape vine which grew over a gazebo at the back of Kate's unit. As usual, Katey would always offer me a cuppa, and we would talk about her life. She had lived an interesting life and was nearly 90 years old. Katey told me that day of a beautiful dream she had the night before, where she thought she was dying. In the dream, she was lying on a beach in the sun, listening to the waves of the ocean. There was a soft, gentle breeze as the waves came up to where she lay, the water seeming to wrap itself around her body. She felt herself floating slowly, at peace, as she floated a little way into the ocean, then back again and placed gently onto the sand. Kate said that happened three times and she thought this must be her dying, but it was lovely and so peaceful that she didn't feel afraid if dying was like that dream.

One summer while working at the village we were all worried about a fire out of control to the west, being fanned with a very hot, strong wind towards the town. I spent the day going up to the top of Red Hill on the eastern edge of the town, observing the fire, which was coming closer, listening to radio reports for people on the west of town to evacuate, and checking in on the village people. At the same time, people were told to have vehicles ready to go, and I made sure the bus and the village station wagon were full of petrol. That was keeping me busy, but I was also worried about my Mum and Dad, as they both would have been in their early 80s, and both still at home. I never forget going down to Dad's as I really was concerned that they should have an evacuation plan. As I drove in their driveway, Dad's four-wheel drive wasn't to be seen and I really expected to see it out ready to go! I peeked through a gap in the shed door which had a steel bar across the door, and it was all locked up, I thought, Dad, you've done no preparation towards a quick getaway. Still with more concern for Mum and Dad, I walked in the back door of the house into the lounge room and there they were, sitting in their two big, easy chairs, the air-conditioner rattling away like an old chaff cutter. It was nice and cool in there, and when I asked what they were doing, they both half looked at me and Dad said, "What do you bloody think we're doing? We're watching the bloody cricket". I just thought to myself, they're not too worried, they had their priorities, and it wasn't the fire threatening the town, it was the bloody cricket. I kept an eye on the fire and the village, and Mum and Dad. Later in the day, the wind changed and started blowing from the south and all was good, as the threat was over. It had worried me, but hadn't worried everyone in town, especially those who really love their cricket.

One day I was driving my VH Commodore up towards the retirement village, and at the intersection near the hospital I noticed an old dear from the village going straight through a give way sign at some speed. I veered out of the way and went for the brakes, but even before my foot could hit the brake pedal, she had driven into my front right guard and the old Commodore spun around. It was like it happened in slow motion, with bits of glass and the front grill seeming to float away into the air and back down to earth. The noise of the collisions and spin seemed to play back in my head. I got the old girl out of her care and took her straight into the doctor's surgery, which we were right in front of. She survived okay and so did I, but the car was written off.

About three months later, I was driving the old dear and her husband to a doctor's appointment at Calvary Hospital in Canberra. I spotted a car on my right come through a give way sign quickly and I braked, took the left lane, avoided a big hit, yelled out "I am sick of trying to avoid dropkicks coming through bloody give way signs, you have to drive for every other bastard these days". That's when it hit me who was sitting in the back seat of the village station wagon, and when I went to look in the rear vision mirror the old dear was lying low so I couldn't see her much, she may have felt a little embarrassed with what I had said: I know I was.

Two more stories about old mate Jack at the village. While he was not well with his leukaemia, we still joked around and he still did a bit of volunteer work at the retirement home. One Sunday, I was reading the paper, and in the sports section was a story and a photo of that bastardly Hopoate. Straightaway, I thought I would take the paper and show Jack the picture of Hopoate sparring in the boxing ring, as he was taking up boxing after football. I showed the paper to Jack, and as soon as Jack saw the photo he said,

"Look at that, that mongrel is at it again: he's still punching some bloke in the ring." Oh well, that was Jack.

Then one day I bumped into Jack in the park on Australia Day amongst a big crowd. Walking past us was Belinda Green, Miss World in 1972. Jack said,

"God, she's beautiful, I'd like to meet her." So, I had to think quick and as she walked past it occurred to me that she wouldn't know I was not part of the Australia Day Committee.

"Excuse me, Belinda. I would like to introduce you to Mr Jack Miller. Jack, Belinda Green." They shook hands and someone yelled,

"Oh, give him a kiss!" Belinda kissed him on the cheek and walked off. Jack reckoned he would never wash that cheek again; he was so happy the old mate. Not too long after that, old Jack was slipping and passed away. Sometime later I bumped into Belinda in Cowra, and I asked if she remembered that day and meeting Jack. She said she did, so I told her Jack knew he didn't have much time left on that day and I thanked her for what she had done for him, as she had really cheered him up. She had made an old man very happy! Thanks Belinda!

In the village we had to do fire drill and practice evacuation procedures, and one evening we had to do it for real when a fire started in a resident's room. I heard the fire siren and from home I thought it went towards the hospital or the retirement village. Most of the residents were out and I was asked to get Big Ron out. Another bloke named Steve helped me get him into his wheelchair. There were five firefighters there, with the fire contained in one room, but the worry was if it got up into the ceiling through the ducting. I was pushing old Ron through the building to get him out when he said I would have to take him back into his room. I could not believe it, and when I asked him why he said he'd left his television turned on. Funny what people think of in some situations eh! Anyway, the fire was contained to the one room, and all was well and when everything was cleared by the Fire Brigade and all repairs were done, the residents could return. I was told one day the fire was caused by an electric bedside light lead being jammed in the moving parts of an electric adjusting lounge chair. I did ask if that chair was one of those Dawson cheers and I had to explain what I was on about, so I said as the chair had caught fire, it must have been one of those Smoky Dawson chairs (an electric adjustable chair promoted by Smoky Dawson an old country music singer in Australia), doesn't matter eh!

Well, here's another snake story that I was called to attend to in the self-contained units at the village. When I arrived at the scene, there was an elderly lady out the back of her unit, and her husband was trying to calm her down. A six-foot brown snake had been on the back veranda of the unit, and the lady saw it go behind the hot water service in a bricked-up corner. I went over the road to my work shed and grabbed a fire extinguisher and my banjo (I mean shovel) while the old bloke and his wife kept watch. I lent my shovel up against the veranda post and fired the cold fire extinguisher around the hot water system, and you wouldn't believe it that brown snake found the hole in the brick wall where the pipe went through from the hot water system was big enough for him to go through and get into the wall in the kitchen of the unit. So now I've got the old girl going off that the snake will come out of the cupboard under the kitchen sink, and she'd never be safe in her unit ever again. They looked at me like I was crazy when I asked if they had some plain flour and went and got some for me which I put a good spread of flour on the concrete floor around and near the hole the snake went into.

I told them to let me know when they saw the flour disturbed so I would check it and know the snake had come out. Then I would seal up the hole so the snake couldn't gain entry again. By now we had an audience of old folk behind their units, and they were all getting a bit nervous about the snake. When I was about to leave, the old bloke yelled he's come out of the wall! I watched him heading off across the green lawn towards some gardens and a couple of old residents. I grabbed my shovel as I then had a real concern for the oldies and took off after that snake, and he was travelling. Then he turned on me with a bit of a charge, so I panicked and accidentally dropped my shovel on his head and sadly that snake was dead. The oldies gave me a good cheer and the old bloke whose unit the snake had visited said he couldn't believe how fast I could move. I must now say you should never chase a snake, just ignore them and they will go away, that's my advice!

As the handyman at the village, I would be asked to do several jobs and one day I was asked to install a new washing machine in the laundry. I was reading the instructions, as you do, those bloody Chinese who make everything, now write some classics. One of the young ladies working at the village came into the laundry and I read her the Chinese instructions on the installation. One bit said, 'Do not sit baby on lid of machine during operation,' then said, 'Load machine evenly so load is balance when operation involved,' there was more rubbish advice as well, and the young lady couldn't believe it, especially when I read out or pretended to read that the instructions said, 'If you do not adjust legs under machine so it would be level and don't load machine, even so, balanced machine could move out of laundry and person who made install bad could suffer by being shot in the morning.'

She shook her head, looked at me and left me there by myself. It may have been she'd had enough of my bullshit, or she feared what the washing machine could do if I turned it on.

I had always enjoyed my time working in the village and the yarns I had with the village people. I was reminded of that old song 'The times they are a changing,' when we had to carry out an exercise in the home of finding where a bomb might be and isolate the area. That made me think how much times had changed, not only for the old folk, but for me in my own life. Imagine kids today hearing about murder, robbery and rape every bloody day. This stuff was rare when I was a kid. I do remember Graeme Thorne, Steven Bradley, and the Beaumont children though. I remember them, as there wasn't a lot of bad stuff going on in those days, and now a days, I had to practice bomb scares at an old people's home. The times they are a changing!

I think it was around 2014 when I left my work at the retirement village after 10 years. I may have been thinking as I was about 62 years old then that I could be looking like I should be booking into the home and becoming one of the village people myself. At the same time, I gave up my work of 10 years, gardening, and handyman for a lady in town which I had enjoyed as I had done a few building jobs there. I had also put some new lawns in the town, and I just gave it all up and just spent my time doing a job I really loved, and that was looking after my Mum and Dad whenever they needed a hand, which, early in the piece was not much, as they built them tough in their day and they were independent old buggers.

I had also for a few years worked part time doing a bush mail run and I didn't mind that job, as I was out in the bush driving about on dirt roads, enjoying myself, and getting paid for it. Reminded me of the 30 years with Telstra. It seemed that I could always get work in way to help provide communication service!

I have been handwriting this now for over fourteen months, so just a little more about my two kids of whom I am very proud. They are a real credit to themselves for the way they worked for their two degrees each, including their Masters.

We understand that myself and my kids have been blessed to have the lives we have, even with those few hard years we had to endure. I also think we all should take the hard times to help shape us into better people who understand others and have compassion for those in need and in trouble at the time of writing our country is in a state of drought and bushfires and it's a time when Aussies can all be proud of all volunteers in this country, we are, after all, a bloody good mob. Any way I have now turned 67, and I have realised an important thing about writing your life story is to try and finish it before you kark it, but to truly be your life story you must write until you go, so I am cutting it short, this book I mean.

So, both my kids found their partners, and now I have a daughter-in-law and a son-in-law, and I must say they made great choices. I looked at it this way, that my family was increasing, and I was happy with that, after all I could still remember the time when I thought my family had only consisted of myself for a while. My daughter was married in Wollongong to Brendon, and they have the pigeon pair: their first born, my first grand-child was about ten weeks early and spent about ten weeks in hospital before he was bought home on New Year's Eve about twelve years back. About three years later a baby girl came along and now they are a beautiful little family. My son was married to Leanne on her parent's property at Narrabri northwest

NSW and as they were married, I looked in the background at Mount Kaputar as I had looked at that mountain many times years earlier while driving cotton pickers. I could never of imagined a day that Mountain would be in my sight while I was watching a son of mine getting married. Matt and Leanne first had a beautiful baby girl and next a little boy. My grandchildren are for Danielle and Brendon, Lachlan then Elice, then for Matt and Leanne, Maleah then Mason. My grandchildren all have a sense of humour, are happy kids and are well looked after by their parents. They will be educated well and one day they will write their own stories as they have encouraged me to do by giving me cards that they make, poems they write, and pens they give me to keep writing, as presents for my birthday and grandfathers day.

Now I will mention my Mum and Dad in getting closer to finishing my writing. After I finished work at the village, I just did a few phone jobs and lived on my superannuation and was there to help my parents in their last years into old age. They were independent people and looked after each other through sixty-eight years of marriage. Dad was Mum's carer, so it was after Dad had a bad stroke that their last three months were spent together in adjoining rooms in hospital. I would always, even when working, just drop what I was doing and help them. If Dad came to me to take him or Mum to Canberra, or Young to the doctors, I would do it: it was another thing I found easy to do in my life, to look after Mum and the old man. Sometimes Dad would come to my work at the village to ask for help, and would cry a little, saying he was sorry for taking me away from my work. I felt sorry for him and would just tell him how much I loved looking after them after they had always looked after me – when I was a kid, or in trouble, or when I was battling to keep my home and win my kids back through the courts. When I got them home, my kids could always count on their grand-parents too.

Through their last years, I took Dad to the doc and asked if I could go in with him. I told the doc he wasn't good and couldn't eat, and straight away that week I took him to Westmead Hospital in Sydney to a specialist. A further four visits, including two sur-geries to repair his oesophagus so he could eat again, and gain weight, as he was looking poorly. Dad came to speak to me at work the day before his third trip to Sydney. He was crying and said he'd had enough. I had to talk him into going to the city again, which we did. After the five trips to Sydney, he was happy and so was Mum, and that kept them together for their last few years.

Mum had a lot of issues in the last few years, including a big operation that I really didn't think she would survive, which gave her a little more time. She had a bad heart and cardio myopa-thy, but those two buggers were determined to stay together and were married for sixty-eight years. Dad used to say sometimes you only get ten years for murder. Only a couple of years before they died, I told Dad I had a mate who could copy old 78 records, Dad asked me to get them done as Mum had a recording of her singing on them when she was only about twenty years old, and she sure could sing. When I dropped in the CDs to Mum and Dad, I put them on the CD player and Mum just leaned on the kitchen bench and listened to them while Dad went to his lounge chair in the lounge room to listen, and I noticed him wiping tears from his cheeks. Dad to most people was a tough old bugger, but I often saw a very soft side of him. As I was leaving to go home, Dad followed me out front to my car and with tears flowing down his cheeks said to me that he wanted those CDs of Mum singing played in the Church at Mum's funeral. Later when Mum and Dad were in hospital and I knew they were both going to step on a rainbow soon, I told a nurse at the hospital about the CDs, and Di got me to get Mum and Dad in the same room and put the CDs of Mum singing on. I would never forget that day, Mum sitting beside Dad's bed, head bowed, listening. Dad lying there just listening to Mum's voice singing, as he had done for many, many years.

Not too long after that, Mum died, and we told Dad Mum had gone. Because Dad could not talk after having a stroke, my older brother Ian asked Dad to squeeze his hand if he wanted to catch up with Mum. Later, another nurse who had looked after the old man, told Dad if he wanted to put on his wings, it was okay to do so: when he was ready, he could fly and catch up with Mum. Dad waited to see his brother Don, who had to get down from holiday in Qld, and my brother Neal, who was the last of his seven kids to see him before he left us to be with Mum, just four days after she had died. They were two tough old buggers and Dad had made eighty-eight years, and Mum had made eighty-six years. All my brothers and sisters, and all the big extended family they had could not have loved them more. Rest in peace.

I started this story with Mum and Dad, and so in my mind I think it's only fitting that it ends on them. After all, if it was not for them, this story would not exist. Something mum used to say to me when I was fighting for my kids just came to mind. There was a song called, "I Won't Back Down" on the radio and she said it always made her think of me. God love you, Mum.

And so, after writing for over fourteen months, the pen must go down and it's funny but now it's hard to stop. My son Matt and daughter Danielle I think are getting this printed up in book form so I decided to get, or should I say commission, a top photographer to take my photo to go on the front of this book so anyone who might read it would have a bit of an idea of the look of the bloke that had been encouraged to think he could write a few stories and yarns of, in and about his life. So, I asked the barmaid in the Returned Services Club in Boorowa to take a pic of me just as I am, and I must say she did a great job, as it is very close to a real likeness now of myself.

Now I worry that I was able to kid myself into thinking I could write a book when I have trouble just to read one. So, to finish up, I hope anyone who has taken the time to read my book may have had a few laughs. I do worry with all the political correctness that some people might have lost their sense of humour, and we should all go out and find it again. Take time to enjoy your life, I have. Cheers.

The End

In Acknowledgement

I want to thank and acknowledge the following people:

My parents and grandparents, for always encouraging me in my attempts at writing and poetry, for teaching us kids to always have a go.

Thanks to my children, Matthew and Daniel, and my beautiful grandkids also. For their encouragement and for paying for my first hand-written 500-page draft to be transcribed to a type-written transcript by a wonderful woman in New Zealand. (The email comments from the lady in NZ to my daughter, Danielle were ever an encouragement as well "send more, your father's a real crack-up.")

Thank you to Bob Spiers, who organised PMG, Telecom & Telstra reunions, for liking my stories of my time on the job and telling me to keep writing it all down.

Thank you to Rosalie Ham, who encouraged me to have my stories published (albeit without having read a word...) I talked to her about how I was doing it for my kids, but that perhaps other people might get a laugh from it too. Rosalie gave me great advice about editing and marketing, as well as sparked the idea of publishing, for better or worse.

Thank you to Chris Keeble for being brave enough to put a poem I wrote about her on her Facebook "Barbering Biker" page after our meeting, and for passing on two other poems to the bereaved families of two special kids that Chris came across in her travels.

Thank you to Novy Rich, who was the first to start editing my words to shape this into a book. Due to Novy's ill health, I had to find a new editor to help me along, for which I also need to thank Karen Smith, of Boorowa.

Finally, I want to thank and acknowledge Anneliese Wilson of Boorowa. Anneliese has worked on editing and finding a publisher for me, while in her little shop 'The Dragonfly Boutique.' Anneliese has put in so much time and effort getting my words into a proper timeline, and my story as I'd meant it from my memories at three years old in Brewarrina to 2020. Thank you to Anneliese's daughter, Lauren Ludwig, for creating the cover art for me, cleverly incorporating all the elements of my story in her drawings.

It's strange that I wanted to write a book and poetry when I don't read much, as I find it difficult with having dyslexia. Still, I've written stories and poems since I was fifteen, even starting a life story at 27 years old, only to lose it all in Jerilderie. I seem to love writing because it is just one word at a time, which I can handle.

Cheers, Steve Oxley 2022

William and Mary Oxley (nee Silk)
William 1844 – 1922 & Mary 1855 – 1933

'Grandfather Oxley & Sons'
Back L-R Leo, Thomas, Steve & Front L-R Jack, William 2nd, William 3rd

'Woodstock Oxleys'
Margaret (nee Hudson), Adeline, Joe, Rupert & Jim
(One of these boys was killed in WW1 France)

Mum (Joan Oxley, nee Howe) as vocalist in the 'Boorowa Embassy Dance Band'
just after the war, with Harry Grosvenor, John Geary, Wally Greig and Gus Chew

Me (Aged 10 yrs) 1962

Collecting wood chips for the Sunday bath, Dry Street house
L-R Lewis, Neale, Caroline, Ian, Paul and Me (all in black just like "Jess Harper")
1963 Or 64

Warilla 1966 – Our housing commission home (FB Holden)

Cotton Trailer similar to one I hauled along stock routes four or more at a time from Merah North to Wee Waa Jinnery

Floods at Wee Waa 1971 – Taking an elderly lady to the doctors

*Floods at Wee Waa 1971 – Me and my brother-in-law Michael Hume –
Water was 4 inches higher than in this photo*

Our wedding 1979
Mum (Joan), Dad (Leonard), Me and the wife,
Flower Girl Meredith Elliott (Mum's niece)

My Son, Matthew 1983 at Grenfell

My Daughter, Danielle 1986 and her thrill seeker cat

Matthew & Danielle 1985 at Orange

Danielle 19XX

Matthew on an appaloosa pony - Orange

Danielle on an appaloosa pony – Orange

Me, Danielle and Matthew...trying hard...clearing a tree at 10 Brial Street

Danielle and Matthew on her confirmation 1999

Danielle and Matthew at Danielle's School Formal 2000

Little Me

Me...at The Three Sisters 2020

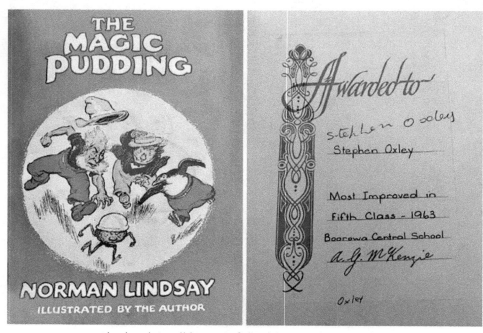

...the book I still haven't felt old enough to read...yet

XXX

CPSIA information can be obtained
at www.ICGtesting.com
Printed in the USA
BVHW071531200223
658845BV00007B/373